SPITFIRE PILOT
FLIGHT LIEUTENANT
JULIAN ZUROMSKI

SPITFIRE PILOT FLIGHT LIEUTENANT JULIAN ZUROMSKI

RAF HERO OR NAZI COLLABORATOR?

COLIN PATEMAN

AIR WORLD

AIR WORLD

SPITFIRE PILOT FLIGHT LIEUTENANT JULIAN ZUROMSKI
RAF Hero or Nazi Collaborator?

First published in Great Britain in 2025 by
Air World
An imprint of
Pen & Sword Books Ltd
Yorkshire – Philadelphia

ISBN 978 1 03613 321 4

Typeset by SJmagic DESIGN SERVICES, India.

Printed and bound in the UK by CPI Group (UK) Ltd.

The Publisher's authorised representative in the EU for product safety is Authorised Rep Compliance Ltd., Ground Floor, 71 Lower Baggot Street, Dublin D02 P593, Ireland. www.arccompliance.com

For a complete list of Pen & Sword titles please contact:

PEN & SWORD BOOKS LIMITED
George House, Units 12 & 13, Beevor Street, Off Pontefract Road, Barnsley, South Yorkshire, S71 1HN, England
E-mail: enquiries@pen-and-sword.co.uk
Website: www.pen-and-sword.co.uk

or
PEN AND SWORD BOOKS
1950 Lawrence Rd, Havertown, PA 19083, USA
E-mail: uspen-and-sword@casematepublishers.com
Website: www.penandswordbooks.com

MIX
Paper | Supporting
responsible forestry
FSC® C013604

CONTENTS

INTRODUCTION

On 28 February 1933, the second president of the Weimar Republic, Paul von Hindenburg, signed the Emergency Decree for the Protection of the German People, also known as the Reichstag Fire Decree, which suspended the democratic aspects of the Weimar Republic and declared a state of emergency within Germany. With the decree in place, the Nazi political regime was empowered to arrest and incarcerate political opponents without charge, dissolve political organisations, and suppress publications. This was to become a permanent feature of the Nazi police state and Germany's withdrawal from the League of Nations and the International Disarmament Conference followed on 14 October 1933. Winston Churchill gave an outspoken warning to the British Parliament highlighting the dangers to peace posed by the evidential growth of German military aviation.

President Hindenburg died on 2 August 1934 and the last remnants of Germany's democratic government was totally dismantled. Hitler combined the role of President and Chancellor into one and the army swore an oath of loyalty to him. He had now fulfilled his ambition in achieving total power over the German states and he was acclaimed as Führer.

Churchill's warning had been a perceptive and well-informed observation. It was made by the man who would later lead Great

INTRODUCTION

Britain as its Prime Minister in war against the aggressing German nation. Few had any concept of what was to unfold across Europe, let alone fifteen-year-old Julian Kazimierz Zuromski from Borysoglebsk in Russia. He had been born into a proud Polish military family that had fought and defended Poland against the Bolsheviks during the Russian Revolution. Tradition and Polish valour would have been a significant component in his early family years and it was very much present during his own military education and service.

In Great Britain, as matters developed within Germany, the regular air force was being bolstered by volunteers from the Royal Auxiliary Air Force. These were recruited within an extension to the military Territorial Associations formed in 1925. The Royal Air Force Volunteer Reserve followed, formed in 1936, initially comprising of civilians recruited at the Reserve Flying Schools. These were young men of between eighteen and twenty-five years of age who undertook part-time training as pilots, observers and wireless operators. This strategic vision of recruitment was to create a reserve of trained aircrew for use in the event of an anticipated war. By early 1939, the imminence of war was fully apparent and joint Anglo-French staff conversations had begun in London. These were intense political and intelligence negotiations based upon events in Europe.

At 1120 hours on 3 September 1939, the German dictatorship communicated with a statement of their position. It related specifically to British Prime Minister Neville Chamberlain's declaration to protect Poland. Germany concluded the communication with the suggestion that His Majesty's government desired the destruction of the German people, with these words: 'We shall answer any aggressive action on the part of England with the same weapons and in the same form.'

Hitler was steadfast with his aggressive military statement. Shortly after, the Prime Minister announced in the House of Commons that Great Britain was at war with Germany. In respect of the RAF, the early volunteers would serve within the three primary Commands: Fighter

Command, with its headquarters at Bentley Priory, Middlesex; Bomber Command, with its headquarters at High Wycombe, Buckinghamshire; and Coastal Command with its headquarters at Northwood, Middlesex.

Commonwealth air crew volunteers from Canada, New Zealand and Australia would be welcomed and they would eventually be recognised by flying in dedicated squadrons. There was also the Allied Polish, Dutch, French, Norwegian, Czechoslovak and Belgian contingents, who would operate within their specifically allocated 300 to 399 squadron numbering. Additional Commands evolved and formed to meet the developing requirements in the aerial war against Germany. The Army Co-Operation Command formed in December 1940, Ferry Command in July 1941, Transport Command in March 1943 and the Second Tactical Air Force in June 1943. The latter was conceived to support the intruding light bomber operations into France and the subsequent air operations in Western Europe. It was principally designed to create the capability of close army support duties; reconnaissance, fighter, and fighter-bomber units that were to operate from independent airfields or forward landing grounds situated close to the fighting fronts.

This book explores several accounts of young Polish aviators and in doing so it provides an overview of their experiences alongside the life and military service of Julian Kazimierz Zuromski. He was a young man who embarked in Polish pre-war military service in the shadow of his father's position as a decorated, patriotic Polish cavalry officer. Zuromski carried his father's forename adjacent to his own forename. He was well educated and held a desire to serve like his father, but he wanted to fly the modern Polish aircraft of that time. He achieved this, but as he did so, he and his fellow aviation cadets witnessed the brewing instability of the German Third Reich. Hitler and the Nazi Party controlled the country, transforming it into a totalitarian dictatorship that developed and eventually spilled out, engaging with yet another Bolshevik invasion of his country. The might of Nazi Germany instigated the aggression and the

INTRODUCTION

Russian invasion followed swiftly, events that ultimately resulted in the execution of Zuromski's father.

Zuromski was on the cusp of becoming a fully qualified fighter pilot when he was forced to escape to France and then to England, which ultimately saw him become a pilot in the RAF Volunteer Reserve. He would have carried understandable embitterment and resentment of the Bolsheviks that impacted his life in many aspects. Zuromski became a gallant Spitfire pilot and endured a unique service life, much of which is comprehensively illustrated through his written words in his log book. His own written account has been fundamental in creating this book. His life as an Allied Spitfire pilot put him in great peril over occupied Europe. With vigour, he attacked enemy aircraft and attained success, but was shot down himself, suffering facial burns before escaping his stricken Spitfire by parachute. His capture and imprisonment by the Luftwaffe exposed his anti-Bolshevik mindset. In the mind of the author, his chosen route to surviving as a prisoner of war is deserving of understanding and contemplation as opposed to judgement or condemnation. Shortly after the war in Europe ended, Sir Archibald Sinclair, the British Air Minister, in his letter to Polish airmen wrote:

> We do not forget that you were the first to resist the aggressor. Neither do we forget that you came after manifold trials to our aid when we most needed your help. Your valiant squadrons fighting alongside our own were in the forefront of the Battle of Britain and so helped to restore the fortunes of the allies throughout the years of struggle. In good times and bad, you have stood by us and shared with the Royal Air Force their losses and their victories.

This is the inimitable account of the life of Polish pilot Flight Lieutenant Julian Zuromski, Polish Cross of Valour (Krzyż Walecznych) and Bar.

PREFACE

During the Second World War, all members of the fighting services who engaged in flying duties were required to keep a personal record of flights undertaken. Log books were issued to all pilots and air crew personnel who flew as part of the RAF or Commonwealth air forces during the Second World War. There were men from Poland, Czechoslovakia, the Netherlands, France and Belgium who had flown in defence of their own countries before they escaped to England in the hope of continuing their fight by serving in the Volunteer Reserve. These men, inevitably by circumstance, held no record of flying service as their log books were lost in battle. One of those Polish pilots was Zuromski. He had flown in Poland as a cadet pilot, then in France, both instructing and defending French ports, and was thereafter regarded as a competent fighter pilot.

Zuromski was issued a log book by the RAF, which was regarded as the property of His Majesty's government. It was bound simply in material, and in it he was required to record all his flying, regardless of the flight's purpose. It recorded his progression during training and assessments of his proficiency, and it would subsequently list all his operational flying.

PREFACE

Proficiency assessments were required to be completed annually and the commanding officers or their deputies were tasked with inspecting and signing these books on a monthly basis. A log book remained with the recipient regardless of where they served and it was composed with continuity. They were of utmost importance to the individual as they evidenced their qualifications and importantly the accumulative hours spent flying operationally. The frequency of submission for inspection and endorsement meant that they were handled often and the card beneath the covering soon became exposed on the corners and the spines became worn. The log books inevitably had the owner's name written on the page edges in order that he could quickly locate his particular book in a large stack after assessment or monthly inspection.

Pilot flying log books were larger in dimension than the observer and air gunner books as they required more detail to be recorded. As you would expect within military service, these books were identified by the unique reference numbers of Form 1767 for observers and Form 414 for pilots. Those men who flew longer periods of service frequently bound additional log books together. The individual's promotion through the ranks was evidenced in the front pages. Lines were drawn through the lower ranks as they progressed towards a commission and subsequent officer status.

Log books were not to be carried in the air. However, this was not strictly adhered to as some Luftwaffe records make mention of such books being recovered from crash locations. Any unfortunate individual who failed to return from operations was regarded as missing in action. Usually, their log books would be dispatched to an Air Ministry central depository. Should any of these men survive, evade capture and then return to their squadron, the log books were always accessible and were effectively reissued. In cases where pilots or air crew were confirmed as killed in action, or lost their lives during training accidents, their log books were often, but certainly not always, offered to their next of kin. A small, printed slip confirming this was normally included in the book.

The vast majority of log books were retained by the Air Ministry on completion of the recipient's service and placed into storage as official documents. The accumulation of logs was substantial and the Air Ministry later let it become known that they could be returned to the individuals upon application. By 1959, in spite of public announcements, the vast majority of log books remained unclaimed. The problem of retention and storage was placed before the Paper Committee, who recommended the destruction of the log books, bar a few selected specimens. This decision induced further announcements, including the BBC broadcast that log books not claimed by 15 September 1960 would be destroyed. Following the advised deadline, the decision of the committee was put into effect. Some historically important log books were selected for preservation but the nation lost thousands upon thousands of them. Those that were claimed or retained by former servicemen represent valuable time capsules of operational duty. They are without distortion of fact or misinterpretation.

Much of this book has been composed around the entries made by Flight Lieutenant Julian Zuromski in his official log book. The survival of his log is an important historical document, and the many signatures within its pages are from men who were required as squadron leaders to endorse the records as being correct. The signatures applied are from both Polish and British commanding officers from within every squadron or unit in which Zuromski served. Many signatories, in particular the Polish commanders, may well have held a mindset of resentfulness towards those who occupied their cherished homeland at that time. Embitterment is a human instinct that can be complex and challenging to understand, however in this instance it may be easy to commiserate with. Open minds and reserved opinions are required before judgement, because only then can a balanced of perspective be achieved, something that is required when reading this book.

Zuromski flew Spitfires in the RAF and fought against a Nazi regime that wanted to destroy much more than territorial boundaries across Europe. There are opportunities to read accounts of the men Zuromski served alongside, fighting Polish oppression and their fates. Zuromski fell from the sky into the hands of his enemy wearing the uniform of an RAF officer, and he then grasped a unique opportunity to also fight against what he regarded as an equal enemy, the Bolshevik communist. The Russian Revolution had enabled Lenin to establish a communist grip over Russia. It led to the creation of a party-driven state that became increasingly authoritarian. Zuromski's father had fought against the initial Bolshevik intrusion into Poland. This would be something that became a justified reason for the Russians to execute him in 1940. His son Julian, while a prisoner of the Third Reich, elected to oppose the Bolsheviks using political propaganda radio transmissions from Berlin. His simple comments against the Bolshevik communist ethos were statements he understandably had few reservations about advocating. At a later time, he embarked upon his personal escape from the control of his captors. It was a personal but driven route to freedom and ultimately he held an eventual desire to return to fly with the RAF once more. However, a spotlight of suspicion fell upon Zuromski and he was suspected of collaborating with the enemy.

The archives relevant to the prosecution and investigation of men suspected of assisting the enemy were obtained from The National Archives. These intelligence files form a significant part of conjecture and evidence within this book. The Judge Advocate General was the ultimate decision maker and prosecutor, assisted by a team of six Assistant Judge Advocates who presided over legal proceedings and assessing evidence with investigations. The Judge Advocate General was the Judicial Head of the Military Service Courts, appointed through the independent Judicial Appointments Commission from the ranks of experienced barristers. When conducting a trial, they wore legal robes, a bench wig and black gown, with a sash in army red and navy blue with air-force blue edges. The Judge Advocate General's decision making, and the evidence heard within the Dulag Luft trials, is included in the hope of understanding the life of Zuromski as a prisoner of war.

CHAPTER 1

THE ZUROMSKI FAMILY 1918-1940

Julian Kazimierz Zuromski was born into a Russian Roman
Catholic family who were living in Borysagtepsk, western Russia.
His father was Kazimierz Zuromski, born 10 June 1895 in Bilca,
on the Romanian border with Ukraine. His mother was Taisa, née
Sidelnikoff, born 8 October 1899.

Julian was born in 1918 shortly after the Bolsheviks came to power
and the Russian Revolution evolved. One of the first concentration
camps in Russia for non-compliant individuals and aliens was
constructed in the Borysoglebsk district where the family resided.
Bolshevik was Russian terminology for 'members of the majority',
one of two factions of the Russian Social Democratic Labour Party,
the other being the Menshevik (minority) faction. The Bolsheviks
were a driven militant party that deployed the slogans of peace, bread
and land for the peasants and eventually became the Communist
Party, which openly advocated the nationalisation of land and assets.
During the Russian Revolution, the Bolsheviks, led by Vladimir
Lenin, seized power in November 1917, and destroyed the previous
tradition of czarist rule over Russia. The significant Polish population
in czarist Russia had been the result of Poland's partition in the late
eighteenth century, with the government consistently pressing for the
Polish subjects to become Russian.

1

Kazimierz Zuromski and his family relocated to the village of Bilka near the town of Zhytomyr in north-western Ukraine. The Teteriv River was in relatively close proximity, situated west of the Ukrainian capital Kyiv. The Zhytomyr region became an area where Ukrainian forces and pro-Bolshevik elements who were seeking to establish and expand Soviet rule came into conflict. Kazimierz Zuromski had served under imperial rule in the Russian army since 1908. He had been in the Cadet Corps in Kyiv and received training at the Military Cavalry School in Yelizavetgrad. Men from cavalry units of the Kyiv, Odessa, and Kharkiv military districts attended this military school. After two years of instruction, the cadets were normally promoted to company-grade officers and sent to the cavalry or horse artillery for further military experience. Kazimierz Zuromski had been promoted to second lieutenant in 1915, and to lieutenant in 1916.

In December 1917, nine months after the demise of the Russian monarchy, the army officer corps finally fell. On 17 December 1917, the Petrograd-based Council of People's Commissars issued an ultimatum demanding that Bolshevik troops be granted the legal right to be stationed on Ukrainian soil. The demand was rejected, resulting in the Bolsheviks launching an offensive on to Ukraine territory. The Civil War induced some foreign intervention but the roots of communism had been established and Polish territory was one of its primary objectives. Only after the First World War when Russia lost its Polish provinces, did the number of Poles living in Russia diminish.

Kazimierz Zuromski continued to serve in the corps and commanded a squadron of the 3rd Silesian Uhlan Regiment, a cavalry unit of the Second Polish Republic from 1917 to 1939. The regiment fought in the post-First World War, 1917 to 1920, war for the restoration of Polish territories.

Another Polish Army officer, Kazimierz Bolesław Jozef Halicki, would feature in Julian's later life. Halicki, born in 1894 in Augustów, was conscripted into the Russian army in 1914. In a similar service to Julian's father, he served in the Polish cavalry, taking part in the battles of Volhynia, Podlasie, Polesie, Galicia and Cieszyn Silesia in the 2nd Uhlan Regiment. Following the First World War, Captain Halicki continued to serve in the Polish Army.

It was January 1919 when the reorganisation of the Polish Army took place. The existent cavalry squadrons were formed into cavalry regiments, which formed under six cavalry brigades. Later a seventh brigade was added and some of the brigades were joined into two semi-independent cavalry divisions. Julian's father had served in the borderland cavalry squadron of Major Jaworski before taking part in the Polish-Soviet War in the ranks of the 19th Volhynian Uhlan Regiment. The newly recreated Polish cavalry units were trained in both cavalry tactics and in trench warfare. After the Polish-Soviet War broke out, they were among the most competent combat-ready troops in Polish service. The cavalry was a decisive weapon in breaking the enemy lines and encircling the Russian units. The smaller cavalry detachments were attached to every infantry brigade and served as reconnaissance and support units. The Polish Uhlans or light cavalry were armed with lances, sabres and pistols, and fought many battles in the twentieth century. The most famous of these, the Battle of Komarów, took place during the Polish-Bolshevik war. Polish cavalry moved using horses but fought using infantry tactics on the battlefronts.

Following Ukraine's signature of the peace treaty of Brest-Litovsk and the entry of German and Austrian troops into the conflict in late February 1918, the combined forces removed the Bolshevik troops out of Ukraine, regaining Kyiv on 1 March 1918. Soviet Russia had little choice but to comply with the articles of the Treaty of Brest-Litovsk and a preliminary peace with the Ukrainian government was signed on 12 June 1918.

Soviet pressure on Latvia, Lithuania and Estonia became an insidious, graduated process. The three Baltic republics, which had achieved their independence during the Russian Civil War of 1918 to

1920, remained steadfast while the Soviets bolstered themselves and started to undermine the Treaty of Riga, which had officially ended the Russian-Polish War of 1920. The treaty, which gave Poland parts of Belorussia and Ukraine, remained in place until 1939.

In 1921 Ukrainian, Belorussian, Bolsheviks and Red Army soldiers crossed the Polish-Soviet border to attack local strategic targets, causing nuisance damage. This caused the formation of the Border Protection Corps or the Polish Korpus Ochrony Pogranicza, referenced as the KOP. It was a military formation of the Second Polish Republic created in 1924 to defend the country's eastern borders against armed Soviet incursions and local bandits. Russia passed a resolution at the Comintern's 5th Congress for East Galicia to be incorporated into the Soviet Union in 1924. Poland had laid claim to this territory over extended and lengthy negotiations.

Eventually, in 1939, Estonia conceded to the Soviets and both Latvia and Lithuania were compelled to admit Russian forces on to its soil. Shortly after all three Baltic states were officially proclaimed Soviet Socialist Republics. Further to the south, Soviet troops invaded the Romanian provinces of Bessarabia and northern Bukovina and incorporated them into the Soviet Republic of Moldavia.

Kazimierz Zuromski had been confirmed in the rank of captain with seniority on 1 June 1919. The service against the Bolsheviks had seen the award of the Order of Virtuti Militari, medal number 4196 bestowed upon him on 11 June 1920. The recommendation for the award was instigated by Lieutenant Colonel Luczynski. Zuromski carried out a counterattack recklessly so that a larger unit of Bolsheviks were temporarily forced to retreat. Thanks to this action, carried out with great initiative under strong artillery fire and at the risk to his own life, the Polish troops had the opportunity to withdraw.

The Treaty of Riga was a peace treaty that resulted in the end of fighting on the Bolshevik front. On 12 October 1920, the preliminaries were signed and the final treaty was signed on 18 March 1921.

It included provisions of the defined borders between Poland and Soviet Russia. The Soviets undertook to respect the rights of Poles living in Soviet Russia and return to Poland cultural property seized during the annexations. The Treaty of Riga concluded on 18 March 1921, and provided for the bulk of Ukraine to remain a Soviet republic, although substantial portions of Belorussia and Ukraine were relinquished to Poland. By stopping the communist invasion in 1920, Poland had defended Europe against Bolshevism. However, Germany would subsequently capitalise on the Polish bravery and seek to destroy Poland and its people in the coming years.

In 1921 Lieutenant Kazimierz Zuromski was assigned to the 20th King Jan III Sobieski Uhlan Regiment. This regiment had been formed in 1920 and was stationed at Rzeszów in the south-eastern corner of Poland, adjoining the territories of Ukraine and Slovakia. In August 1924 Zuromski was transferred to the 26th Cavalry Regiment of Greater Poland Uhlans and for the following six years he served in the 19th Uhlan Regiment and the 2nd Mounted Rifle Regiment in Hrubieszów in south-eastern Poland. During the spring of 1929, a new reorganisation of the cavalry units took place, with three of the four cavalry divisions being disbanded and new brigades created from their regiments. Kazimierz's son Julian was now eleven years of age and the family had grown with the birth of another son, Edward.

Similar to Julian's father, in 1920 Captain Kazimierz Halicki was also awarded the Order of Virtuti Militari. Promoted to major, he was appointed deputy commander of the 20th Uhlan Regiment where Julian's father was serving at that time. In 1926, by order of the Department of Cavalry of the Ministry of Military Affairs, the Cavalry Reserve Cadet School was established as part of the Cavalry School Camp and Major Halicki was appointed as the school commander. The school began operating in September 1926 and the student cadets included graduates who, having passed their secondary school exams, could volunteer to join the army. The training lasted eight months and field service skills on horseback were still regarded as fundamental for the Polish Army. Graduates of the Cavalry Reserve Cadet School received the rank of senior uhlan or platoon cadet of the cavalry reserve.

In January 1927, Kazimierz Halicki was promoted to the rank of lieutenant colonel and returned to service as deputy commander of the 7th Lublin Uhlan Regiment. Julian's father, Kazimierz, was at this time serving in the 2nd Mounted Rifles Regiment in Hrubieszów. In September 1930, Captain Zuromski left his posting and on 28 February 1931, it appears that he retired, residing in the Poznań district with his wife and two sons, Julian and Edward. He registered as a responsible person for reserve military deployment in the event of emergency or wartime deployment. Kazimierz Zuromski was the recipient of the Silver Cross of the Military Order of Virtuti Militari, the Cross of Valour twice, the Commemorative Medal for the War of 1918–1921 and the Medal of the Decade of Regained Independence.

The Polish Army began to mobilise its forces in March 1939 when Germany and Hungary invaded what was once Czechoslovakia. It is unknown if Captain Kazimierz Zuromski was engaged in any aspects of the mobilisations. The occupation of Bohemia and Moravia by Germany on 15 March 1939 was a flagrant breach of the Munich Agreement of September 1938 between Hitler, Mussolini and the British and French Prime Ministers in Munich. This was an agreement by which Czechoslovakia was required to acquiesce in the cession of the Sudetenland to Germany. This agreement was brought back to Great Britain by the British Prime Minister, signed by himself and Hitler, expressing the hope that for the future, Britain and Germany might live without war. In light of the breach of the Munich Agreement, Great Britain gave an assurance to Poland on 31 March 1939, that in the event of any action that clearly threatened Polish independence, and which the Polish government accordingly considered it vital to resist with their national forces, Great Britain would feel itself bound at once to lend Poland all the support in its power. The French government took the same stand.

On 23 August 1939, the Foreign Ministers of Germany and the Soviet Union signed a non-aggression treaty. This became known as the Molotov-Ribbentrop Pact, which included an additional secret protocol whereby the parties agreed to settle the territorial map of their interests in the event of any future territorial and political rearrangement of the then independent countries of Central and Eastern Europe, including Poland. According to the protocol, the eastern part of Polish territory was to fall to the Soviet Union. On 31 August 1939, a general mobilisation was announced in Poland, the first step in preparation in the event of war with Germany. However, the next day German troops attacked Poland, effectively commencing a sequence of events starting the Second World War.

After the publication of the news of Herrvon Ribbentrop's visit to Moscow, British Prime Minister Chamberlain wrote a letter to Hitler making a clear statement of the British obligations to Poland:

> Whatever may prove to be the nature of the German-Soviet Agreement, it cannot alter Great Britain's obligation.

He added that:

> it has been alleged that, if His Majesty's Government had made their position more clear in 1914, the great catastrophe would have been avoided. Whether or not there is any force in that allegation, His Majesty's Government are resolved that on this occasion there shall be no such tragic misunderstanding.
>
> Having thus made our position perfectly clear, I wish to repeat to you my conviction that war between our two peoples would be the greatest calamity that could occur.

Hitler replied:

> The question of the treatment of European problems on a
> peaceful basis is not a decision which rests with Germany,
> but primarily on those who since the crime committed by the
> Versailles Diktat have stubbornly and consistently opposed
> any peaceful revision. Only after a change of spirit on the
> part of the responsible Powers can there be any real change
> in the relationship between England and Germany.

On 1 September, German military forces invaded Poland. The
following day, the Prime Minister made a statement in the House of
Commons, in the course of which he said that no answer had been
received to a message sent to the German government the previous day
requesting the cessation of German aggression and the withdrawal of
German troops from Poland. The following day, 3 September, Britain
and France declared war on Germany.

On 17 September, the Soviet Red Army marched into Polish
territory, allegedly acting to protect the Ukrainians and Belarusians
living in the eastern part of Poland because the Polish state had
collapsed under the German aggression and Poland could no longer
guarantee the security of its own citizens. Stalin in fact invaded the
part of Poland already granted to him under the Molotov-Ribbentrop
Pact. The Russian fighting forces surging into Poland were made
up largely of ethnic Ukrainians. Following the Russian invasion of
Poland, Germany broadcast in English a joint Nazi-Soviet declaration:

> The German and Russian Governments have declared
> that in accordance with the spirit of the Russian-German
> pact, the action of their armies consists in the restoration
> of law and order in Poland which has been destroyed by
> the disintegration of the Polish state. Numerous meetings
> in the Soviet Union have passed resolutions endorsing

the policy of the Government. The White Russian and Ukrainian minorities regard themselves as coming back into the fold of the Russian family. The Pravda says that in accordance with Soviet ideals, Russia is remaining neutral and has only liberated brethren from Polish oppression.

In 1939 Poland had only one effective motorised brigade, while a second was in transition, both based upon a traditional cavalry brigade. Despite possessing light motorised equipment, they were identified as cavalry brigades. The Russian Ukrainian commander, Semyon Timoshenko, was himself from a cavalry corps background and had studied at the Soviet Military Academy. He commanded a significant strength of force. His men were told by their political commissars that they were entering Poland not as conquerors, but as liberators. Leaflets were distributed explaining that he had come to rid them of their oppressive Polish rulers.

The Polish Army defended valiantly. In September 1939, there was an estimated sixteen traditional cavalry charges by the Polish Uhlans or light cavalry. At Krojanty they surprised German troops in an assault that could be regarded as effective as it was reported as having halted an advance. The battles of Mokra, Lasy Królewskie and Husynne were bloody engagements. At Krasnobród, the Polish cavalry engaged with German cavalry on horseback. Uhlans typically wore a double-breasted jacket and a distinctive square-topped Polish lancer cap. The Italian official press agency correspondent Mario Appelius apparently witnessed and reported upon the Polish cavalry charge in Wólka Węglowa on 19 September 1939, an action where the Polish cavalry cleared the way for their army to retreat. He reported in the newspaper *Il Popolo d'Italia*, which was founded and owned by the Italian dictator Mussolini:

There was a heroic advance of several hundreds of Polish Uhlans who all of a sudden appeared from the bushes.

They advanced with their banner. All German machine guns stopped shooting, only artillery was covering the field with shells over a distance of 300 metres in front of the German defence. Poles were attacking like it was in mediaeval pictures with their commander with his sabre raised. The distance between the attacking cavalry and the wall of German shelling was diminishing with every second. It was unthinkable to continue this charge against certain death. But the Poles went through …

Appelius eventually came to voice criticism of the Italian fascist regime, something that resulted in Mussolini dismissing him from his position of influence. In Germany, Hans Fritzsche was the director de facto of the Reich press until 1942. He controlled the newspapers and radio channels, which consistently fed political propaganda to the population.

During the first few weeks of the war, in Great Britain the single BBC station available was the Home Service. Daily broadcast of several hours of recorded music was supplement by ten daily news bulletins, at least an hour of public service announcements and ministerial broadcasts. This and the daily newspapers were the only avenue to gather news of the developing war. The BBC Overseas Service was used as an attempt to counter Nazi propaganda, but opinion was often voiced that the British public got many reports on the radio from Germany and very few home reports. Propaganda was a valuable weapon in itself, which was well recognised by Germany.

Poland's defence against the German strong advances were ineffective by virtue of their strength, surprise and effectiveness. The Soviet Bolsheviks' strength on the second front was just as effective. The Polish commander-in-chief, Marshal Edward Rydz Smigły, ordered his men to head to Hungary and Romania in an effort to save lives. Nearly 40,000 Polish military personnel were successful and were interned in Hungary and Romania. An estimated

8,000 Polish airmen, representing a significant proportion of the Polish air personnel in 1939, were located in Romania and a much smaller representative number were in Lithuania. However, immense numbers of Polish military personnel were captured by the Bolsheviks, with approximately 125,000 uniformed personnel held from within the territory they had invaded on the eastern sectors of Poland.

A high proportion of those detained were handed directly to the German forces. They were effectively Polish personnel from within the pre-agreed territories allocated to Germany. The two belligerents shared both the spoils and the captured people of Poland. The Russian forces were at that time very focused on securing both military personnel and others assumed or regarded as a threat to communism. Captain Kazimierz Zuromski was taken prisoner by the Soviets, something that was to put in motion terrible consequences for his life. Whether a Polish soldier was captured by German or Russian troops in many cases was to become literally a matter life or death. Captain Zuromski, as an anti-communist, was imprisoned in Starobielsk.

On 9 October 1939, the Russian forces commenced actions to identify and confine all Polish officer corps personnel at secure guarded camps at Kozelsk in Russia, and Starobielsk in Ukraine. The Polish non-military functionaries, including police officers and prison guards, were detained in Ostashkov, Russia. All leading Polish intellectuals were regarded as potential enemies against the Soviet Union and they were likewise selected for segregation and imprisonment. The Russian forces released most of the privates and non-commissioned officers of Polish origin from within the areas occupied by their forces.

Under a prisoner of war exchange agreement, those captured from the territories occupied by the Germans were handed over to the Third Reich, while Germany handed over captured Polish soldiers that were mainly of Ukrainian and Belarusian nationality from territories annexed by the Russian forces. Both the Germans and the

Soviets had begun arrest, deport, and execute orders against Polish intellectuals in their occupied zones of Poland. Their policies differed in no significant way.

Russia annexed all of the territory under its control and in November 1939 declared that the estimated 13.5 million Polish citizens who lived there were henceforth Soviet citizens. It is thought that 17,000 Polish military officers were identified and imprisoned by the Bolshevik NKVD, known as the People's Commissariat for Internal Affairs, the predecessor of the KGB. They instigated four significant deportation campaigns from within the Polish territories it had annexed. The definitive numbers cannot be established but an estimated 320,000 Poles were exiled deep in the Russian homelands primarily for forced labour. They were taken by cattle trucks to the most inhospitable and isolated areas within Russia. They were secured in camps known as gulags and kolkhozes where conditions were appalling, with sub-zero temperatures and where work quotas had to be fulfilled to receive even a meagre ration of food. As a result of these conditions, many perished from starvation and disease.

Kazimierz Halicki, the commander of the reserve of the Volhynian Cavalry Brigade in Hrubieszów, could be regarded as more fortunate, falling into the hands of the German forces. He commanded a cavalry group of six horse squadrons, two cyclist squadrons and a heavy machine gun squadron. The Volhynian Brigade fought as resolutely as possible and it was not until 25 September 1940, when Halicki fell into German captivity.

The camp in Starobielsk held Polish officers, together with civilian prisoners thought to be a threat to the Soviet rule of power. Officers of rank, i.e. colonels, lieutenant colonels, majors, captains and cavalry captains, were specifically transported to the camp. Many of those remaining were detained by the Soviets and sent on to other internment camps. These mass internments were intended to undermine Poland's will to resist communist domination.

THE ZUROMSKI FAMILY 1918-1940

On 5 March 1940, Lavrentiy Beria, head of the NKVD, wrote to Stalin, Secretary General of the Russian Communist Party, proposing that the men secured in the special camps should be declared guilty of offences against Russia and be deemed as threats to communism. He urged that approval be given for the shooting of Polish prisoners of war on the grounds that they were all enemies of the Soviet authorities. The proposal specified the prison camps that held 14,736 former Polish officers, officials, landowners, police officers, gendarmes, prison guards, settlers and intelligence officers, as well as the prisons in the western regions of Ukraine and Belarus. These accommodated a further 18,632 former Polish citizens who had been arrested, all of whom were regarded as threats to the communist state.

Among the 3,845 men held in Starobielsk camp in March 1940, there were 1,303 Polish officers and 2,231 reserve officers, including 600 members of the air force and thirty warrant officers and cadets. There were also more than twenty university lecturers, 400 doctors, several hundred lawyers and engineers, teachers, writers and journalists, and many staff members of the Polish reserve army.

The Politburo of the Central Committee of the Russian Communist Party was the highest governing body of the Soviet Union. They took the decision to implement special procedures and employ capital punishment by the shooting of the 14,736 former Polish officers held in the prisoner camps. This decision was signed on 5 March by all the members of the Politburo, including Stalin, Voroshilov, Mikoyan, Molotov, Kalinin and Kaganovich.

The Kozelsk camp was in western Russia, 150 miles south-east of Smolensk. The site was an old, dilapidated monastery and the Polish officers were interrogated at the site. During the first week of April 1940, the NKVD counted 4,599 prisoners, predominantly military officers in the camp. The liquidation of Kozelsk began on 3 April 1940. On that day the first transport of seventy-four Polish officers was taken to Gnezdovo, and from there to the Katyn Forest. Similar transports departed almost every day in April. The last transport was sent from the camp on 20 May. The prisoners were escorted by the 136th Independent Battalion of the NKVD Transport Troops stationed in Smolensk. They travelled by train from Kozelsk to Gnezdovo station, near Smolensk. Then they were taken to the Katyn Forest, just west of Gnezdovo, shot and thrown into mass graves.

On 8 April 1940, the number of prisoners in the Ostashkov camp in eastern Russia was 6,364. In the Starobielsk camp on Stolobny Island in Lake Seliger, there were 3,894. Starobielsk camp was in the north-east of Ukraine. The site was an old monastery with two churches and barracks. Starobielsk held the greatest number of high-ranking officers, including eight generals. On 5 April 1940 came the first liquidation of Starobielsk. From that day until 25 April, transports of between 60 and 260 prisoners were sent to UNKVD Kharkiv oblast in eastern Ukraine every day. The UNKVD was the administration unit of the secret police.

The killings of camp prisoners took place during April and May 1940. Prisoners from Starobielsk were shot in the Kharkiv prison and their bodies were buried near the village of Piatykhatky. The police officers from Ostashkov were killed in Kalinin prison and buried in Mednoye. For various reasons it appears that nearly 400 men were selected or excluded from the execution procedures and placed in Yukhnov internment camp on the Kola Peninsula, in the extreme north-west area of Russia, It held more than 2,000 prisoners, mostly Poles, Ukrainians and Belarussians, who were put to work forcibly. Starvation rations barely kept inmates alive. NKVD propaganda glorifying the achievements of the communist system was imposed upon the prisoners, all of whom had committed no crimes; they were simply regarded as intellectual and anti-communist.

The circumstances of the execution of the prisoners from the prisons in western Ukraine and Belarus remain unclear. However, by the spring of 1940 the prison camps were effectively empty. The prisoners from the three special camps had been murdered, shot on the orders approved by the Politburo on 5 March 1940. There were

14,552 executions, a number generally accepted by historians in the post-war era.

Captain Kazimierz Zuromski was murdered by the People's Commissariat for Internal Affairs. He was executed in Kharkiv and buried in a mass grave among hundreds of fellow Polish casualties that had been held at Starobielsk. The executions were carried out in the late evening and during the night. The bodies were loaded on to trucks and taken to a forest near Piatykhatky, near Kharkiv. The surveys of the death pits conducted fifty years after the crimes had been committed revealed that 4,302 Polish soldiers were buried in the Kharkiv Forest. Among thousands like them, Julian and his brother had lost their father to an atrocity of war. Julian as a young man had witnessed sufficient to harbour the need to fight both the Bolsheviks and the German state that had consumed much of Europe for its own desires and objectives regardless of boarders or humanity. As a military cadet in the Polish Air Force, his life journey so far had no doubt created significant embitterment. He was uncertain of the events that had befallen his father, who had been arrested and removed from society simply because he had been a decorated officer who had fought in the Polish-Soviet War.

The independent Polish state had been eliminated, and its territory seized by the Third Reich and the Soviet Union. The onslaught of NKVD executions upon the creative potential of intellectual and military men was undertaken to prevent a sovereign Polish state being rebuilt. The German plan was for Poland to be totally wiped away and its people to act as slaves until their eventual elimination as a race within forty years or thereabouts.

Julian Zuromski's mother Taisa survived the Russian onslaught upon Poland. It appears that prior to 1940 she had remarried, her second husband being Kazimierz Halicki, the commander of the reserve of the Volhynian Cavalry Brigade. Halicki had been exceptionally lucky to have avoided the Russian retribution cast upon the Polish military. Having been imprisoned by the German forces, he had been transported to Oflag VII-A at Murnau in Bavaria, along with an initial intake of 1,000 Polish officers captured in the September 1939 campaign.

Following Germany's invasion of its former ally, the Soviet Union on 22 June 1941, it turned erstwhile allies and accomplices into enemies, and vice versa. A Polish-Russian military agreement was signed on 14 August 1941 that granted the Polish prisoners of Russia an amnesty, allowing them the freedom to leave both the prisoner of war camps and gulags, and also the distant kolkhozes in the remote Russian territories.

In 1943 the German Army discovered mass graves of murdered Polish Army officers in the Katyn Forest. This information was seized upon by Germany's Propaganda Minister, Joseph Goebbels, who embarked upon a cynical publicity campaign to spread before the world the perils of Bolshevism. Berlin radio announced the grim find on 13 April. The Soviet Union denied all responsibility for the Katyn massacre and placed the blame on Nazi Germany. The long and gory accounts given of the findings in the forest by the Germans were clearly determined efforts to convince listeners throughout Europe of the horrific fate that awaited them at the hands of the Bolsheviks.

The Polish government in exile in London asked the International Red Cross to investigate. This was supported by Germany but opposed by the Soviet Union. The Red Cross declined to investigate without the support of all the interested parties. However, with the consent of the Polish government in exile, the Technical Committee of the Polish Red Cross were authorised to operate in Katyn and the Germans established an International Medical Commission. They invited leading experts in forensic medicine from nine countries of German occupied Europe and one from neutral Switzerland to conduct their own investigation into the mass graves. This commission reported in May 1943:

> The way in which the hands of the victims were tied is similar to that observed in the case of corpses of Russian

civilians, also exhumed in Katyn Forest, but buried much earlier ... The Commission observed that the uniforms of the exhumed bodies, especially in respect of buttons, badges of rank, decorations, boots ... etc. were typically Polish. The uniforms in question were winter ones ... [concluding] that the victims were buried in the uniforms worn by them up to the moment of their death ... From statements made by witnesses, as well as from letters, diaries, newspapers, etc. found on the bodies, it follows that the executions took place in March and April 1940.

The Germans began their excavation of the mass graves in March 1943. They found 3,000 bodies in the first grave. The Polish Red Cross Commission later identified 2,733 out of more than 4,243 exhumed bodies.

Stalin had broken off relations with the Poles in April 1943 when the Germans found the graves at Katyn and accused the Russians of murdering the Polish officers. The Polish government was put in an impossible situation, unable to accuse the Russians outright. There were also pressing issues across many fronts. For example, in early 1943, the Polish High Command was advised that in the Middle East approximately 1,500 Polish boys aged between twelve and fifteen had reached the area as orphans or assumed orphans. Many had lost their parents in the invasion of Poland by Soviet Russia, or had been separated while held in various camps.

A report by the German police in June 1943 stated that:

The work of exhuming, examining and identifying the bodies of Polish officers came to an end on 7 June 1943 ... The seven mass graves of murdered Polish officers which have been cleared cover a relatively small area. Of 4,143 exhumed bodies, 2,815 have been definitely identified ... In many cases identity cards, documents and considerable sums in zloty banknotes were sewn into the legs of their boots … From the translation of diaries, of memoirs, and other notes found with the bodies, it was proved that the officers who had been taken prisoner by the Soviet army in 1939, were sent to various camps. Kozielsk, Starobiels, Ostashkov, Putiviel, Bolotov, Pavlishchev Bor, Shepyetovka, Gorodok.

The majority of those killed in Katyn Forest had been in the Kozielsk camp (south-east of Smolensk on the Smolensk-Tambov railway line). With a few exceptions, all the bodies evidenced pistol shots in the head and many of the dead men had their hands tied behind their back.

The precise numbers of murdered prisoners were given in a note that Alexander Shelepin, Chairman of the State Security Committee, wrote on 3 March 1959 to Nikita Khrushchev, Secretary General of the USSR Communist Party:

> All in all, on the basis of decisions of the Soviet NKVD's special troika, a total of 21,857 persons were shot, 4,421 of them in Katyn Forest (Smolenskiy district), 3,820 in the Starobelsk camp near Kharkov, 6,311 in the Ostashkov camp (Kalininskiy district) and 7,305 in other camps and prisons in western Ukraine and Belarus.

A joint committee of historians was formed in 1987 to explain further the anomalies surrounding the facts in the history of these murders. The Russian researchers Natalia Lebedeva, Vladimir Volkov, Yuri Zoria, and Valentina Parsadanova fortunately found some relevant NKVD documents and compared them with the German exhumation papers to expose a definitive correlation of facts.

On 13 April 1990, Soviet President Mikhail Gorbachev finally admitted that the 25,000 Polish prisoners of war killed in the spring of 1940 were murdered by the Soviet Secret Police (NKVD). Fifty years of denial were finally over.

The Soviet – later Russian – Katyn investigation, begun by the Soviet Military Prosecutor's Office in 1990, dragged on for years. In September 2004 it was unofficially made known that it had discontinued the investigation and that no one would be charged with any crime. Finally, on 11 March 2005, the head of the office, Aleksandr Savenkov, announced that the investigation had been closed and no one would be condemned because all the accused were dead. He qualified Katyn as a 'common murder' subject to the statute of limitations.

This statement caused outrage in Poland. In January 2006, the senior Russian military prosecutor rejected a request for rehabilitation on political grounds, submitted years previously by the widow of an officer shot at Katyn, because documentation indicating the relevant paragraph of the Soviet Criminal Code had been destroyed. Thus, he ignored the published Politburo decision of 5 March 1940, citing political reasons, and confirmed that the prisoner of war files had been destroyed in 1959. The conclusion was that there was no evidence that genocide had been committed by the Soviet Union against Poland. The Katyn massacre thus remains a crime without punishment. The reference 'rehabilitation on political grounds references' applies to those who had been repressed or criminally prosecuted without due basis. It restored the person to the state of acquittal. In many cases, rehabilitation was posthumous, as thousands of victims had been executed.

On 26 November 2010, the State Duma, the lower chamber of the Russian Parliament, adopted a statement entitled 'On the Katyn tragedy and its victims', which read partly as follows:

> Seventy years ago, thousands of Polish citizens held in
> the prisoner-of-war camps of the NKVD of the USSR
> and in prisons in the western regions of the Ukrainian
> SSR and Belarusian SSR were shot dead.

The official Soviet propaganda attributed responsibility for this atrocity, which has been given the collective name of the Katyn tragedy, to Nazi criminals … In the early 1990s our country made great strides towards the establishment of the truth about the Katyn tragedy. It was recognised that the mass extermination of Polish citizens on USSR territory during the Second World War had been an arbitrary act by the totalitarian State …

Copies of many documents which had been kept in the closed archives of the Politburo of the Communist Party of the Soviet Union have already been handed over to the Polish side. The members of the State Duma believe that this work must be carried on. It is necessary to continue studying the archives, verifying the lists of victims, restoring the good names of those who perished in Katyn and other places, and uncovering the circumstances of the tragedy …

The published materials that have been kept for many years in secret archives not only demonstrate the scale of this terrible tragedy but also attest to the fact that the Katyn crime was carried out on the direct orders of Stalin and other Soviet leaders.

The fight for the truth and dignified commemoration of the victims of the Katyn crimes committed by the Soviet regime on officers of the Polish Army and other functionaries of the Second Polish Republic was unreservedly complex and deceitful. Nevertheless, exhumation from the actual death pits and the relocating of the found remains did provide some definitive answers.

Between 1998 and 2012, four cemeteries were constructed in Kharkiv, Katyn, Mednoye and Bykivnia. The Polish War Cemetery in Katyn was solemnly opened and consecrated on 28 July 2000. The bodies of 4,415 prisoners of war from the Kozelsk camp, murdered in April and May 1940 in Smolensk, now lie in this cemetery.

Julian Zuromski's father was among the bodies of those who had been put in the ground at Katyn. He is now officially recognised as one of the many who suffered such terrifying circumstances in the purge by the Soviet leadership in 1940. His remains were eventually identified and were reburied in the Cemetery of Victims of Totalitarianism in Piatichatki, Kharkiv.

The Polish Minister of National Defence announced in Warsaw on 9 November 2007 a posthumous promotion for Kazimierz Zuromski to the rank of major.

Back to 1940, Julian's Zuromski's mother Taisa appears to have made her way as a displaced person from Poland, travelling south into France. It would be a safe assumption that Julian had proffered advice or possibly assisted his mother in replicating his movements through France to reach the southern regions in a period whereby the fall of France became a reality. The French southern ports were identified as evacuation centres for escaping Allied service personnel and historical documentation confirms that they also evacuated civilians.

Julian Zuromski sailed from Bordeaux on 17 June 1940 with a group of both Polish and Czechoslovaks and the vessel made for Falmouth. His mother at that time was also in southern France. On 23 June 1940 the British destroyer HMS *Keppel* departed Port-Vendres for Sète, both of which were French Mediterranean ports, to organise the evacuation of Czechoslovak, Polish military personnel and refugees. The British destroyer HMS *Velox* was sent to Port-Vendres from Gibraltar, arriving at 0600 hours on 23 June. Involved in the evacuation of Port-Vendres and Sète were the British steamers *Apapa*, *Coultarn*, *Gartbrattan*, *Viceroy of India*, *Ashcrest*, *Saltersgate*, *Northmoor*, *Neuralia* and the Egyptian steamers *Rod El Farag* and *Mohamed Ali El-Kebir*.

At Port-Vendres approximately 200 Czechoslovak and Polish airmen had gathered. They had been serving with the French Air Force mainly in the Bordeaux area. These men, together with a small group of Belgium airmen and other refugees, boarded *Apapa*. One of the Polish pilots was Stanisław Wandzilak, a student from the same graduation course at Deblin with Julian Zuromski. Stanisław, born in 1917, obtained his high school leaving examination in 1937 and had gliding lessons as part of military aviation training. He underwent infantry training before being admitted into the Aviation Cadet School in Deblin in January 1938. In September 1939 he escaped to Romania, where in October he got to Beirut on a Greek vessel ship and then on to a French vessel to Marseille. Once in France he joined the Polish air base at Lyon-Bron. On 1 March 1940, he moved to Étampes for training on French aircraft, after which the pilots were sent to Lyon and then Salon. In June 1940 they flew north to Clermont-Ferrand, where on 19 June orders to evacuate allowed some of the pilots to fly south to Port-Vendres. The British steamer *Apapa* was berthed at Port-Vendres and the Polish pilots managed to board for the departure to Gibraltar on 26 June 1940. Thereafter the convoy passage was to England.

By sheer coincidence, Zuromski's mother, Taisa was also on board *Apapa*, having been accepted as a refugee. A much later connection between these two people would create another turn of unexpected events. It is possible that Zuromski's mother made efforts to communicate with the Polish pilots who had been on board *Apapa* in the hope of finding news about her son's whereabouts. Stanisław Wandzilak, of course, became well known to Zuromski.

Apapa had been built at the same shipyard as the famous RMS *Titanic*, and shared some identical fixtures with the liner when it was built in 1927.

The destroyer *Keppel* departed Sète with the Egyptian steamer *Mohamed Ali El-Kebir* and joined the destroyer *Velox*, which had departed Vendres at 0300 hours on 26 June with *Apapa*. The ships travelled in company to Gibraltar, where they arrived later that day. The convoy departed Gibraltar on 2 July with twenty-seven ships escorted by four French Navy destroyers. *Apapa* sailed with

457 Polish officers, 215 Czechoslovak officers, 20 Belgian officers, 16 French officers and 395 civilian refugees.

Apapa arrived at Liverpool on 7 July 1940. The Czechoslovak personnel including the airmen were taken to Beeston Castle in Cheshire and thereafter to Cholmondeley Park in Cheshire. President Beneš, who headed the Czech government in exile, visited Cholmondeley Park on 27 July. Beneš was an advocate of forming new RAF squadrons from Allied personnel who had been evacuated from France. The Air Ministry Document No. 2514/PDO details that three bomber squadrons were to be formed; 304 and 305 Squadrons with Polish personnel and 311 Squadron with Czechoslovak personnel, and the same policy of intent existed for fighter squadrons.

On 15 November 1940, four months after sailing to Liverpool, *Apapa* was in convoy from Freetown to Liverpool carrying general cargo including palm oil and gold bullion, along with 261 passengers and crew. The convoy was sighted at 1000 hours by a Luftwaffe Fw 200 Condor long-range patrol aircraft. *Apapa* was targeted and by two bombs were dropped on it. One missed but the other penetrated the deck and exploded, blowing out some port hull plating and destroying the engines. The palm oil caught fire and the order to abandon was given. The catastrophic damage eventually broke the vessel in two and it sank about 200 miles west of Achill Head, County Mayo, Ireland.

On 21 September 1941 Stanisław Wandzilak was posted to 308 Squadron. Despite both Zuromski and Wandzilak both serving with this unit, they were never on the same pilot strength at any one time. In 1941 Wandzilak flew over France on operations but at the end of the year he was admitted for surgery in an Edinburgh hospital. He returned to flying in March 1942 and the following year was posted to 303 Squadron. In June 1944 he was posted back to 308 Squadron, where he took command of 'B' Flight. On 26 August, during an attack on German troops, his Spitfire was hit by anti-aircraft fire and he parachuted to safety. He managed to avoid capture and was provided shelter by the French until he found an advancing Allied unit. In January 1945, he was appointed adjutant to General Marian Kukiel, who reported directly to General Władysław Sikorski. The two generals had been established friends for many years. As head of the Polish Ministry of Defence, on 17 April 1943, Kukiel had communicated with the International Red Cross in Geneva and had demanded investigations into the circumstances of the deaths of Polish officers in Katyn.

Wandzilak served as Kukiel's adjutant until 1947. In exile, Kukiel became a co-founder of the General Sikorski Historical Institute, now the Polish Institute and General Sikorski Museum in London. In 1948, with the rank of Polish captain and British flight lieutenant, Wandzilak joined the RAF and served until 1972, when he retired with the rank of group captain. During his long service in the RAF, Wandzilak was awarded the Distinguished Flying Cross, Order of the British Empire and the Air Force Cross. Wandzilak was awarded the Virtuti Militari number 10794, the Cross of Valor three times and the Air Medal three times. For his social work, he was awarded the Commander's Cross of the Order of Polonia Restituta. Probably the most extraordinary development within Wandzilak's life was his marriage to Taisa, Julian Zuromski's, mother in 1971.

CHAPTER 2

DEBLIN, POLISH AIR FORCE 1938–1940

Following the Polish-Soviet War, Poland's aviation pilot training facilities consisted of four flying schools and four observer training schools. The investment in facilities and student aircrew was undertaken to rebuild the Polish ability to defend itself. General Władysław Sikorski was the Military Affairs Minister. His ambition was to separate the Polish flying units from the Polish Army. However, in 1928, Sikorski was removed from his post and his desired intentions did not materialise until much later. The title or name the Polish Air Force was effectively established in Great Britain in 1940.

In 1935, 6,000 young men competed for just 100 places at the Polish Air Force's Aviation Cadet School at Deblin, north-west of the large city of Lublin and some 20 miles south-east of Warsaw. General Sikorski had been a visionary in the development of the Polish Air Force. He had served in the First World War and became the commissioner of the Polish Legion, which built the fighting strength of Poland. He fought in the Polish-Soviet War, later becoming Chief of the Polish General Staff in 1921 within the newly independent Poland. In the interwar period, the selection of candidates to serve at Deblin gradually evolved. After 1935, candidates had to have secondary education with a high school diploma and have completed a basic pilot course at a flying club or other establishment. Obviously that was not open to all potential students and another route to qualifying existed at the Military Gliding Centre in Ustjanowa in southern Poland. Clearly, most of the candidates came from intellectual, well-educated and in particular military backgrounds.

The eligible candidates took an entrance examination consisting of a written general knowledge test and an oral test as well as a foreign language exam. A personal medical examination was undertaken, providing a certificate of fitness for service in aviation, issued by a military medical board. These measures saw the foundation of principles that saw the evolution of a comprehensive model of aviation training. The principal of practical training, based solely on Polish aircraft and equipment, ensured that the graduates of Deblin would be thoroughly prepared in all aspects of military aviation and possess high ethical and moral levels.

In 1936, Zuromski had been a high school student studying political science. His studies and research engaged with areas well beyond the field of Polish historical research and connected closely with the politics and political thought of other nations. Poland had deep-rooted history in European political conflict, which may well help in understanding the events and situations that engaged Zuromski in his later years. In political science, propaganda is understood as a deliberate and systematic attempt to shape perceptions, manipulate cognitions, and direct behaviour to achieve a response that furthers the desired intent of the propagandist. To what depth Zuromski studied such subjects will undoubtably remain unknown. However, propaganda was to become a positive factor in the latter years of his life.

Flying attracted Zuromski and aviation challenged the traditional reliance upon the gallant cavalry officers of his country. His father's cavalry service was deeply rooted in tradition and had maintained its strength of purpose over many years, but the air force provided opportunities Julian wanted to investigate. Opportunities were limited and training was demanding. The traditional Polish Army staff officers remained the most influential in decision making and opportunities for potential pilots were only available after completing three months' service in the infantry. That service was designed to be physically and mentally challenging to every applicant. Zuromski proved to be a successful cadet; he passed all his examinations and as a result he gained a position as a flying student at Deblin. On 15 October 1937, Marshal Edward Rydz Smigły handed over to the then commander of the Aviation Cadet School, Lieutenant Colonel Stefan Sznuk, a banner for the School of Eaglets. Thereafter the reference to the Eaglets of Deblin became recognised across Poland.

Zuromski commenced pilot training in January 1938 and, aged twenty, he graduated in the thirteenth class of cadets. He possessed the basic skill of a fighter pilot, however, the instruction for cadets focused on both bomber and fighter training, with two separate course structures at Deblin. Lieutenant Colonel Jerzy Bajan was the commandant of the Aviation Cadet School in Deblin at that time. Polish military personnel were issued with identity tags, which were to be worn around their neck at all times. They were constructed of a light alloy designed in an oval shape and impressed with the required information to identify the owner. The shape allowed the disc to be bent and easily separated into two half sections. In case of death this allowed for one half to remain with the body, with the remaining half to assist with the registration and administrative process. Zuromski wore such a tag throughout his military service.

At 0355 hours on 15 March 1939, Czechoslovak President Dr Emil Hácha had ceded control of his country to Hitler. The demands of both Hitler and Mussolini had been of such consequence, he felt it was the only way to avert terrible bloodshed. Dr Hácha signed the documents to permit German occupation and ordered that his troops were not to resist. At 0500 hours that same morning, Prague radio broadcast the following orders of the President of the Republic and Minister of National Defence:

> The German army infantry and aircraft are beginning the occupation of territory of the Republic at 0600 hours. Their advances must nowhere be resisted. The slightest resistance will cause the most unforeseen consequences and lead to the intervention becoming utterly brutal.

The Protectorate of Bohemia and Moravia had been created four days previously and Slovakia had declared independence and become a puppet state and ally of the Germans. Slovak airmen were restricted to two hours of flying a day but due to the close proximity of the Polish border, aircraft were only permitted to carry enough fuel for them to make a training circuit of the airbase. However, on 7 June an escape was planned at one airfield. The fuel bowser was unguarded and four aircraft were filled with fuel. The aircraft flew over the town of Žilina, where the Germans fired on them. The aircraft then headed towards the town of Kraľovany and flew over the High Tatra mountains into Poland. Hence, Deblin witnessed the unexpected arrival of the flight of Czechoslovak aircraft carrying Jan Lazar, Karel Valach, Jozef Kana, Frantisek Knotek, Imrich Gablech, Josef Rehak, Jozef Hrala and Ludevit Ivanic.

These Czechoslovak pilots and airmen had ignored orders, desiring to fight Germany from Polish soil. The price of failure in any escape attempt was severe and to be captured would inevitably have resulted in execution. The eight Czech airmen were initially taken to Warsaw, where they were interviewed before being returned to Deblin. However, the Polish authorities could not lawfully accept citizens of a foreign country into its military forces in times of peace. The pilots' only option was to sign a commitment to enter the French Foreign Legion. This explains why a plethora of cases exist recording both Polish and Czech aircrews serving officially with the Legion.

The declaration stated that in the event of war being declared, they would be released and would be able to fight for their own forces. In Great Britain, concern was raised because the agreement included the following:

> I promise that, after arrival in France, I will enter the Foreign Legion if, for any other reason, it is not possible to deploy me to another part of the army. Currently, I am aware that if I do not adhere to this commitment, I will be sent home across the German border.

The Poles insisted that any arriving Czechoslovak airmen must negotiate with the French authorities. On 15 June 1939, a ceremony took place at the aviation school in Deblin for the completion of the training of 150 cadet pilots and observers. Those airmen were swiftly transferred to line units for further training on combat aircraft. While that was happening, in July 1939 the probability of the German invasion of Poland was increasing. In light of this, the Poles had a change of heart and now offered any Czechoslovak airmen who were preparing to sail to France the option of joining the Polish Air Force. Each and every Czechoslovak who accepted carried the knowledge that Germany did not look upon any Czechoslovak military man in exile as an enemy combatant; they were specifically regarded as traitors. This was because, following the German occupation, they were citizens of the Protectorate of Bohemia and Moravia, part of the German Reich, and therefore Czechoslovaks who took up arms were officially threatened with death.

Political bantering purporting to avoid war with Germany was prevalent, however on 24 August all Polish military forces were put on to readiness for war duties. At this time, the personnel strength of the Polish Air Force was around 10,000 and with the activation of the reserves, it reached just over 12,000. The Polish government ordered a general mobilisation on 30 August, but many reservists were making efforts to join their organisations and some units were in the process of movement to defensive positions when the Wehrmacht commenced operations. The operational aircraft strength within Poland on or around 31 August was just under 400 combat aircraft. Additionally, there were many training and auxiliary types but overall the vast majority were obsolete. The numeric strength of Polish aircrews at that time is thought to have been 1,181 pilots, 497 observers and 219 gunners. Orders were received for all operational combat aircraft to be dispersed to camouflaged airfields.

With the outbreak of the war on 1 September, all graduates of the thirteenth pre-war pilot and observers' course at Deblin immediately received the rank of lieutenant. Zuromski and his fellow student aircrew were now required to fight and defend the Polish homeland. The School of Eaglets had by that time passed out 266 pilots and 707 observers during its fourteen years of existence. Lieutenant Zuromski was now among an elite few who retained the status of being an Eaglet from Deblin. The terrors of war would see all 973 men who had passed through Deblin fight in Poland, France and Great Britain. Some of the accounts of those pilots will be recounted in the story of Zuromski, all linking with the wartime adversity they endured.

When Germany invaded Poland, six ships sailed from Gdynia to France carrying 1,212 Czechoslovak military personnel, including 477 pilots. The German Air Force commenced hostilities against Poland at 0440 hours on 1 September 1939 with aerial bombing. The main aerodromes at Warsaw, Grudziądz, Toruń, Łódź, Częstochowa, Radom, Katowice, and Kraków were bombed heavily, destroying numerous aircraft and facilities. The district of Deblin was bombed in the early hours, as was the cadet training airfield near the town. The bridge over the Vistula River was deliberately targeted in the bombing, which continued for eight days. The entire country and its military capabilities began collapsing. On 2 September, Lieutenant Colonel Jerzy Bajan was injured as a result of a bombing raid on Deblin, suffering terrible injuries to his lower left arm and in particular his hand. He escaped to France and later to Great Britain, where in June 1942, he was appointed head of the personnel department of the Polish Air Force Inspectorate. The following May he became liaison officer at Fighter Command, eventually holding the rank of group captain in the RAF.

The Czechoslovak pilot Imrich Gablech who flew into Deblin in March was among those who succeeded in escaping at the very last moment. However, several days after the bombing, he and the others in his group of escapees had reached the Polish town of Horodenka near the Romanian border. The Soviet troops were advancing towards that district and eventually all the aviators were rounded up by the Red Army. Inexplicably the Russian NKVD charged Gablech with espionage and he was sentenced in March 1940 to five years' forced labour in a Soviet correctional labour camp.

By 8 September 1939, the Polish Army had retreated from the Deblin district, leaving only a small garrison to guard the nearby ammunition dump. Within three days, however, the entire military contingent had retreated from the area. The hope that French units would support and fight for Poland and the promises of aircraft deliveries to the Polish from the docks in Romania diminished completely. Several hundred polish aviation personnel made their way into Romania and as many pilots and trainees as possible had flown from the aero school at Deblin. Their instructions were simply to escape to distant airfields. The Polish air units and the ground troops were pushed towards south-eastern areas of the country, where it was hoped that a defensive action could be mounted. However, by 17 September, the Soviet offensive made these hopes impossible when they advanced on Polish soil. The regular units of the Polish Army fought on as bravely as possible, terribly disadvantaged by both their strength and armament against Hitler's forces.

By 18 September, any aircraft capable of flight had been evacuated across the border to Romania. Among those who had escaped were some of the pilots who had flown from Deblin including, Zuromski.

They were all interned on landing because at that time King Carol II had declared Romania a neutral country. However, their conditions were more than reasonable and the availability of an active Polish embassy in Bucharest created opportunities to escape. Many Polish forces moved towards Romanian ports, avoiding security checks in the hope of regrouping as a fighting strength in France or the British Isles. Only in September 1940 did King Carol II abdicate, primarily because of the imposed and enforced loss of the northern Transylvania territory to Hungary. A coalition government of radical right-wing military officers then came to power and on 20 November 1940 Romania formally joined the Axis alliance.

More than twenty Polish reconnaissance bombers had escaped to Romania. However, the Polish Air Force had lost an estimated 100 aircraft that had been shot down by the Luftwaffe in the September campaign. In addition, thirty Karaś light bombers had also landed in Romania, having crossed the border on 16 September. It is highly possible that these aircraft had flown from Deblin.

Among the young pilots was Alojzy Baltazar. He had joined the Aviation Cadet School in Deblin, graduating as an air observer in 1939. He had flown several reconnaissance flights as an air gunner in the September campaign before his internment, after which he eventually reached France, intent on continuing the fight against the German Air Force.

Ludwik Krempa was another young man among the group. He had been a qualified glider pilot who had been conscripted into the army in January 1938, serving at the Cadets School of Communication near Warsaw. His gliding qualification saw him placed into the reserve officers pool at the Deblin school. He graduated as a pilot in June 1938 and was attached to the 6th Air Regiment as a reserve pilot. He worked in a civil capacity as an engineer while maintaining his flying part-time with the 2nd Air Regiment based at Rakowice airfield near Kraków. With war imminent, he was posted back to the 6th Air Regiment, where he took part in exercises and by the end of August 1939 he was based at Lublinek aerodrome near Łódź. An illness in early September saw him taken to hospital in Lublin. The hospital staff warned him that the Germans were closing in on the city and, despite being unable to walk properly, he made a difficult escape. He witnessed the Soviet attack on 17 September that encircled the Stanisławowo area, but he managed to escape by train. In desperation he worked in the mines in south-eastern Poland until the spring of 1940.

Ludwik Krempa crossed into Hungary on foot in the company of others, only for them to be detained and sent back to Poland. In November 1938, Germany had annexed Czechoslovakian territory that had formerly belonged to Hungary and handed it back. This had been undertaken in order to build an alliance between Hungary and Germany. In August 1940, Germany also gave Hungary possession of northern Transylvania, taken from Romania. The annexation was completed by 13 September, and that territory was incorporated into Hungary under a law passed by the Hungarian Parliament on 2 October 1940, the same month in which Hungary joined Germany in an Axis alliance.

Krempa made a second attempt to cross into Hungary in the summer of 1940. On this occasion he reached a refugee camp for displaced Poles at Záhony. In a further escape, he travelled on to Budapest, Belgrade, Greece and Turkey, where he boarded the Polish steam ship *Warsaw*, bound for Haifa in Palestine. In the late summer of 1940, he joined the Polish Independent Carpathian Rifle Brigade. The brigade was formed in French Syria and composed of Polish soldiers in exile. Good fortune saw him reach England, eventually reporting to the Polish Air Force Depot at Blackpool on 26 October 1940. He was reunited with fellow Polish airmen who had also escaped, few of which had undertaken such a complex escape as the one he had experienced.

In November 1940, he joined the Elementary Flight Training School at Carlisle, followed by another flight training school at

Newton in Nottinghamshire. On 1 February 1942, Krempa was commissioned into the RAF as a pilot officer and shortly after attended the Operational Training Unit at Bramcote in Warwickshire.

The integration for young Poles was a challenging process. Any flying skills were subject to lengthy examination, creating in some cases a protracted transition towards operational flying. In October 1942, Krempa received a posting to join 304 Squadron in the company of several Polish aircrew. This was effectively a Polish squadron based in Dale in Pembrokeshire, Wales, as part of Coastal Command. Flying duties included anti-submarine patrols and convoy protection. The squadron also supported Bomber Command operations and Krempa's first operation to the French Channel port of Bordeaux came on 26 January 1943, where his unit bombed the infrastructure. No. 304 Squadron later served at Davidstow Moor in Cornwall, where on 10 September 1943 Ludwik was promoted to flying officer, flying with a more regular Polish contingent, including twenty-five-year-old Sergeant Jan Jozef Zientek. He had experienced a similar escape route from Poland through Romania to France until he made his way to England via North Africa. In September 1943 he was posted into 304 Squadron and completed a full tour of operations over the Atlantic Ocean, the Irish Sea and the Bay of Biscay. Krempa served until 1949 and lived in England thereafter. In 1988 he returned to Poland, where he died in Kraków, aged 100, on 3 January 2017.

Another graduate of the Deblin school was Władysław Szulkowski. In 1939 he was an instructor at the nearby Advanced Flying School and in September he flew as a fighter pilot in the Polish campaign before escaping from Romania and into France. He arrived in England and served as a commissioned pilot officer. After flying assessments and training, he was posted to 65 Squadron at Hornchurch in early August 1940. Szulkowski was one of the fighter pilots who took part in the Battle of Britain.

Josef Szlagowski, a fellow escapee from the Deblin school, managed to escape to Romania in a light aircraft with an air mechanic.

Their exploits saw them eventually board a vessel bound for the Beirut seaport in the Black Sea before eventually reaching Marseilles. The collapse of France saw a further escape to England, where Szlagowski joined 234 Squadron at St Eval on 3 August 1940. On 8 August, after an aerial fight with the Luftwaffe, his Spitfire, N3278, force landed after running out of fuel at Pensilva near Liskeard. Szlagowski was uninjured. Szlagowski was also one of 'the few' who took part in the Battle of Britain.

Stanisław Pietraszkiewicz was twenty years of age when he saw service at the Aviation Officer School in Grudziądz. After several months of training, he was promoted to observer second lieutenant. In May 1930, he started a pilot course at the Aviation Officers Training Centre in Deblin and later to Grudziądz to attend the Aviation Shooting School. In August 1936, he was appointed as a tactical officer and the following year he was appointed to the Aviation Cadet School in Deblin and he held that position until the outbreak of the war. After the evacuation of Deblin, he crossed the border into Romania and thence to France to the Aviation Training Centre in Lyon-Bron. It was here that the gathering Polish airmen were forming, but a lack of aircraft was prohibitive in establishing any real strength.

French documents dated 24 January 1940 identify a contingent of Polish pilots who came from Lyon-Bron, were assigned to the Ecole de pilotage in Versailles near Paris. They flew from 2 March at nearby Villacoublay. Zuromski was confirmed as being sent to the school of observers and machine gunners on 2 March and he was then directed to the pilot school of single-engine aircraft. The identified Polish airmen at Versailles during March 1940 were Capitan Pietraszkiewicz, who commanded Ryszard Koczor, Antoni Dziegielewski, Olgierd Ilinski, Julian Zuromski, Bernard Buchwald, Tadeusz Aspir Zmijewski, Tadeusz Socha and Jan Pawlikowski.

Zuromski and the Polish contingent of pilots were transferred to Saint-André-de-l'Eure aerodrome, located west of Paris, on 15 March 1940. This aerodrome was used extensively by the French

Air Force, with numerous units flying operationally against the advancing German Forces. The movements of the French Air Force were sporadic, by example the French Bomber Group 1/63 flying Martin 167F aircraft were at Saint-André-de-l'Eure for just ten days in June 1940 before being ordered to withdraw.

By the end of April, 8,678 Polish airmen had reached France or Britain. The bulk of airmen that reached France arrived through Marseille and congregated at Lyon-Bron. The official dates for the Battle of France were 9 May to 22 June, however the numbers of Polish airmen who fought is unknown as most of the documentation, equipment and log books were destroyed.

After a German attack on 11 May, the pilots and pupils were sent to the French reserve airfield at Saint-André-de-l'Eure. Between 28 and 31 May, a further move ordered the Poles to Bordeaux and swiftly then on to Bussac, just east of Bordeaux. Here the Polish pilots became part of a fighter patrol with nine pilots, one of whom was Zuromski. They flew eight old French aircraft: four Spad S.510, single-seat, single-engine biplane fighters and four Dewoitine 501, low-winged, fixed-undercarriage fighters, all of which were flown according to their serviceability. These aircraft patrolled the French skies as much as possible during the seventeen days in which the Polish pilots defended Bussac, and the north-east region of Bordeaux. Zuromski and his friend Bernard Buchwald seized every opportunity to fly, with Zuromski calculating that his flying time within both the Polish and French Air Forces accumulated to a total of 460 hours.

Zuromski was entitled to be awarded the French 1939–1945 commemorative war medal, which was awarded to all military personnel serving under French authority or under a French government in a state of war against the Axis nations, those who had fought against the Axis forces or their representatives and to foreign military personnel who served as Frenchmen in formations at war against the Axis forces. The medal was created post-war in May 1946 and awarded to military personnel who participated between

3 September 1939 and 8 May 1945. The medal could receive several bars. Zuromski's medal subsequently displayed the bars France, Great Bretagne and Liberation, illustrating his operational flying in those three areas of conflict.

Polish design and aviation production workers who also escaped to France with diplomas of excellence became employed in the factories at Argenteuil near Paris. The large contingent of Polish aviation engineers who had escaped to Romania and later arrived in France were distributed across several factories. It is thought that their strength had reached over 700 by March 1940. By example, at the Argenteuil facility, eighteen Poles headed up a design team working on the twin-engine, multi-purpose SE.100 fighter. At the Ambérieu facility more than 100 Poles were employed working on the LeO 451 bomber. Polish engineers were deployed in many factories across France producing aircraft components. However, their commitment to productivity was to be of little consequence as the French resistance began to falter. The temporary Polish headquarters established in Paris in February 1940 would soon be in jeopardy.

During the Battle of France on 23 May, several flights took place from Croydon aerodrome near London to Merville, France. These were undertaken by assorted aircraft both civilian and military. The second pilot on board one of the DC-3s was Flying Officer Benson Freeman, and his crew was a mixture of personnel, including a Belgian pilot, Raymond Chartier, with Piet Vrebos his flight engineer. Their navigator, from the civilian British Overseas Airways Corporation, was Captain John Hoare. The crew were tasked alongside other aircraft to deliver emergency supplies and recover evacuees and injured personnel from France and return them to Croydon. Many assorted aircraft were crossing the English Channel. It had been planned that there would be fighter protection for the transports but that was problematic. Anti-aircraft gunfire and rounds from vessels off the French coast were haphazardly targeting the numerous aircraft, and it was a rather chaotic environment. Having loaded in France,

Freeman's aircraft took off from Merville and commenced the return flight. Over Calais, it was hit by anti-aircraft gunfire. The damage to the DC-3 was sufficient to cause the crew to force land near Arques on the Pas-de-Calais. The navigator had been killed and some wounds were sustained by the passengers on board. The survivors faced capture by the German forces. The pilot was shot as he attempted to escape, while the second pilot, Freeman, was detained and later interrogated at the Dulag Luft centre. There he openly disclosed his fascist tendencies with the Luftwaffe staff. It appears from his behaviour that he agreed to work with the Luftwaffe interrogators and later engaged in writing propaganda to be transmitted from Germany. Freeman would later become a person known to Zuromski. The Belgian sergeant pilot, Raymond Chartier was initially buried at Arques but was later exhumed and reinterred at Ixelles, Belgium, in 1950. The body of Captain Hoare remains in the Arques churchyard. His Commonwealth Graves headstone carries the rarely seen crest of the BOAC airline above his commemorated name.

The remnants of the Polish Air Force command that was still located in Paris departed on 12 June, relocating to the Château de Londigny, south of Poitiers. On 16 June, French Premier Reynaud resigned. He was replaced by Marshal Pétain, the French First World War hero, who swiftly proposed an armistice with the German forces. Pétain subsequently commanded what became the Vichy government across the south-eastern area of France in collaboration with the German forces. Late on 18 June, General Sikorski flew from France to England and, following a meeting with Churchill on 19 June 1940, he broadcast instructions for all Poles to make towards the French ports. Both British and Polish ships were dispatched to pick them up, and the contingent of Polish aviators at Bussac made for Bordeaux.

Hitler presented harsh surrender terms to France on 21 June. At the same time at Bordeaux, many Polish escapees were boarding the steam ship *Kmicic*, formerly the Polish cargo ship named *Robur III*. The vessel steamed down the Gironde estuary carrying both Czechoslovak and Polish airmen in a route which took them out into the Atlantic before changing course east to the port of Falmouth in Cornwall. Zuromski was on board that vessel. He had survived and finally left mainland Europe not knowing what had befallen his family and in particular his father. His friend Bernard Buchwald was at his side, both having graduated at Deblin. Bernard Buchwald later flew with 316 Squadron where his Spitfire was shot down in combat on 12 April 1942 over France. He landed unscathed onto the beach where he was captured becoming a prisoner of war in Stalag Luft III. Later becoming involved in the escape tunnel digging for the great escape which took place from that famous camp.

Churchill announced that the escaping continental airmen were to join the RAF and that Britain and its allies were committed to continuing and winning the war. The first Poles had in fact arrived in Britain on 8 December 1939 as a result of an agreement negotiated the previous October between the British and French air ministries and General Zajac, the commander of the reconstituted Polish Air Force in France. In December 1939, Eastchurch had become a training centre for Polish pilots. This was an air base on the Isle of Sheppey, north of Chatham in Kent. By March 1940, 1,300 Polish airmen were stationed there. The location conveniently provided both a receiving and training centre for Polish Air Force personnel. The station soon became overcrowded and with the threat of a German invasion on the south coast, the men were moved to Blackpool in May 1940. Squires Gate Aerodrome in Blackpool became the home of the free Polish Air Force and established the Polish Air Force Headquarters and School of Technical Training. Thousands of Polish Air Force personnel passed through Blackpool, which remained functional during the entire war period. It was where several Polish Air Force squadrons were formed up for operational service. By the end of July 1940, 8,383 Polish airmen had reached the United Kingdom. Polish camps were in place at Blackpool, Gloucester, Kirkham and Weeton in North Yorkshire.

The British accepted 300 pilots and 2,000 Polish personnel for flying training. An agreement between the Polish and British governments declared an intent to form two Polish bomber squadrons, and they encouraged Polish men to join them. In the meantime, the Poles formally enlisted in the RAF Volunteer Reserve. The British Air Ministry insisted under the direction of the Minister for Air in the Chamberlain government, Sir Kingsley Wood, that all Polish personnel who were to being transferred from France to the United Kingdom for air duties were for administrative reasons to be enrolled in the Volunteer Reserve and take an oath of allegiance to the king. This was later amended under the terms of the Anglo-Polish agreement of 5 August 1940, which afforded the Polish Air Force independent status and henceforth its personnel swore loyalty to the Polish Republic and were permitted to wear Polish Air Force badges on their uniforms. Sikorski and Churchill signed the agreement, the first article of which declared:

> The Polish Armed Forces (comprising Land, Sea and Air Forces) shall be organized and employed under British command, in its character as the allied High Command, as the Armed Forces of the Republic of Poland allied with the United Kingdom.

The largest contingent of Polish airmen, over 4,000 in strength, had left France through the southern Mediterranean ports of Vendres and Argelès between 21 and 25 June. Among them were both French and Polish men from the Lyon base. A significant contingent of Czechoslovak airmen also sailed from Vendres in late June, with the Czech Air Force High Command finally departing from Bordeaux on 25 June. The Air Ministry made a decision to commission all exiled air force officers to the lowest RAF officer rank of pilot officer. This was undertaken before assessing any Polish officer's previous rank or suitability for promotion. This created dissent and instability, which was an unintended result for a situation that in hindsight was rather predictable. General Sikorski had objected to the suggestion at the time but he had been unable to influence a change. The Anglo-Polish agreement did resolve several issues and as time passed further changes were made and incorporated into the Air Ministry structures.

Polish airmen billeted in Blackpool were frequently sent to the Goodwood Hotel in Hornby Road for debriefing and registration prior to any squadron assignments. The Lansdowne Hotel in Blackpool became the Polish Air Force headquarters and both venues were of significant importance to the airmen. In November 1940 the highly experienced pilot Stanisław Pietraszkiewicz was assigned from Blackpool to 616 Squadron stationed in Kirton-in-Lindsey. In January 1941, he took command of 315 Squadron at Acklington in Northumberland flying the Hurricane fighter. In the summer, that squadron moved to Northolt, having converted to Spitfires, and they prepared for offensive operations over occupied France. On 21 September 1941 Squadron Leader Pietraszkiewicz led 315 Squadron to France, providing fighter cover for Circus 101, a flight of twelve Blenheim light bombers to Gosnay in the Pas-de-Calais. A Circus was the code name given to operations where bombers, with a mass escort of fighters, were sent over continental Europe to bring Luftwaffe fighters into combat. On the way to the target, the Spitfires and Blenheims were attacked by Luftwaffe Fw 190 fighters. During the fight, Pietraszkiewicz suffered a damaged engine and was forced to land in France, where he was immediately taken prisoner and ended up in the famous Stalag Luft III prisoner of war camp until the end of the war.

A fellow Polish pilot, Henryk Skalski, who had also passed through Blackpool, met up with Pietraszkiewicz in Stalag Luft III. On 9 October 1940, Pilot Officer Skalski had found himself posted to 607 Squadron at Tangmere in Sussex, an airfield that played an important role in the Battle of Britain. He then moved to North Weald and Acklington. On 27 August 1941 he was flying his Spitfire with

72 Squadron taking part in Circus 85, which was a diversionary sweep towards Saint-Omer, when he was shot down. Following his capture and interrogation at the Dulag Luft, he became a prisoner in Stalag Luft III prisoner of war camp and, like Pietraszkiewicz, also remained there until the end of the war.

Zuromski recorded in his log book that he was stationed at the Polish Depot in Blackpool from 19 October 1940 to 7 April 1941. Blackpool, being a central location, was where pilots were often reunited. In many cases, these men had been flying students or instructors at Deblin. Another of the Polish airmen from Deblin who took part in the Battle of France was Henryk Franczak, who had experienced a prolonged escape initially by making for Romania on foot. He had been captured but managed to escape, moving through Lithuania, Latvia, Sweden and Norway using false identity papers before reaching Lyon-Bron. After the fall of France, he reached England and joined the Polish forces at the Blackpool depot, where he trained as a radio operator despite requesting to serve as a pilot. In August 1941, he was posted to 304 Squadron and flew on his first combat mission to bomb the docks at Rostock. He flew a full tour of operations, over thirty flights to Germany and occupied Europe, and was promoted to flight lieutenant. In 1943 he was recommended for pilot training and qualified in October 1944. After the war, he remained in flying service as an instructor until December 1948. He subsequently accepted a three-year contract to serve in the Royal Pakistan Air Force and was alongside Zuromski when they fought in the first Kashmir War. He was in a transport squadron based at Peshawar, flying Douglas Dakotas, and thereafter he flew for Orient Airways in Pakistan.

Franczak died while living in the United States in July 2006. His wish for his ashes to be buried in the Military Cemetery at Warsaw were carried out. Henryk had three brothers with only one, Jozef, surviving the war. Jozef had been captured by the Russians and spent two years in Siberia. One brother, Edek, an officer in the Armia

Krajowa or Polish Home Army, had been executed by firing squad by the Russians in 1944, while Stasiek lost his life in a Liberator of 1586 Flight, which was shot down over Senta in Yugoslavia on a supply drop to Warsaw during the Home Army uprising on 11 September 1944.

Another radio operator deserving of mention is Kazimierz Czlapka, who endured an escape through the Balkans, Portugal, Spain and Gibraltar. At Blackpool he was trained at the radio telegraph school and then posted into the RAF training infrastructure before serving in the Polish 301 Bomber Squadron. Czlapka responded to a request for Polish radio operators to be trained in special duties and to be parachuted into Warsaw to fight in the Polish Home Army. The Home Army was the main resistance organisation of the Polish Underground, and joining its ranks required the swearing of the oath:

Before God Almighty and the Blessed Virgin Mary, Queen of the Polish Crown, I hereby put my hand on this Holy Cross, the sign of the Passion and Salvation, and I pledge allegiance to my Fatherland, the Republic of Poland. I pledge to steadfastly guard Her honour, and to fight for Her liberation with all my strength, even to the extent of sacrificing my own life. I pledge unconditional obedience to the President of Poland, the Commander-in-Chief of the Republic of Poland, and the Home Army Commander whom he appointed. I pledge to resolutely keep secret whatever may happen to me.

The person accepting the oath would respond:

I hereby accept you into the ranks of the Polish Army, fighting its enemy in conspiracy for the liberation of the Fatherland. Your duty shall be to fight with arms in hand. Victory shall be your reward. Treason shall be punishable by death.

Czlapka became a 'Cichociemni', a title for membership in the Polish special operations paratrooper force, recognised by the Polish Army in exile. He was parachuted into Warsaw by the RAF on 19 February 1943. His duties were to operate at the radio station at Żoliborz, north of central Warsaw. He had previously completed seventeen bomber operations over mainland German targets, experience that assisted him in his duties that involved aerial supply drops by the Allies. But possibly more importantly, communication lines needed to be kept open for occupied Poland to stay in touch with London and the Polish commander-in-chief. This was ensured by means of clandestine radio transmitters manned and operated consistently night and day while tracked constantly by enemy interception measures. Czlapka was injured in battle and captured by the Germans at Żoliborz on 30 September 1944. Very fortunate to have escaped with his life, his identity as a member of the Polish Cichociemni had not been established. He was among 317 elite Polish special operations paratroopers parachuted into Poland to fight in the Home Army.

Following the fall of France in June 1940, airmen from occupied Europe who escaped to England had negotiated many routes in order to continue the fight against Hitler's Germany. By August 1940 there were some 8,400 Polish and 900 Czechoslovak air force personnel being embedded into the RAF. Britain was then their 'Wyspa Ostatniej Nadziei', their Island of Last Hope.

The Polish and Czechoslovak governments in exile in London were keen for their airmen to see action. However, very few spoke English and they came from countries with quite different flying qualifications and flying skills from those embraced within the RAF. On 19 July 1940, Hitler went before the German Reichstag to warn in a public address that, if the war continued, the British Empire would be destroyed. It was that same day the first Polish aerial victory occurred when Pilot Officer Antoni Ostowicz of 145 Squadron shared in the destruction of a Heinkel He 111. Tragically, three weeks later he became the first of his countrymen to be killed in the Battle of Britain on 15 September 1940, a date now celebrated as Battle of Britain Day.

Despite the European military exiles being screened by British intelligence on arrival in England, at least one Czechoslovak pilot, Sergeant Augustin Přeučil, proved that not everyone held the same desire to fight against the German occupation of their homeland. At the time of the German invasion of his home country, he was serving as a reconnaissance pilot in Air Regiment 1 of the Czechoslovak Air Force. Following the German invasion in March 1939, he volunteered to join the Luftwaffe but was rejected because he was not a German national. It appears that the Germans later recruited him and engaged in a plan for him to join the ranks of Czech pilots and report upon the activities of other Czechs trying to join the Polish forces. After the declaration of war in September 1939, Přeučil was accepted by the French to join a fighter pilot training course at an airfield near Chartres. He saw service throughout the invasion of France and escaped to England. Serving as a pilot in the RAF Volunteer Reserve, he received training but was not posted operationally and he eventually flew in an instructor capacity at 55 Operational Training Unit at Usworth. Zuromski had been resident at Usworth receiving instruction in preparation for operational flying at that time. In all probability, Zuromski and Přeučil had known each other. The author will return to Přeučil within the following chapters; his actions, however, illustrate to some extent the required restraint undertaken by the Air Ministry, who shielded the Poles and Czechoslovaks from being entrusted with detailed information about the workings of the radar defensive infrastructure across Britain at that time.

After an uncertain start, the RAF developed trust with the Poles and Czechoslovaks, who repaid that with significant vigour in the aerial fight over occupied Europe. The king visited the Polish

303 Squadron at Northolt and the RAF built on the success of the exiles in the Battle of Britain. Further dedicated Polish squadrons were formed and gained significant reputations for efficiency across the various commands. Throughout the war, the Polish and Czechoslovak airmen continued to serve with distinction and were respected for their cultures and traditions. They grew to attain complete equality with British nationals in terms of rank, pay and career development.

The contribution of Polish and Czechoslovak airmen to victory in the Battle of Britain and thereafter was without doubt significant. It must be remembered that in 1940 there were other airmen from other occupied European countries serving in the air in far less significant numbers. These were Belgian, Dutch, Norwegian and Free French. Their wartime flying experience was evident but their desire to fight for their occupied countries and families under persecution was in the forefront of everything they undertook. It should not be forgotten that mastering the English language to an acceptable standard for the RAF was in itself a challenging situation and for the majority exemplified their fighting spirit. It should be acknowledged that because of the geographical location of Poland and the borders surrounding it, many pilots spoke French, some of them spoke German and of course several spoke Russian.

The British newspapers published articles extensively upon the arrival of the Polish, Czechoslovak and Free French aircrews into Great Britain. Accounts of individual escapes were exposed and they reported on the fact that these men were going to make an immediate and effective contribution to the war effort. The Poles were also highlighted as the reason why the country was at war with Germany. No doubt some material was British propaganda and politically motivated. The British public were made aware that, regardless of country or circumstance, all the European escapees were to serve in the RAF Volunteer Reserve and wear the uniform of the RAF, distinguished simply by shoulder insignia.

In August 1940 the British and Polish governments made the considered agreement to rescind the necessity for Polish airmen to attest into the RAF Volunteer Reserve. The established Polish Air Force structure became sovereign and any allegiance was made specifically to the Polish government in exile. Polish buttons and cap badges were worn on the uniforms, along with British and Polish rank insignia. Sikorski was frustrated that the Air Ministry stood firm by not allowing Polish decorations to be worn as brevets. Likewise, the Air Ministry were frustrated by the fact that the Polish held the rights over any award recommended to any Polish pilot or air crew by the British. The most significant and visual element of the Polish agreement with the Air Ministry was the permission to fly the Polish Air Force ensign with official consent at appropriate airfields and stations. It was agreed that the flag was required to be flown on aerodromes across the various commands positioned below the RAF flag. Also, that individual aircraft piloted or flown by Polish crews could, from that moment forward, also feature the square Polish red and white chequerboard symbol. This was effectively the Polish equivalent of the RAF roundel. This Polish sign consisted of four squares, two white upper left and lower right and two red lower left and upper right. Around the edges were the same inverted but opposite colours. On 20 August 1940, Churchill said in the House of Commons:

> The gratitude of every home in our Island, in our Empire, and indeed throughout the world, except in the abodes of the guilty, goes out to the British airmen who, undaunted by odds, unwearied in their constant challenge and mortal danger, are turning the tide of the World War by their prowess and by their devotion. Never in the field of human conflict was so much owed by so many to so few.

This extracted portion from his speech that day has since become the epitome of gratitude bestowed upon Fighter Command pilots who flew in the Battle of Britain. Four days after that speech the Luftwaffe bombed the airfields of North Weald and Hornchurch before concentrating upon central London, Birmingham, Liverpool, Bristol and South Wales. Much more was to follow and by the end of 1940, German bombing raids had killed approximately 25,000 British civilians. The emergency services structures, underground shelters, precautionary and managed evacuations, and anti-aircraft defences played their part in protecting both the people and industry, enabling the war to continue. No doubt the escaping Allied airmen who had joined the RAF and witnessed this most significant defiance to Hitler would have reflected upon having seen their own countries' crumbling defences fail and fall without such strength, spirit and determination.

CHAPTER 3
AIR TRANSPORT AT WHITE WALTHAM, GRADING COURSE AT HUCKNALL

The Air Transport Auxiliary was founded at the beginning of the Second World War and was primarily staffed by civilian men and women. These pilots were assigned to Reserve Command and attached to RAF flights. Their duties were to ferry aircraft from factories, maintenance units and storage units on to operational RAF stations, effectively releasing operational pilots from engaging in time-consuming but necessary flying duties. The Air Transport Auxiliary's Central Ferry Control centre was based at Andover, with a ferry pool of pilots established at RAF White Waltham, near Maidenhead in Berkshire, which began operating on 15 February 1940. The entire establishment of pilots at this time was no more than 100, and among them would be many mature people with the required qualifications holding an Air Ministry Certificate of Competency and Licence to Fly Private Flying Machines.

A young Polish female pilot, Jadwiga Piłsudska, the younger daughter of Marshal Józef Piłsudski, the Chief of State of Poland, became a pilot and studied aviation engineering. In September 1939, Jadwiga, together with her mother and sister, worked in the Praga district of Warsaw helping injured civilians. By mid-September 1939, they were surrounded by Russian forces. They managed to get to Latvia, from where they flew to Stockholm. They eventually reached England, where Jadwiga commenced studying architecture at the University of Cambridge. As a student, she wrote several times to the Air Transport Auxiliary and was eventually assessed and accepted as a competent pilot.

Most of the German and Austrian immigrants living in Britain when war was declared were refugees who had fled from Nazi oppression. The British government wanted to avoid a policy of mass internment and hoped to use the refugee community to support the British war effort. Tribunal hearings were set up around the country to interview all enemy aliens; an unfortunate title, as very few were of 'enemy' status. The intention was to classify them into three categories: 'A', considered a threat to national security requiring immediate internment; 'B', considered suspect and subject to certain restrictions; and 'C', considered to be a genuine refugee from Nazi oppression. Until May 1940, British authorities saw no reason to intern the large numbers of enemy aliens in categories 'B' and 'C'. However, after the fall of France the threat of invasion of the British mainland became a very real prospect, so it was felt prudent to intern all male enemy aliens, regardless of classification, between the ages of sixteen to sixty. All women in category 'B', sometimes with their children, were also interned. There was a serious matter to consider as the Abwehr or German military intelligence in Hamburg were controlling German agent deployments into Great Britain to spy and report to Berlin. In 1940 an estimated twenty to twenty-five spies had been inserted into Britain and Ireland by various means. The department of B Division at MI5 operated from Latchmore House at Ham Common in Surrey. They were the spy hunters trying to dismantle the German espionage system, but they did so with an advantage. The pre-war efforts undertaken by MI5 had established a network of intelligence and surveillance on some known German agents, which led to further identification of suspects. Any suspect arrested had the option to become a double agent, which did happen, and eventually, when they were of little use for what could have been many reasons, they found themselves in internment camps. Wulf Schmidt was parachuted into England near Cambridge in the late summer of 1940, and after capture he transmitted misleading information to the Abwehr until the end of the war. Those who refused and became known individuals who had engaged in serious intelligence successes for the Abwehr faced a probable legally imposed death sentence after trial.

It appears that after Zuromski's arrival at Falmouth from France on 20 June 1940, he swiftly passed through the Polish reception centre. The RAF administration had a plethora of forms, including the Service and Release Book, described as Form 2520A, which contained a Certificate of Service. The certificate was effectively the central two pages within the booklet. It is assumed that for identity purposes Polish personnel at the reception centre were issued this essential booklet following the essential identification scrutiny that was in place.

Zuromski was sent to join the Air Transport Auxiliary at White Waltham, and no doubt this was far removed from his expectations of flying offensively against the Luftwaffe. He arrived at White Waltham on 10 September 1940 when the London Blitz was taking place. The previous night the Luftwaffe had attacked London with approximately 200 aircraft. A time delay bomb dropped at Buckingham Palace caused damaged when it exploded long after the raid. There were other Polish pilots deployed as Air Transport Auxiliaries. Jerzy Drzewiecki was a civilian pilot born in Warsaw in 1902 and educated at Warsaw University of Technology. He became an aircraft designer who fled the German-Soviet occupation of Poland and escaped to England. His qualifications were immediately in evidence and he was employed at the Westland Aircraft Company as a draughtsman. With over 1,000 hours' flying experience, it was not long before this was recognised and he was posted to fly within the Ferry Pilot Pool for the Air Transport Auxiliary at various stations. On 24 November 1941, Drzewiecki was landing a Bristol Beaufort at Llandow when both engines failed unexpectedly. He crashed and hit a tree at a farm adjacent to the airfield, suffering significant injuries.

Zuromski was at White Waltham for a brief period before being posted back to the Polish Depot at Blackpool on 19 October 1940. On that night, the Luftwaffe bombed London, Liverpool, Manchester and Coventry. It was the week in which Hitler met Marshal Pétain in occupied France to discuss Franco-German collaboration in the governance of France. In November 1940, a campaign began in Germany to enhance domestic morale, which included large numbers of meetings in factory and workplaces as well as the usual press and radio broadcasts. A prolific poster campaign with slogans of 'Victory is with our Colours' and 'We are beating England, and Victory is Certain' were prominent everywhere. Germany proclaimed it was prepared for the methodical and steady strangulation of the British Empire. Anti-Semitism continued to be a factor within much of the Nazi propaganda in the Blitz period. It was a weapon that the Germans used in several ways; the Jews were portrayed as directly responsible for the war and therefore for the bombing of English targets.

When Zuromski was issued his RAF pilot's log book, he made an initial entry that his flying time attained in both Poland and France had reached 460 hours. This was accepted by the RAF, and it was duly recorded as correct. Zuromski also wore around his neck the British military identity discs. These differed from the Polish ones he previously wore in that there were two fibre board discs. The material was to be fire proof, with one green and another red. They were embossed with the required information to identify the wearer at all times. The identity disks were hand stamped with the surname, initials, service number and religion of the holder and, if in the air force, the initials RAF were present. The disks were worn on a length of cotton cord. If the wearer became a casualty, the green disc was left with the body and the red disc would be submitted for the registration process. This was easy to do as the cord around the neck connected the green disc, while a separate cord connected the red disc to the upper green one.

Zuromski now wore the RAF uniform but sewn across each upper shoulder on the tunic arms were the titles 'Polish'. Also, but not uniformly, Polish collar rank star tabs were worn in addition to the braiding rank for RAF officers, which was always sewn on the lower sleeves. The preferred tunic buttons were those manufactured with the Polish eagle if they were available. The Polish pilot wing was a cast metal design in the form of a flying eagle holding a laurel crown in its beak, suspended from a chain, unique to the Polish Air Force. Officers were able to purchase these from the recognised jewelers Firmin or Gaunt and Spink, each made from the original design of the manufacturer, Jan Knedler in Warsaw. It was, however, not unusual to just see the RAF pilots' wings worn on the left breast of uniform jackets.

By the end of July 1940, the numbers of Polish airmen on British soil had escalated to an estimated 8,384. After processing these men into the RAF through the established facility at Blackpool, the pilots in particular needed to understand how to measure speed in miles and not kilometres and fuel in gallons instead of litres. Height was a most important conversion for the Polish pilots, and as 1km equated to 3,280ft, it was far from a natural equation to relate to. Even more difficult were temperature calculations. Also, all Polish aircraft had throttles that operated in a backwards motion, while British designs used a push forward to accelerate. This was a fundamental issue of safety, likely to be forgotten in an emergency situation. The PZL P.11 was the Polish aircraft that most fighter pilots had flown and were familiar with. It was an all-metal, gull-winged fighter that Poland had exported to countries like Romania, Bulgaria, Turkey and Greece. Polish pilots had also been part of their army's infrastructure, which was different to the RAF; another situation to understand at Blackpool and in training.

By early 1941, the Polish Air Force in Britain listed thirteen squadrons: eight fighter, four bomber and one reconnaissance. Polish squadrons came under 1 Group's command between 1940 and 1941. In January 1941, the Polish Flying Training School was established at Hucknall. It was composed of an Elementary Flying Training Squadron, an Intermediate Training Squadron and a grading and testing flight. This centralised all of the requirements in establishing trained and competent Polish pilots for integration into the RAF.

Candidates with flying experience were admitted and were proficiency tested in the Elementary Flying Training Squadron. This involved two to three hours flying in Tiger Moths and a theoretical examination. Results determined whether the student was sent on to the Intermediate Training Squadron, or to the grading and testing flight. In general, only pilots who had been fully trained in Poland were directed to that flight, which was equipped with Fairey Battles and then from April 1941 also Airspeed Oxfords. During the first half of 1941, 150 pupils passed out from the grading and testing flight and approximately fifty pilots officially received their pilot wings. Courses for those sent to the Intermediate Training Squadron lasted approximately four months. Along with an average of fifty hours of flying instruction, they underwent theoretical and practical instruction in airmanship, navigation, meteorology and armament. After a conversion course of approximately a further ten hours, students were then normally posted to an Operational Training Unit. At the beginning, all the commanding officers of the Polish school were British with Polish understudies. Some of the instructors, the majority of whom had completed special short refresher instructor courses at the Elementary Flying Training Squadron near Carlisle, were Polish.

Zuromski was posted to a grading course at Hucknall in March 1941. He commenced recording flights in his log book on 9 April flying a Magister, a two-seat monoplane basic trainer built by the British aircraft manufacturer Miles Aircraft. The following day he flew Magister L5929, undertaking circuits and landings at the airfield. Sergeant Stanisław Knapik was flying Oxford R6385 also at Hucknall when a collision occurred when Zuromski was landing the Magister at 1545 hours. The subsequent accident investigation disclosed that the Oxford was damaged and beyond repair. Zuromski's Magister suffered damage to a fin and rudder assembly and he had suffered a minor injury to his leg. The accident investigation record AIR 81/5808 fails to disclose the circumstances but it appears that the Oxford landed and careered into Zuromski's aircraft. Fortunately he had been the only occupant.

Zuromski resumed flying three days later and progressed on to flying the larger Battle aircraft on circuits and landings flights. On 23 April 1941, the officer commanding the Polish Flying Training School at Hucknall signed Zuromski's log book as proficient and he was posted to flying duties. Shortley after Zuromski departed the Polish Flying Training School, the facility was expanded with additional grading and testing capability. It undertook the RAF model for training new recruits and was staffed by an all-Polish contingent.

CHAPTER 4

ROYAL AIR FORCE STATION AT DUMFRIES

Pilot Officer Zuromski was posted for flying duties to the RAF station at Dumfries, a large airfield in south-west Scotland. In the summer of 1940, the airfield became a bombing and gunnery school for both bomb aimers, air gunners and navigators, and was equipped with Fairey Battles and Hawker Henleys, with Armstrong Whitworth Whitleys used for bombing exercises. The instructor staff included both pilots and other aircrew in order to deliver the various training components for the respective duties that engaged both bombing and air gunnery students. Dumfries airfield controlled satellite landing grounds at Stranraer, Haddington and Cumbria, which were all used for repair facilities and aircraft storage for the maintenance units. Dumfries also controlled several frequently used bombing and gunnery ranges in the area.

Zuromski had not expected to be posted and tasked with delivering training. His ambitions to fly fighters offensively against the Luftwaffe had been thwarted as he returned to fly the Battle light bomber once again. In addition, from 9 May 1941, he flew the Henley, which was smaller and lighter. The Henley had been developed in the pre-war years as a light bomber but proved disappointing in performance and design. The aircraft was subsequently deployed into production as a target tug. There was a need for a fast target-tug aircraft to provide realistic speeds for the Spitfire and Hurricane fighters, which were being developed with ever-increasing performance. Henleys were produced with drogue-towing equipment, which was operated by a windmill motor system that protruded from the side of the fuselage. As a target tug the Henley's Merlin engine required running at high speed over long periods, which induced greater engine wear. The Henley's coolant radiator was efficient for normal flying, but when towing a target at high-engine speed the drag was immense and the radiator was insufficient to keep the engine cool, resulting in frequent overheating.

During the late evening of 10 May, a most unusual event took place. A solitary Messerschmitt Bf 110 aircraft was detected by the Chain Home radar flying into Scotland's airspace from the east. An attempted interception by scrambled fighters was not successful, primarily because of the low height and most probably intermittent radar plotting. In the darkness the Luftwaffe pilot was trying to locate Eaglesham Moor. This pilot was Hitler's Deputy Führer, Rudolf Hess. The influential Nazi was intent on reaching Dungavel House on the moor to locate the Duke of Hamilton. Eaglesham Moor was only 70 miles north of Dumfries airfield, where Zuromski was resting after his first day on duty.

Hess was able to ascertain his whereabouts and gained sufficient height to parachute out and carry on his endeavours by foot. He was prepared to some extent, having a torchlight in his flight suit pocket. There was a sound reason in his wish to meet the Duke of Hamilton at their ancestral home. The aristocratic family had been involved with the Anglo-German Fellowship during the interwar years. The Fellowship, and its sister society in Germany, the Deutsch-Englische Gesellschaft, had promoted good understanding between England and Germany. Hess had held a dream of an Anglo-German alliance and it was the Fellowship connections he hoped to kindle in Scotland. It has to be assumed that Hess's intent was to bypass the diplomatic process of engaging with Churchill's government and use the influence of those who belonged to the since passed Anglo-German Fellowship Association and his own to bring about peace. However, for Joseph Stalin, news of this event heightened what he most feared; that Hess might indeed be successful.

When the Hess came down on his parachute, having suffered a minor injury, he initially gave the false name Hauptmann Alfred Horn to an attending local and asked to see the Duke of Hamilton. The duke was himself an accomplished pilot and held the rank of wing commander, serving in the RAF. Ironically he was responsible for the air defence of Scotland and stationed at Turnhouse, close to Edinburgh. It was reported that the duke, having being contacted by the authorities, visited the German pilot in hospital and Hess revealed his true identity. The Duke of Hamilton reputedly communicated directly with Churchill on the evening of Sunday, 11 May. After the solitary Messerschmitt had intruded into Scotland that same night, central London had been subjected to a heavy Luftwaffe bombing raid. Some 1,212 people had lost their lives and 1,769 were seriously injured. An estimated 2,000 fires raged among the carnage and the House of Commons was also badly damaged by both bomb explosions and fire.

On 14 May *The New York Times* reported that 'British sources' had 'intimated that Herr Hess, in deciding to fly to the enemy, felt that Germany should make peace with Britain rather than co-operate with the Bolsheviks'. This no doubt will have stirred Russian fears of an Anglo-German alliance, which they had contemplated intensely for a long period and was still very much evident. Hess was one of the few people in Hitler's inner circle who knew that the Third Reich was about to invade the Soviet Union. The instructions and strategic plans were in place, crafted by Hitler himself as a Führerbefehle, (Hitler's directive). Within the Nazi military structure, Führerbefehle's were binding and were to be followed without compromise. Hess was well aware of such definitive orders being imposed upon the Third Reich. Many believe this may have been the primary reason for his actions. The National Archives files on the Scottish incident exist with heavy redactions and omissions. They disclose that on Friday, 16 May, Hess was moved to the Tower of London for a short duration, but later detained as a prisoner of war at several other secure locations. Hess eventually stood trial at Nuremberg in 1945 and was sentenced to life imprisonment in Spandau prison, Berlin. He became the longest-serving war crimes prisoner to be guarded at Spandau by the Allied powers. His death, reportedly by suicide, at the age of 93 came in 1987.

The Duke of Hamilton came under pressure from the press to explain his role in the affair, with suspicions being raised that he might have been in prior contact with Hess. Questions were also asked in the House of Commons and on 22 May, Sir Archibald Sinclair, the Secretary of State for Air, gave this statement to the House:

> When Deputy-Fuhrer Hess came down with his aeroplane in Scotland on 10 May, he gave a false name and asked to see the Duke of Hamilton. The Duke, being apprised by the authorities, visited the German prisoner in hospital. Hess then revealed for the first time his true identity, saying that he had seen the Duke when he was at the Olympic Games at Berlin in 1936. The Duke did not recognise the prisoner and had never met the Deputy-Führer. He had, however, visited Germany for the Olympic Games in 1936, and during that time had attended more than one large public function at which German Ministers were present. It is therefore quite possible that the Deputy-Führer may have seen him on one such occasion. As soon as the interview was over, Wing-Commander the Duke of Hamilton flew to England and gave a full report of what had passed to the Prime Minister, who sent for him. Contrary to reports

which have appeared in some newspapers, the Duke has never been in correspondence with the Deputy-Führer. None of the Duke's three brothers, who are, like himself, serving in the Royal Air Force, has either met Hess or had correspondence with him. It will be seen that the conduct of the Duke of Hamilton has been in every respect honourable and proper.

The *Aberdeen Evening Express* published articles on Hess's arrival, and without doubt the event would have been a hot topic at the Dumfries aerodrome. The wreckage of the Messerschmitt could be easily seen about 12 miles west of Dungavel House before they were removed on 13 May. Also that day, the German newspaper *Der Führer* published an article reporting that 'Rudolf Hess has met with an accident'. It was the first mention of his name to the German public for several months and thereafter it was suppressed.

Among all the news speculation and the plentiful theories, the truth behind Hess's mission remains a mystery. The Air Ministry Directorate of Public Relations was based in Whitehall with offices in the Ministry of Information building. Some 371 staff were employed handling press enquiries, press releases and, most importantly, questions of censorship. C.P. Robertson and Group Captain Lord Willoughby de Broke were Deputy Directors of Public Relations at the Air Ministry. The Air Ministry News Service output by May 1944 had seen 13,000 news bulletins published. No doubt the censorship in relation to the speculation over Hess in 1941 was robustly managed in relation to security and public news.

Zuromski had been in close proximity to these unfolding events in May 1941. He had embarked on his new duty, which had its own difficulties to endure because both instructors and student air gunners were subjected to the cancellation of flights at short notice due to inclement weather. The RAF had a special meteorological section known to everyone in the service as the Met Flight. No matter how foul the weather over their own aerodrome, these special pilots managed to go up and bring back the information that was so vital for all of the operational and training commands. Two distinct types of weather flights were undertaken. One was the altitude flight, where weather readings were taken at about 23,000ft or higher if possible. The other were the long-range flights out over the Atlantic. Ideally both pilots obtained readings at around the same time for the weather experts to predict the oncoming weather situations, as well as what weather would be arriving in the short term.

When flying the air gunnery Battles at Dumfries, the aircraft carried a pair of student air gunners and their training apparatus, which often included cine camera guns to record the student's aerial targeting. The Battle also served as a target tug. The first trainer version, known as the Battle T, flew in October 1939. This aircraft was noticeably different in that it had two individual cockpits, while the other Battle trainer variant used for gunnery training had a rear turret installed.

The target-towing Battle carried a winch operator, who let out and withdrew the long cable attached to the fabric target. Once in the air, the pilot flying the student's aircraft would make a rendezvous in an allotted firing zone over the firing range. The target-towing aircraft pulling the large truncated cone shaped-drogue deployed from the aircraft by means of wire was some 1,200ft behind the towing aircraft. By firing on the moving drogue, the gunnery students gained the perspectives of aerial gunnery using deflective shooting skills on a moving target.

Zuromski flew with many target tow operators. These men were normally corporals or leading aircraftsman who had volunteered for that duty. They were responsible for ensuring that the distance of the target from the towing aircraft was sufficient for students to practise air-to-air firing without any possibility of them hitting the towing aircraft itself. Once the exercise was completed, the target drogue was drawn back towards the aircraft and stowed for landing. Each sortie required the drogue to be repacked and made ready for deployment.

Clearly safety was an important factor as live ammunition was being fired at the targets. Important as these duties were, for a frustrated fighter pilot, it was more than likely not particularly rewarding.

Sergeant Henryk Skowron, a fellow Polish pilot who had arrived at Dumfries for flying duties on 8 April 1941, lost his life performing these training duties on 18 July the same year. Zuromski's log book evidences that he flew a search flight on that day after Skowron's aircraft was reported missing. His Battle, serial L5775, was later found, having crashed into the Solway Firth off Blackshaw Bank, to the south of the Merse salt marsh, approximately 10 miles south-east of Dumfries. The target tow winch operator on board was nineteen-year-old Leading Aircraftsman William Weatherburn, who also lost his life in the unexplained accident. He is buried in Tweedmouth Cemetery, Northumberland. Skowron was buried in St Andrew's Cemetery, Dumfries, and is additionally commemorated on the Polish War Memorial at Northolt.

Pilot Officer Roman Hrycak was another Polish pilot serving at Dumfries. He had introduced the requirements of towing a drogue behind the Battle to Zuromski on 12 May 1941. Hrycak later flew Spitfires with 317 Squadron and on 15 March 1942, returning from France in poor weather with diminishing fuel, he parachuted out of his Spitfire at Bolt Head, south of Salcombe, on the south coast. In doing so, he sustained some injuries but survived his rather perilous escape.

On 18 June 1941, Zuromski was given the opportunity by Flying Officer Martin to take control of the gunnery school's large twin-engine Whitley. It was a welcome opportunity as the Whitley was by far the largest aircraft he had piloted. It was the first British bomber to have a retractable undercarriage and the first Bomber Command aircraft to operate over Germany. When used in training the Whitley would carry six student gunners, who in turn would fire the fixed forward guns and the power-operated Frazer-Nash rear turret. Zuromski took control of the Whitley and gained a very different perspective of flying. That same day he also had the opportunity to fly the later model of the Whitley, which was fitted with a power-operated front gunner turret. The flights in the two Whitleys are among the more unusual entries made in his log book.

There were a great many aerial air gunnery exercises flown over England. Rudolf Marczak was a Pole of German descent who had received some pre-war military flying experience. Reaching England as a pilot, he was posted to fly target-towing duties at the Air Gunnery School at Morpeth in Northumberland. Many Polish air gunners trained at Morpeth, and Marczak flew both Lysanders and Battles vibrantly painted in yellow and black, a design feature to assist with clear identification for the student air gunners firing at the targets they towed. Squadron Leader Biaby, a Polish liaison officer, and Squadron Leader Sasinowski, the Polish chaplin, visited Morpeth to support the large Polish contingent there. Leading Aircraftsman Leonard Ashton spent endless hours operating the winch mechanism and stowing the equipment in the aircraft flown by Marczak.

Safety was a significant matter for the flying crews engaged in this area of flying training. Safety guidance in relation to the firing of guns by the student air gunners was based upon the rule of firing only when the guns were 20° above a horizontal position. A bullet fired from a gun in that position should travel 2.5 or 3 miles before becoming spent of energy and follow the laws of gravity and drop to the ground. A Whitley bomber engaged in aerial gunnery training was flying over the Newbury area, south of Oxford in the summer of 1942. The target was a drogue towed by a Lysander aircraft and there were no concerns expressed during the exercises undertaken. Below in the general area was Highclere School, where eleven-year-old Mary Hazel Russell was playing cat's cradle knitting in the playground. It was lunchtime and Mary was with several friends. Her best friend, Sylvia Stacey, of the same age, was standing alongside her when she suddenly collapsed without warning. She fell to the floor at Sylvia's feet, and her sudden death was at that time unexplained. An inquest took place whereby a pathologist revealed that a small wound was present in her right upper shoulder. The pathologist, Doctor Newcombe, also gave evidence that he located a bullet in the child's heart, which was the cause of her death. He reported that the bullet probably entered her body nearly vertically. Squadron Leader Walters, the chief armaments instructor serving at an undisclosed location, gave evidence that there were aircraft practising gunnery training in the area when the incident occurred. The coroner ruled that Mary's death was one of misadventure. Walters, representing the commanding officer of the station and the crew of the aircraft concerned, expressed sympathy with the girls' parents. Mary was later buried in Highclere Chapel on the estate, where her father worked as a chauffeur and mechanic. Two airmen attended the funeral.

It was a return to the mundane target-towing flights in the Henley for Zuromski in June. On 22 June, news broke of German forces launching a surprise attack on the Soviet Union, Germany had embarked upon a deeply penetrating and wide-front attack upon what had been its ally. The news was very unexpected and Churchill later broadcast to the nation: 'Any man or State who fights against Nazi-ism will have our aid.'

A month later, on 22 July, Squadron Leader Ashworth signed Zuromski's log book, endorsing his completion of service at the Bombing and Gunnery School. The squadron leader recorded him with an assessment of 'Average' with no areas of flying noted. This was credible and reflected well on his time flying the rather uninspiring duties he had undertaken. That night, news broke that the Luftwaffe had bombed Moscow with an estimated 150 aircraft. Eight days later, on 30 July, the Secretary of State for Foreign Affairs, Anthony Eden, addressed the Houses of Parliament. His words must have had an impact on the Polish personnel who listened to the subsequent announcements. He told his parliamentary colleagues:

I must apologise to the House for trespassing on its time, but when an international event of importance occurs, I think it right that the first public announcement of that event should, if possible, be made in Parliament itself. I am very glad to be able to inform the House that an Agreement between the Soviet Union and Poland was signed at the Foreign Office this afternoon. Under that Agreement the Soviet Government recognise that the Soviet-German Treaties of 1939 as to territorial changes in Poland have lost their validity, while the Polish Government declare that Poland is not bound by any agreement with a third party directed against the Soviet Union. Diplomatic relations will be restored at once and Ambassadors exchanged. The two Governments agree to render each other support of all kinds in the war against Hitlerite Germany. The Soviet Government agree to the formation of a Polish Army on Soviet territory. This Polish Army will be subordinated, in an operational sense, to the supreme command of the Soviet Union. Attached to the Agreement is a Protocol by which the Soviet Government grant an amnesty to all Polish citizens now detained on Soviet territory, either as prisoners of war or on other grounds, as from the resumption of diplomatic relations. Here, perhaps, I may say that arrangements for immediate resumption are being made.

After the signature of the Agreement, I handed General Sikorski a note in the following terms:

On the occasion of the signature of the Polish-Soviet Agreement of to-day's date, I desire to take the opportunity of informing you that in conformity with the provisions of the Agreement of Mutual Assistance between the United Kingdom and Poland of 25 August 1939, His

Majesty's Government in the United Kingdom have entered into no undertaking towards the U.S.S.R. which affects the relations between that country and Poland. I also desire to assure you that His Majesty's Government do not recognise any territorial changes which have been affected in Poland since August 1939.

He added:

I want to say a word in connection with the Note which I handed to General Sikorski. It is stated in paragraph one of the Soviet-Polish Agreement that the Soviet Government recognise the Soviet-German Treaties of 1939 concerning territorial changes in Poland, as having lost their validity. The attitude of His Majesty's Government in these matters was stated in general terms by my right hon. Friend the Prime Minister in the House of Commons on 5 September 1940, when he said that His Majesty's Government did not propose to recognise any territorial changes which took place during the war, unless they took place with the free consent and good will of the parties concerned. This holds good with the territorial changes which have been affected in Poland since August 1939, and I informed the Polish Government accordingly in my official note. As to the future frontiers of Poland, as of other European countries, I would draw attention to what my right hon. Friend said in the speech to which I have referred. I am sure the House will agree with me that both parties are to be warmly congratulated on the signature of this Agreement. This is an historic event. It will lay a firm foundation for future collaboration between the two countries in the war against the common enemy. It will, therefore, be a valuable contribution to the Allied cause, and will be warmly welcomed in all friendly countries, and not least, I feel sure, by public opinion throughout the British Empire.

Zuromski had witnessed Russian military aggression upon the Polish Army and how it had been complicit with Hitler in annexing significant parts of pre-war Poland. The Polish people had been subjected to terrible repression. The Russian forces had entered Poland and had inflicted imprisonment on tens of thousands of people, and the expulsion and exile of hundreds of thousands to forced labour camps. The fate of over 20,000 Polish officers including Julian's father, who had been taken prisoner, was still unknown. The Russian NKVD had been responsible in the spring of 1940 for inflicting a huge atrocity against men like Zuromski's father. Now his son was required to embrace Russian forces as an allied partner during the same war. It is impossible to understand the impact such news had upon him. The obvious resentment and embitterment towards the Russian aggressors that prevailed in his mind at that time cannot be established or understood. The turmoil was enhanced further when he received orders to then serve in yet more training duties at 55 Operational Training Unit. However, this was for his own benefit because it was to be the last step in his own qualification and assessment to be ready for operational duties as a fighter pilot. He departed Scotland for the relatively short transit into North-East England.

CHAPTER 5

55 OPERATIONAL TRAINING UNIT

In February 1941, units from 55 Operational Training Unit at Aston Down moved to Usworth, near Sunderland, in the North-East of England. The entire unit was on site by early March and commenced operational training duties thereafter. The unit trained fighter pilots on Hurricanes. An assortment of aircraft at Usworth provided the services of target towing, attack training and other tasks to ensure the pilots were trained effectively and ready for operational squadron postings.

The development of Usworth airfield had commenced in September 1939 with the construction of two concrete runways. Both were 2,800ft in length running north-west to south-east and north to south heading. A new perimeter track was laid along the airfield boundary with eight dispersal points and hard-standing areas for aircraft. Accommodation blocks were constructed along with airfield buildings and an operations room provided good facilities for the station. It became effectively a fully operational fighter station.

Zuromski arrived at Usworth in late July 1941 to progress through his own pilot training. The RAF was invested in all the pilots who had escaped across Europe and who were capable of flying to the standards and procedures prescribed in air force regulations. Zuromski carried with him his log book, which held the official endorsements as confirmation of the acceptance of his previous flying experience to have totalled 597 hours and 50 minutes. It also accepted that the earlier records had been lost when evacuating from France. It should be noted that the vast majority of RAF personnel who had flown in France in the Advanced Air Striking Force did so without returning with their log books. Those men flying Battle light bombers suffered terrible casualties, trying to stem the German invasion across the Low Countries and into France while engaged in low flying.

At Usworth, Zuromski met two fellow Polish pilots whom he had known at Deblin. Tadeusz Czerwinski had been an instructor there, and he would once again take on the role of teaching Zuromski, but this time in the skills of flying a fighter aircraft operationally and aggressively against the Luftwaffe. Pilots of many nations were trained at Usworth, including Polish, Czech, Canadian, Australian, American and smaller numbers from New Zealand. Operational training was dangerous. During 1941 alone thirty-two pilots were killed. Pilot Officer Ignacy Makomaski of the Polish Ferry Flight was one of those who died when he was delivering Hurricane N2494 to Usworth on 3 June 1941. He struck high-tension cables at Coxhoe, County Durham; an example of the dangers that existed in all types of ancillary flying during the war years.

Zuromski flew a Hurricane from Usworth for the first time on 5 August 1941. He had signed a certification in his log book to the effect that he knew the fuel, oil, ignition and coolant system, and that the actions required in the event of a fire were known to him. This was a prerequisite safety certification required for all types of aircraft. Gaining experience on the Hurricane for eighty minutes on that day had set him free for the first time as a fledgling fighter pilot. The flight for Zuromski had been uneventful but that same Hurricane, serial V7400, took the life of Sergeant Ronald Graham White Carter at Usworth in January 1942. The aircraft dived into the ground west of Castle Eden Dene from 7,000ft during a combat fight exercise. The pilot was later buried at Castletown Cemetery near Usworth. During the war Castletown Cemetery was used by the RAF for casualties sustained at the Usworth Operational Training Unit. There are forty-eight war burials in the cemetery. Family requests obviously resulted in other burials elsewhere.

Another pilot from Zuromski's course at Deblin and also resident at Usworth was Władysław Kuryłłowicz. He was of Polish Siberian origin and could converse in Russian, Polish, French and English. He was among the pilots who escaped to Romania from Deblin and, like so many, he had made his way into France and then on to Great Britain, arriving in February 1940.

On 7 August, Zuromski took Hurricane W9186 on another local sortie from Usworth. Once again it was an uneventful flight but he spent seventy-five valuable minutes in the air. Five days later Pilot Officer Stanisław Roman Swiderski flew that same Hurricane and lost his life when it crashed into the ground. That same fateful day, Stanisław Karubin, who had instructed Zuromski in a Miles Master trainer the previous day, was instructing on a Hurricane formation training exercise from Usworth. He was with another Polish pilot flying over Cumberland. Due to low cloud cover, both Hurricane aircraft flew at high speed into a cloud-enveloped hilltop at Horn Crag, Scafell, in Cumberland. Karubin was a most experienced fighter pilot and had been credited with shooting down seven enemy aircraft during the Battle of Britain. He had been awarded the Distinguished Flying Medal but a simple misjudgement in cloud took his life. Karubin was buried at Castletown Cemetery. The Polish student pilot killed was Pilot Officer Zygmunt Hohne, also buried in the same cemetery.

Canadian pilot Frank Stamp lost his life at Usworth when his Hurricane, V7608, flew into the ground on 15 August, and another Canadian, John Parker, was killed on 28 August when Hurricane Z4046 spun into the ground at Washington, Durham County, now in the City of Sunderland. Between those dates Zuromski had been flying simulated air attacks, and low-flying and formation attacks in Hurricanes, all of which were completed satisfactorily. Henryk Jozef Trybulec had instructed Zuromski in aerobatics and low flying in early September 1941. He was a most experienced Polish pilot, having served as an instructor at Poznań and fought in the September campaign of 1939 flying over German Panzer columns advancing towards Warsaw.

Usworth was a busy training base, with intense flying sorties undertaken whenever the weather permitted and making as much use as possible of nearby RAF Ouston in Northumberland, which was available to Usworth as a satellite airfield. The personnel, both instructing and student, were from diverse backgrounds. Pilot Officer Lewis Benjamin Louden was an American from Tacoma, Washington, who volunteered to fly for the Canadian Air Force and found himself at Usworth. He was killed on 15 September 1941 flying Hurricane P3665, which dived into the ground at Low Pittington, County Durham. He was buried in Castletown Cemetery.

A Czechoslovakian pilot, Augustin Přeučil, was stationed at Usworth as an instructor. He was a conscripted military airman who had experienced being captured by the Germans in 1938 (see Chapter 2). Conjecture exists over his experiences at that time, however, he became one of many pilots who fled to Britain when France fell. At Usworth, he met Muriel Kirby of Sunderland in July 1941. The 1939 war emergency census indicates that she was living at 2 Haughton Road, St Hildas Terrace, Durham. Muriel and Augustin married in the September quarter of 1941, in Sunderland, and they were recorded as then living in Hill View Gardens in Tunstall, Sunderland, a short distance from RAF Usworth.

Zuromski has no log book entries that directly reference Přeučil as instructing or flying with him. However, 18 September 1941 is a date that correlated with both airmen because Zuromski took off from Usworth in Hurricane W9122 and recorded the flight as formation flying. Sergeant Augustin Přeučil also took off in Hurricane W9147, apparently to practise aerial combat with a Polish student. It is possible that the student was Zuromski. The operational record book thereafter recorded Sergeant Přeučil 787344 as missing, due to a flying accident. It appears that he was flying off the coast of Sunderland and reported his aircraft developing problems before subsequently disappearing in vaguely reported circumstances. These circumstances led to him being posted missing, believed killed, and no doubt this was officially recorded thereafter.

In fact, it appears that Přeučil's actions were intentional and his ambition was on flying to occupied Europe in order to present himself to the German forces. This intent may have been for financial gain and reward or political belief. He betrayed his homeland and the RAF thereafter for nearly four years. The circumstances of his actions were directly connected to the loss of life of those civilians he betrayed. In Prague, he began work with the Gestapo, producing lists of identifiable Czechoslovaks fighting against the Germans. He also engaged in the interrogation of shot-down Czech airmen, making no attempt to conceal his identity. He engaged with some pilots he had met in RAF service and, knowing their background and his squadron, used that information to the advantage of the German forces. In 1947, after trial, he was found guilty of high treason and hanged by the Czechoslovakian authorities.

There were varying circumstances where under-training pilots and aircraft failed to return to Usworth, however the case involving Přeučil was without doubt the most astounding. More frequently, aircraft simply became incapable of flight, such as Hurricane V6701, which suffered engine failure on 26 September 1941, forcing Pilot Officer Zarebski to escape by parachute. He sustained injuries that prevented him completing his operational training.

Zuromski flew his last sortie from Usworth on 16 October, flying Hurricane P2906 on an engine test. This completed his operational training requirements in the Hurricane and on 20 October he presented his log book for an authorisation of his accumulated flying hours. His log was signed by Wing Commander Gough, the officer commanding the Training Wing and 'C' Squadron in which he had been serving. Zuromski's grand total of hours flown was now 703 hours and 15 minutes. He then received orders to travel to his next posting, which was to a Polish squadron equipped with the Spitfire, and to report for operational flying. His log book by this time had acquired the bold naming Zuromski upon the closed book paper leaves, enabling the book's ownership to be located easily when it was in a stack and submitted collectively for assessments.

Zuromski and Władysław Kuryłłowicz had once again parted company within a few weeks of each other. Both pilots were posted to serve operationally flying Spitfires, but in different squadrons within Fighter Command. Like the vast majority of Polish pilots, Zuromski and Kuryłłowicz would have received their postings from Squires Gate, commonly referred to as Blackpool. They would, however, meet up once more after some passage of time. Both would fly from Northolt and, unknown to either, they would experience very similar fates.

CHAPTER 6

306 SQUADRON, SPEKE

Squires Gate had grown to become the training and dispersal depot for all Polish pilots and ground crew to the Fighter, Bomber, Coastal, Special Operations and support squadrons located across Great Britain. In July 1940, the facility had seen over 8,000 men arrive from France and by the summer of 1941 Blackpool held the title of the Revised Establishment of the Polish Depot.

Squires Gate provided a ground training centre, medical, interpretation, chaplain, translation and printing service in addition to the commissioning of ranks of flying personnel and their distribution and postings. The significant tower at Blackpool served well as a radar mast and the intensity of Polish personnel in the area saw many types of signage reproduced in Polish language. The 1st Polish Fighter Wing comprised 303, 306 and 308 Squadrons, which were based at Northolt. No. 1 Polish Wing was part of 11 Group, Fighter Command. Flight Lieutenant Tadeusz Rolski, while based at the Polish Depot in Blackpool, was requested to form 306 Polish Squadron, which then moved to Northolt in the spring of 1941 and spent six months flying offensive sweeps into occupied France. The station was commanded by the newly promoted Wing Commander Rolski from the Polish Depot in Blackpool.

Germany had invaded the Soviet Union at dawn on 22 June 1941, and thereafter the offensive by Hitler into Russia was referenced as the Eastern Front. Churchill anticipated a distinctly changed period of the war; in particular, the assumption that the Luftwaffe would have a diminished presence as it stretched its strength towards the east. The Russian forces had suddenly become an ally to the British, something Zuromski and vast numbers of personnel from across occupied Europe would have had to accept with mixed emotions. Stalin, alongside Hitler, had previously swept into territory across Poland and had forcibly inflicted terrible retribution against those who attempted to resist. The Polish fighting forces were now required to regard the Russian forces as allies, no doubt creating emotional turbulence for Zuromski and the other Polish people who had been so abused by Russian brutality.

The Polish and Soviet Union governments had mutually agreed to render aid and support of all kinds in the war against Germany. The Soviet government granted amnesty to all Polish citizens detained on Soviet territory, either as prisoners of war or otherwise, and the resumption of diplomatic relations was immediate. It would be Blackpool where the first Polish prisoners of war released from the Russian camps would arrive in July 1941. The Soviet-Polish Agreement was in retrospect responsible for saving a considerable number of lives.

Returning to Zuromski's posting to 306 Squadron, the first Polish pilot to be lost over France with that unit occurred on 28 June 1941. Pilot Officer Zulikowski was shot down while flying fighter protection for light bombers. He was presumed to have lost his life, however, he had escaped from his Hurricane. Despite a brief period of capture, was able to escape and evade, crossing into Spain to eventually reach Gibraltar and return to England by ship. The official recommendation for an award of a Mention in Despatches explains further:

> This officer, flying a Spitfire, was attacked by enemy fighters and was compelled to bale out over Calais on 28 June 1941. He dislocated his left arm on landing.

He remained in Calais whilst receiving treatment for his arm until 15 July. He then left for Marles les Mines and crossed the Line of Demarcation on 25th July. He was arrested by the French authorities the next morning and interned in St. Hippolyte. He escaped from St. Hippolyte on 27 September and on 6th October was taken to a camp for foreign workers. From here he went to Perpignan on 10 October and crossed the Pyrenees, reaching Barcelona on 21 October. He was repatriated from Gibraltar on 30 December.

Fighter Command's 11 Group and Bomber Command's 2 Group were creating most effective results with combined operations. The fighter aircraft supporting light bombers were undertaking Circus sorties daily, taking advantage of the lengthening hours of summer daylight and mild weather. The Poles from Northolt and North Weald were often engaged in flying close escort to the light bombers intruding over France and the Netherlands. These operations were often referred to as 'Circus' in log books. On 23 July, a Circus operation saw the Northolt pilots attacked by several Luftwaffe Bf 109 fighters. In the short engagement, the Poles of 306 Squadron claimed two enemy fighters but lost two themselves, as well as another who had to bail out into the English Channel. This pilot was rescued, while Flying Officer Witold Pniak, a successful Polish Battle of Britain pilot, ran out of fuel and crash-landed in Richmond Park, Surrey.

On 27 August 1941, Flying Officer Radomski of 306 Squadron was attacked by a Luftwaffe fighter over Calais. The cannon fire struck his Spitfire and tore into his left arm between the shoulder and the elbow. The loss of blood and tissue damage was significant but despite that, he flew across the Channel and landed in a field near Deal in Kent. In hospital, the amputation of his arm saved his life. He would no longer fly but later served as a controller at Northolt, with his uniform jacket left arm always tucked into his lower left pocket.

Zuromski knew Radomski during their shared service at Northolt. Two days later, 306 Squadron lost its commanding officer, Squadron Leader Slonski-Ostaja, who was killed on a Circus to the railway yards at Hazebrouck, France, having only been in command for some fifteen days.

The three squadrons within the Polish Fighter Wing changed locations periodically. One squadron normally rested in a posting to the north of England. The establishment of a Polish fighter squadron at this time normally held a strength of fourteen pilots, which allowed for the inevitable conversion training on to differing aircraft and for pilot assessments. In addition to the squadron code, each aircraft displayed the distinctive Polish red and white chessboard insignia on the forward section of the fuselage. When examining any Polish fighter pilot's log book, it invariably lists additional training on arrival at any station. This is understandable as many pilots had endured several ad hoc postings and were not able to evidence consistent training and assessments of ability. In the summer of 1941, the 2nd Polish Fighter Wing was formed with 302, 316 and 317 Squadrons. They were tasked with defending the south coast ports and Exeter, combined with convoy protection duties. It is worthy of note that by December 1941 all the Polish fighter squadrons had been converted to Spitfires.

In October 1941, 306 Squadron moved to Merseyside, where it performed defensive duties from Speke, effectively a rest from offensive operations into France. Speke, a suburb of Liverpool, saw 306 Squadron revert to flying training while providing two aircraft sections for convoy patrols. Several new pilots appeared in the unit records at this time, among them Zuromski, having arrived from Usworth. The new pilots all received training whenever the weather permitted. Zuromski's opportunity to fly the Spitfire resulted in him entering formation flights, interception flights and dog fighting into his log book, all of which accumulated over ten hours' flying time. He was soon thereafter posted, departing 306 Squadron, destined to join

308 Squadron. Not long after Zuromski's departure, a fatal accident occurred when Sergeant Ottan Pudrycki went down in poor weather conditions flying Spitfire P7749 near Squires Gate on 5 December. He crashed in the grounds of King Edward School. He was reported to have bravely made every effort to avoid hitting the school before he lost his life.

No. 306 Squadron's rest period at Speke ended on 12 December 1941. By that time Zuromski had arrived at Northolt and was about to fly operationally into occupied France. An expectation existed that any operational fighter squadron would fly at least twenty days a month and engage with twelve to eighteen sorties a day if possible. As December 1941 drew to a close, the year had claimed the lives of almost 700 Polish Air Force personnel, 341 of which had been killed in action. The air force had 126 fighter aircraft on its strength by the end of 1941, with Polish fighter pilots in the skies over occupied Europe alongside their British, Canadian, Australian, Dutch and Belgian allies.

An offensive operations policy document was issued by Fighter Command around this time and provided guidance to station commanders upon the numbers of sorties to be flown per week by the fighter pilots. It emphasized that these were advisory and they did not require close compliance. Circus operations were suggested to take place around six times each month, with each operation engaging with an eighteen to twenty-four combined squadron strength. Ramrod operations, escorting bombers against fringe targets across the Channel, were advocated at between six to eighteen squadron participation, according to the target chosen. Roadstead operations on shipping targets with fighter support, targeting the enemy's flak ships, were very much left as discretionary for the fighter group leaders.

CHAPTER 7

308 SQUADRON, NORTHOLT

No. 308 Polish Fighter Squadron had been formed at the Polish Depot, Blackpool, on 9 September 1940. Among the Polish personnel at that time were men who had served in the 2nd Aviation Regiment in Kraków, a unit with such historical connections it became the pathway for 308 to become named the Krakówski Squadron. Hurricanes were received at the depot in October 1940. A squadron emblem derived from the badge of the Kraków Regiment soon appeared on their aircraft, and the unit became operational in December 1940.

Zuromski was posted to 308 Squadron a Northolt on 16 November 1941, commencing a lengthy operational posting with the unit until 21 February 1943. By coincidence and good fortune, Stanisław Wandzilak was also posted into the squadron. He had been with Zuromski at Deblin and they had graduated together. The connections between Polish pilots that had been at Deblin were relatively prevalent, created by the consolidation of men from Poland being posted to limited squadrons. It created a bond between many pilots who were reunited following their various escapes to England. On 18 December, Zuromski took up a Spitfire to fly a local sortie from Northolt. The Spitfire was without doubt the desired aircraft to fly for the vast majority of fighter pilots. He gained further experience on the type during two formation flying sorties in which he was accessed for his competency in the air and in particular in the Spitfire.

The commanding officer at Northolt was Squadron Leader Pisarek, who wore the medal ribbon of the British Distinguished Flying Cross on his tunic. His signature appeared in Zuromski's log book when it was submitted for examination during his early service with the squadron. No. 308 Squadron had been continually active flying against the Luftwaffe during the preceding months before Zuromski arrived and there had been noticeable losses of pilots. It has to be assumed Zuromski was among the replacements for these men.

During spring 1941, 308 Squadron had received orders to fly daylight raids and fighter sweeps over northern France. Circus sorties provided fighter escort to a small strength of bombers, with a strong fighter presence. The Circus operations were directed by intelligence officers flying into the regions most saturated with enemy fighters. It was effectively created to induce the Luftwaffe into attacking the light bombers. If that should happen, waves of fighters reacted according to their height or position in regard to the bombers they escorted. The fighter aircraft were divided into close cover, escort cover, high cover and top cover. One section or wing flew slightly behind and above the other. These operations would on occasion also be provided with forward or rear support, which operated freely as part of the overall operation, allowing for differing capabilities or reactions to any enemy fighter attacks. No. 308 Squadron flew fifty of these sorties in 1941.

A further development of the Circus sorties were Ramrods, Rhubarbs, Roadsteads and Rodeos, all of which were variations on the original theme. A Ramrod was similar to a Circus but the primary objective was the destruction of the target. A Rhubarb was a small-scale attack by fighters using cloud cover or surprise with the object of destroying German aircraft in the air or striking at ground targets, mostly aerodromes and radio or radar stations. A Rodeo consisted of a fighter sweep over enemy territory with no bombers, whilst Roadsteads were sorties directed against shipping and coastal traffic. Fighters in those instances provided escort and attacked vessels and enemy flak positions. Zuromski commenced entering code references for operational sorties in his log book within days of joining 308 Squadron. On 8 December he received a briefing for 'Sweep to France', which proved uneventful. That statement was not applicable for ten Spitfire pilots across several squadrons who failed to return from Ramrod sorties that day. On 23 December, Zuromski received a briefing for 'Ramrod 12' and on 27 December he received a further briefing for a longer sortie identified as a 'Rover to Calais France'.

As 1941 drew to a close, orders were received to the effect that Circus operations were to be reduced. The guidance advised commanding officers to reduce the intensity of sorties by flying just two or three per month. These measures were to reduce losses and temporarily consolidate both aircraft and operational flying crews. The statistics for the second half of 1941 indicated that Fighter Command losses had been around 600 in total. Circus operations for the year had claimed nearly 300 fighter pilots' lives. They had been costly but it was acknowledged at the same time they had been effective.

No. 308 Squadron was about to be rested from operations when news of the remarkable survival of Sergeant Pietrasiak arrived. He had been one of the pilots lost and assumed killed over France in August 1941. His survival and actions in evading capture induced the recommendation for his award of a Mention in Despatches for his escape:

> This airman, flying a Spitfire, was hit by anti-aircraft fire and compelled to bale out over Dunkirk on 19 August 1941. Whilst descending he was fired on by machine guns but was not hit although he hastened his descent and hurt his arm and leg on reaching the ground. He managed

to evade capture by fording a canal and hiding in a copse. He then made his way alone to St. Omer which he reached on 20 August. From here he was taken to Lille on 23 August and left the Zone Interdite at Abbeville on 2 September. He travelled via Paris and Tours and crossed the Line of Demarcation on 3 September. He arrived in Marseilles on 5 September and, as he was not well enough to continue the further journey, remained there until 12 September when he left for the Spanish frontier. While crossing the Pyrenees he lost his way and wandered about for three days but eventually managed to find his way to Barcelona. He was repatriated from Gibraltar on 30 December 1941.

Air Marshal Trafford Leigh-Mallory personally visited Northolt, where he decorated Squadron Leader Pisarek with his Distinguished Flying Cross award. The air marshal addressed the personnel of 308 Squadron, acknowledging that they had achieved remarkable results. He stated that between June and December 1941 they had attained the most significant numbers of victories within Fighter Command. The commanding Polish officer, Marian Pisarek, left 308 Squadron to take up a Headquarters Group posting as the Northolt Polish liaison officer. Promoted to wing commander, he took every opportunity to continue flying. He lost his life on 29 April 1942 when leading the 1st Polish Wing over France in Spitfire BM307.

At Northolt, Zuromski met another pilot he had flown alongside at Deblin. Kazimierz Budzik was also the son of a career Polish Army officer, an infantry captain. With little doubt, much reflection on the invasion of Poland and the disappearance of many military men like their fathers must have united them both. Budzik had escaped Poland and followed orders to make towards Romania. After initial internment, he made his way to Syria and eventually arrived in France in March 1940. In June, he escaped to England. Budzik's and

Zuromski's service had followed the same path. Both were posted initially as ferry pilots before additional training. Pilot Officer Budzik reported for flying duties with 303 Polish Squadron in September 1941, and thence to Northolt to serve with 308 Squadron alongside Zuromski.

Another officer who had served at Deblin was Walerian Zak. In September 1939, he had fought in the Deblin Group, defending the airfield and surrounding area before reaching France via Romania. From 26 May 1942, he commanded 308 Squadron and during his service received both Polish and British flying decorations. Another highly decorated Polish pilot who had trained at the Air Force Cadet Officers' School in Deblin was Tadeusz Kotz, who from June 1942 to February 1943 was a flight commander in 308 Squadron. His luck nearly ran out on 3 February 1943 when he was shot down over northern France. However, he survived and with assistance of the French managed to return to England by the end of that month.

During December 1941, Zuromski was promoted to flight lieutenant, due to time served in the previous rank and for his efficiency and good conduct. The winter period of 1941 prohibited a lot of flying, and it was the coldest December for some years. Pilot Officer Edmund Krawczynski lost his life in an accident after encountering adverse weather on 21 December. His Spitfire, P6183, crashed near Lytham, Blackpool. Zuromski recorded a flight in Spitfire P8183 that day, flying to Blackpool, quite possibly looking for the missing Krawczynski.

No. 308 Squadron moved to Woodvale, north of Liverpool, in December 1941. The airfield had been built as a fighter airfield for the protection of Merseyside following the Luftwaffe winter raids of 1940 and 1941. The living quarters were basic for 308 Squadron, who were the first operational squadron to be resident on site. A bombing decoy site was built at Great Altcar to lure the enemy bombers away from the airfield. The night-time decoy displayed a series of lights to simulate an airfield. The control building housed a power generator and contained a communications and operations room and shelter for the decoy crew. Decoy sites without doubt proved effective in deceiving the Luftwaffe night bombing operations when targeting mainland airfields.

In January 1942, 308 Squadron was required to patrol the Liverpool districts and protect the important shipping passages. They were also required to fly at night in an attempt to make contact with the Luftwaffe bombers targeting Liverpool and the dock infrastructure. Several training flights were undertaken to prepare for those unusual duties. Zuromski experienced his first night flying in circuits undertaken on 6 January. Three nights later, Squadron Leader Marian Wesołowski and Kazimierz Dolicher flew into the night sky but both Spitfires collided. Wesolowski was killed, however Dolicher was only slightly injured and was able to land his damaged Spitfire, P7745, at Woodvale. Their accident clearly illustrated the additional dangers faced when flying Spitfires offensively at night. Zuromski flew several night protection sorties in January, in addition to shipping protection. He was scrambled on one occasion for a daylight interception that was inconclusive in its outcome.

February involved several duties engaged with instruction and training. Air firing exercises were always beneficial and normally honed the skills of any fighter pilot. News reached 308 Squadron that the permanent war rank of flying officer was to be granted to a number of pilots who had previously been granted the Polish equivalent rank. This did not affect Zuromski as he already bore the more senior rank of flight lieutenant by that time.

That winter period saw the Irish Sea constantly becoming the source of fog and mist that enveloped the area. The inability to fly saw the development of what were called 'weather runs' into Blackpool for entertainment. On 9 February Squadron Leader Nowierski, Pilot Officers Pietruski and Ilinski in company with Flight Lieutenant Zuromski set off for Liverpool in one of the many cars that had been accumulated on the station for such weather runs. Unfortunately, they crashed and, with the exception of Zuromski, all received some injuries, which were treated at Southport hospital. Olgierd Ilinski's injuries were such that he did not return to the squadron immediately. He later lost his life flying a Rodeo sortie on 16 August 1943.

Zuromski flew Spitfires at Woodvale on varied training sorties, including towing targets. His log book indicates that there were several flights towing a target in Spitfire BL482. The use of Spitfires for such duties is rarely seen and it can only be speculated as to the type of targets they towed. No. 308 Squadron was operating over the Altcar firing ranges, which lay at the mouth of the River Alt, towards the southern end of the Sefton Coast sand dune system. Twelve miles north of Liverpool, the village of Hightown was the closest residential area. The squadron records indicate that moving trams were seen on occasions in the firing ranges, which caused concern. On 25 March, squadron records note that Zuromski's Spitfire collied with a lorry parked on the runway during dusk. No reference to this was recorded in his own log book. In the absence of a red endorsement in his log book, something that was used when a pilot received a caution or warning for his actions, it has to be assumed the incident was not worthy of any reprimand. The rest period at Woodvale was closing for the squadron and preparations were under way for a posting to Exeter on the south coast.

Between April and June, there was a new wave of bombing from the Luftwaffe on the south coast of England. These operations were launched on Hitler's orders in retaliation for the RAF raid on the German city of Lubeck in March. Exeter was the first place to be targeted, and it was bombed over three consecutive nights in April. The attack on Sunday, 3 May was the heaviest the city had suffered, with approximately thirty bombers dropping 54 tons of bombs in an attack that lasted just under an hour. The following day German radio broadcasted,

> Exeter was the jewel of the West … We have destroyed
> that jewel, and the Luftwaffe will return to finish the job.

No. 308 Squadron had moved to Exeter at the start of April, having been delayed by dangerous weather at Woodvale. The planning of moving an entire squadron from one end of the country to the other required some ingenuity, combining both land and air movements. The first two days were spent unpacking and settling into Exeter. The pilots did get airborne at the first opportunity to fly locally and gather an understanding of the landfall around them. A bombing decoy station at Aylesbeare Common was in place to draw the Luftwaffe bombers away from attacking the aerodrome at Exeter. It was a target that had been among the Luftwaffe's prime objectives during the 1942 raids.

No. 308 Squadron was part of the 2nd Polish Wing at Exeter. There Zuromski was confronted with operational offensive flying with some intensity, and his log book records a flurry of entries. Frequently the unit began its day with a flight south to the adjacent 11 Group airfields, where its aircraft were fuelled for sorties over the Continent. Often two or three such missions were flown during one day, with pilots and aircraft logging long hours. In addition, the squadron carried on with defensive patrols over Exeter. Often forgotten is the fact that lengthy hours in the air created more servicing and additional ground crew duties, which impacted on almost everybody stationed at a base.

Zuromski flew on 4 April undertaking convoy protection. That same day news broadcasts reported the bombing of Darwin, Australia, by the Japanese. It was a disturbing development for the war raging on the other side of the world. Zuromski scrambled on 6 April but once in the air he was diverted to provide convoy protection. On 10 April there was another unproductive convoy protection scramble. Zuromski's name did not appear on the orders for the Circus on 14 April. On that operation the squadron flew as top cover to twelve Boston light bombers returning from France when they were attacked by Messerschmitts and Fw 190s. Squadron Leader Antoni Wczelik and Flying Officer Edward Jankowski were both shot down in the sudden but short aerial battle. On 16 April, Zuromski flew to

Tangmere in Sussex and later escorted Bostons over France and flew a sweep before returning to Tangmere. Three enemy fighters were claimed as shot down by the Polish pilots that day. It was also the day on which Malta's heroism and endurance under ceaseless enemy air attacks was rewarded. It was announced that the island was to receive the George Cross, a unique occasion in military history.

On 22 April, a sweep was flown to provide rear fighter cover to aircraft returning from France. Flying Officer Tadeusz Stabrowski and Pilot Officer Stanisław Madej of 308 Squadron damaged a Ju 88 on a defensive patrol that day. Zuromski was scrambled once more on 23 April dispatched to Bolt Head, and to the same destination the following day. Bolt Head was a satellite airfield for Exeter, effectively an emergency landing ground. It was also the location of an important radar interception site. Bolt Head became important as it lay in the usual flight path of the Luftwaffe hit and run bombings upon Torquay and Exeter. At Bolt Head there was a daylight scramble capability of two pilots strapped in their Spitfires ready for immediate take-off. Such measures were necessary in order to rapidly take to the air and chase or attack the marauding Luftwaffe Ju 88s and intruding Fw 190s. Exeter was once again the chosen target of the Luftwaffe on the night of 24 April, when several people died in the bombing. Twenty-five bombers struck in what was a reprisal raid on the orders of Hitler to have the greatest possible effect on civilian life.

On 25 April Zuromski recorded another Spitfire escort mission to escort bombers returning from France. Thirteen Spitfires took off from Exeter at 0840 hours. The log book holds a red ink entry by Zuromski illustrating a swastika with the comment 'One Me 109 probably destroyed'. He additionally noted on the same page, 'Flight Lieutenant F. Szyszka, One Me 109 Destroyed'. All thirteen Spitfires returned safely at 1005 hours. It was normal to immediately provide information to the station intelligence staff by way of debriefings. Strangely, 308 Squadron records provide little if any record of engaging the Luftwaffe on 25 April, simply noting several

Messerschmitts seen, but that results were unobserved. Post-war research at the Imperial War Museum archives disclosed that the wing guns carried on Zuromski's aircraft on 25 April had been fitted with automatic cameras. The cameras filmed any operation of the guns after the firing button was pressed by the pilot. Known as the G45 gun camera, it was designed and manufactured by the Williamson company of London and Reading. The cameras used 16mm orthochromatic film supplied in 25ft lengths. They operated with a frame speed of twenty exposures per second, corresponding to the rates of fire of the Browning machine guns. The cameras were fitted in the wings of many Fighter Command aircraft and controlled by an automatic electrical switch operated by the gun-firing pneumatic system. The film that was exposed during Zuromski's engagement with the Bf 109s that day was processed and developed, identified as film numbers 112 and 113. Both films had been indisputably fully exposed in the air on 25 April. The only missing detail was the failure to record the exposure time, which was the duty of the photographic technician. The film evidence clearly identifies damage caused to one Bf 109 and that on two occasions the target attacked by Zuromski had been identified as a Luftwaffe Bf 109. This is indisputable evidence supporting the credibility of the log book entry. For reasons unknown, the combat report of events submitted by both Zuromski and Szyszka were not accepted, which appears to be unjust.

Feliks Szyszka was an experienced Polish fighter pilot who had flown against the Luftwaffe during the bombing of Poland in September 1939. Szyszka experienced the terrifying circumstances of being shot down and while suspended on his parachute he was shot at and injured while unable to defend himself. He was captured and placed in a hospital, where he received treatment for his callously inflicted injuries. With great fortitude, he escaped from the hospital and made his way through occupied territory until he eventually reached France and then went on to England. He regained fitness and returned to operational flying with 308 Squadron.

Some Polish airmen serving in Bomber Command enjoyed the status of flying in one of very few predominately Polish-manned squadrons. Pilot Officer J. Fusinski was a pilot on 300 Squadron. His Polish crew were shot down three days after Zuromski celebrated his success protecting the bombers returning from operations over France. On 27 April, among a stream of bombers, Fusinski reached Belgium on his way to bomb Cologne. He had the misfortune of being attacked by a Luftwaffe night fighter and had to instruct his crew of five fellow Poles to abandon their Wellington. The events that followed were of such fortitude that once known Fusinski was officially recommended to be Mentioned in Despatches. It stated:

> Baling out over Belgium he successfully evaded capture, and although injured in the knee from his parachute jump, immediately commenced his journey southwards. Finally, too disabled to walk, he decided to venture a journey by train. Displaying great initiative and boldness he successfully reached Brussels. Obtaining information for his further journey, almost from the enemy himself, he succeeded in crossing a frontier river and reached Paris. He continued by train to the area of demarcation where he was compelled to hide for a period and suffer great privations. Although now very weak from lack of food, he nevertheless succeeded in swimming a river into unoccupied France and proceeded immediately to Lyon. Content with only a short rest he made his way into Spain, whence he was repatriated on 19 August 1942.

The next day, 28 April, saw Zuromski flying a sweep into France. The target area was Guînes, a historical town about 10 miles from Calais. Twelve Spitfires left Exeter at 1420 hours and returned safely after a flight of one hour and forty minutes. As the month closed, Zuromski flew a sortie protecting a convoy and another on 1 May. As the new month arrived, the Luftwaffe once again returned to attack Exeter. Bolt Head received a brazen attack by five Bf 109s on a 'tip and run' bombing. At 1,000ft they dived and dropped two bombs close to the dispersed fighters on the ground. The other Bf 109s shot up at any target they saw, while a further bomb also fell. Sergeant Henryk Marchewicz of 306 squadron suffered a facial injury while still on the ground that caused the end of his service as a fighter pilot.

The Luftwaffe sent in the region of twenty-five further 'tip and run' attacks that month. A Ju 88 was claimed destroyed when a pair of Spitfires flown by Flying Officer Stabrowski and Flight Sergeant Władysław Majchrzyk chased the aircraft all the way back to Cap de la Hague on 3 May. Each pilot officially claimed the destruction of the bomber. Sufficient evidence was presented to the intelligence officer whereby a half claim was credited to each pilot. The squadron had been on alert during the night bombings of Exeter and on 4 May four Spitfires were scrambled to intercept the German raiders. Squadron Leader Nowierski and Flying Officer Retinger managed to make contact with the bombers but they were thwarted in inflicting any damage upon them. The raid on that night killed more than 150 people and injured nearly 600. Many ancient buildings including the cathedral were damaged or destroyed in the flames. In total, the raids on Exeter resulted in a great many deaths and the casualties were buried in a mass grave in Higher Cemetery at Heavitree.

The Polish contingent of 308 Squadron, having witnessed the devastation of Exeter, left the airfield after five weeks. During that time the squadron had participated in many offensive sweeps and bomber escort missions over occupied France, as well as the more routine shipping and convoy patrols over the ports and sea lanes and standing combat patrols. They had also endeavoured to protect Exeter as best possible from the night bombings and daylight intruders.

On 6 May, the squadron received word that their flight commander, Feliks Szyszka, was to be promoted to squadron leader and he would take command during the following day. The squadron departed

Exeter for Hutton Cranswick, near Driffield in Yorkshire, where their main duty was to defend the eastern coast of England along what was known as the Hull–Whitby line. The Luftwaffe had been a constant threat to Allied convoys and whenever it was possible to fly, a pair of Spitfires patrolled over the passing convoys from dawn until dusk. Other pilots were kept at scramble readiness at Hutton Cranswick. On 17 May, Szyszka, the pilot denied the combat claim with Zuromski in April, was flying in a formation exercise with other pilots of 308 Squadron when he collided with another Spitfire flown by Sergeant Witold Knott. Both aircraft, BL534 and AB250, fell to the ground, killing both pilots. The 308 Squadron records make reference to the funerals, but little definitive detail exists on the accident. Both pilots were buried on 21 May and the Battle of Britain veteran Squadron Leader Walerian Zak took over command of the squadron and would lead the unit for the following months. Both 306 and 308 Squadron were ordered to fly out over the North Sea in the early hours of 31 May to provide extended fighter protection for the bomber crews returning from the first 1,000-bomber raid upon Germany.

The month of June saw an absence of flying entries in Zuromski's log book. This may well have been leave or illness, however, Squadron Leader Zak's signature appeared in his log book when it was submitted for inspection at the end of the month. July would see Zuromski return to dusk flying, interception training and another long convoy protection sortie. The Luftwaffe crews operating from bases in Norway constantly probed the east coast waters searching for convoys. Whenever they were spotted, the Luftwaffe tactics were to avoid and evade any engagement with the RAF. A formation flying exercise over Godstone in Surrey on 6 July resulted in 308 Squadron suffering further losses through another aerial collision, Pilot Officer Julian Kawczynski was killed, while Sergeant Witold Herbst suffered serious injuries. The Polish pilots applied white stripe markings on the noses of selected Spitfires in an experiment to aid instant recognition but it received no approval from the RAF. Interestingly, this white stripe principle was actually adopted for application on the wings of Allied aircraft to provide recognition in the June 1944 invasion of Europe.

At 1830 hours on 24 July, Zuromski was to lead with two Spitfires undertaking a weather reconnaissance flight. This was simply to fly out over the waters at height in order to ascertain weather front activity. The weather conditions often dictated if any intrusions were likely to be undertaken by the Luftwaffe. His second pilot was Pilot Officer Adam Habela, a man who had previously encountered a frightening experience when his Miles Magister broke apart in the air due to catastrophic structural failure, and his parachute saved his life. Habela and Zuromski both received radio interception instructions shortly after taking off from Hutton Cranswick. They were about 60 miles out over the sea and were effectively scrambled to the navigation vectors provided, which disappointingly only resulted in the sighting of a British Beaufighter. Subsequent vectors were also given that resulted in another sighting for the pair of Spitfire pilots as approximately 3 miles distant an aircraft was heading away from their position. Full boost was applied to the Spitfires' engines, effectively giving extra speed that was produced by the supercharger, as the suspect aircraft was seen to commence a turn to starboard. This provided an opportunity to head off the aircraft and they closed rapidly to 1,000ft. As he did so, Zuromski's Spitfire, P8746, came under gunfire from the aircraft he was chasing. Closing further, the aircraft was identified as a Ju 88. Habela was ordered to attack after the confirmed identification as Zuromski opened fire and closed even further upon the bomber. He made two attacks from starboard, finishing dead astern before crossing to the port quarter, when Habela then attacked. Zuromski had previously seen the bomber's starboard undercarriage leg drop and hang loosely, and that the starboard engine was smoking. The gunners in the Luftwaffe bomber were targeting Zuromski's Spitfire but as Habela attacked they stopped firing. Zuromski turned into the Ju 88 and this third attack used up his ammunition completely. Habela attacked as the German flew into cloud. The Ju 88 was listing to starboard, seriously damaged. Both Spitfires had used up all their ammunition and damage was seen inflicted during their attacks. Both pilots considered that the Ju 88 was incapable of returning to its base.

After returning to Hutton Cranswick, the armaments officer reported that Zuromski had fired 120 cannon rounds and 640 machine gun rounds. Additionally, his number one port gun had jammed after 72 rounds and his number two port gun had jammed after 90 rounds. Habela had fired 116 cannon rounds and 380 machine gun rounds. His number one port gun had jammed after 18 rounds. Both Spitfires were not carrying camera guns. Zuromski added another swastika motif into his log book, claiming one Ju 88 destroyed. Officially both Polish pilots were credited with half each.

On 30 July, 308 Squadron was transferred back into 11 Group, creating another posting that saw them moving back towards Northolt, but based at Heston in Middlesex. Fighter Command was continuing to engage with Circus and Rhubarb sorties in the long summer daylight periods. Returning from the adventurous Dieppe Commando raid on 19 August, Sergeant Czachla of 306 Polish Squadron was low on fuel. On the approach into Northolt airfield, his engine cut with Malvern Avenue laying in front of him as he lost height. The pilot tried to land on the roadway between the houses in an effort to avoid damaging the houses and to save his Spitfire aircraft. He escaped injury but some houses and his aircraft were damaged. Zuromski took his Spitfire on an offensive patrol across the Channel into France on 24 August and another on the 29th; both flights being of nearly two hours' duration.

On 6 September, 308 Squadron sent twelve Spitfires on a large Circus operation to France. Boston light bombers were escorted by four fighter squadrons and 308 Squadron joined up with the wing in mid-Channel. Once positioned about 7 to 10 miles distant from the French coast, a dinghy was spotted by 308 Squadron. A radio message was made reporting the dinghy's position and 308 Squadron detached a Spitfire to circle the area, remaining above the dinghy. Zuromski was by this time in the air, accompanied by Pilot Officer Mach, and orbiting over Dungeness to provide the usual rescue patrol flight for the Circus operation. Hearing of the dinghy, the pair flew towards Dieppe and sighted the circling Spitfire, which peeled off as they arrived. Zuromski and Mach protected the occupied dinghy and ensured its position was not lost while they awaited an air-sea rescue flight. Having been in the air for nearly two hours, Walrus W3076 arrived with its usual escort protection. The amphibious biplane had flown from Shoreham in Sussex, piloted by Flight Sergeant Barber and Sergeant Healy of 277 Squadron. Below them in the dinghy was Flight Sergeant Mason, a Spitfire pilot from 64 Squadron who had been shot down during a Circus operation on 5 September. He had been floating off the French coastline for thirty-seven hours. Unfortunately, he was by this time floating in a German minefield area, which could be seen by Zuromski. There were strings of mines stretched out but the Walrus flying boat was skilfully landed on the water between them. The weather was getting rougher and the prevailing winds hindered the rescue but the Spitfire pilot was successfully dragged aboard. After three attempts to take off, the Walrus eventually succeeded with enemy gunfire by that time being directed towards them from the French coastal batteries.

Zuromski had witnessed a most daring and brave rescue of a fellow Spitfire pilot who had parachuted into the sea and sat in the tiny inflated one-man fighter pilot's dinghy over many hours into nightfall and thereafter. Zuromski and Mach were by now low on fuel and navigated to the nearest landing site, which was Friston, on the chalk cliffs near Eastbourne, Sussex. Having obtained fuel, they arrived back at Heston a full three hours after having taken off.

At 0900 hours the following day, Zuromski took off in a Circus diversionary sweep. Twelve 308 Squadron Spitfires met with the

Northolt squadrons and the entire wing with the bombers made for Ostend. Another Spitfire escort wing came from 11 Group. Reaching the French coastline, they made towards Dunkirk, with their target the shipyards at Rotterdam. Before returning across the Channel, the uppermost squadron saw four Luftwaffe Fw 190s dive and attack. Pilot Officer Zdzitowiecki of 302 Squadron received serious damage to his Spitfire, which forced him take to his parachute and he was rescued from the Channel. Sergeant Edgar Lawrence Dickerson of 64 Squadron suffered a similar fate in his Spitfire, however his parachute failed to operate correctly and he lost his life in the fall. Dickerson was just nineteen years of age and now rests in the Bruges General Cemetery in Belgium.

On 26 September Zuromski entered 'Rear Rover to bombers' in his log book. Twelve Spitfires had flown to the aerodrome at Middle Wallop for this operation. No. 315 Squadron led the sweep, which made for Cherbourg. No. 308 Squadron at the rear was overflying the Isle of Wight as orders were received cancelling the operation, so they returned to Middle Wallop and then returned to Heston. As 1942 was drawing to a close there were escort operations involving upwards of fifteen squadrons. These various missions did not always succeed in their purpose of drawing enemy fighters into an aerial battle. The Luftwaffe often allowed large formations of Spitfires to fly unmolested over northern France and at times were prepared to ignore the light bombing raids rather than risk engaging in actions under what they regarded as unfavourable conditions. The Spitfires' range was always limited and these intrusion attacks were no doubt regarded mainly as nuisance raids by the Luftwaffe. They were, however, most impressive sights, with many aircraft forming up and crossing the shores of the south coastal cliffs to cross the Channel waters.

Without doubt, among the most unusual orders ever received by a fighter pilot were given to Zuromski on 10 October. He was required to fly his Spitfire over central London, concentrating on Wembley football stadium. Wembley was providing temporary accommodation for blitzed victims and refugees, but it also staged wartime football cup finals and internationals for the Red Cross and other charities. That day Scotland and England were to play an international game with an attendance of 75,000 visitors. The famous post-war football manager Matt Busby played for Scotland in the match. He was a soldier, serving in the King's Liverpool Regiment, Army's Physical Training Corps, and had been given permission to participate. Zuromski flew above the stadium, his presence being both practical and serving to enhance morale in protecting the public in the stadium. The 308 Squadron record book holds a cryptic comment that states:

> Twenty-two members of the island race kick a ball at the Wembley Stadium, whilst the squadron plays 'nanny' and keeps out any intruders.

Two days later, the entire Polish wing of thirty-six Spitfires patrolled over the Channel. No. 308 Squadron departed from Northolt with ten Spitfires but later landed at Tangmere in readiness on the south coast. Among the 308 Squadron Polish pilots was the newly arrived Pilot Officer Karol Marschall. Like so many, he had endured the training duties of towing targets for an air gunnery school before being provided the opportunity to fly the Spitfire at an operational training unit. Zuromski's final shipping patrol of the year took place on 15 October.

An operation to Cherbourg was cancelled at the last minute on 2 November, while Zuromski flew an air-sea rescue sortie on 7 November. Two further Circus operations to the French coastal areas took place on 8 and 9 November, and there was an eventful close escort for Boston bombers to Le Havre on 10 November. Interestingly there are two combat gun camera film exposures, number 2887 and 2886, held in the Imperial War Museum archives where Zuromski had selected and fired his guns at ground defences posts and a sea mine during that operation to Le Havre. There is no mention of those events in the log book entry for that day. This camera film appears to be slightly obscure evidence, not expected for the duties of a Spitfire pilot flying close escort duties. However, the squadron operational records provide an explanation. Flying with 302, 306 and 315 Squadrons, the Spitfires crossed the Channel and 308 Squadron saw a dinghy and an antenna mine. Clearly this will have been the mine the gun camera film recorded as being exploded by gunfire from Zuromski's Spitfire. During this Circus operation, two Bostons collided and both crashed into the sea but nothing else of note was recorded. It has to be assumed that Zuromski also took the opportunity to strafe the ground defence position on or in close proximity to the target area that day.

RAF combat reports were written by pilots who engaged in aerial combat with the enemy. They are the official reports that cover offensive action by the squadrons, wings and groups serving within all Commands. The records that survive are now held at The National Archives in series AIR 50. During the war the pilots composing these reports were most unlikely to know that the information was actually providing significant intelligence that was cascaded down to a plethora of official departments. The methods of attack and the weapons and ammunition deployed were of obvious importance. The height and general location of where the encounter took place and any identifying aspects of the aircraft attacked also revealed intelligence that was useful in many aspects of the service.

No. 308 Squadron sent two Spitfires on a free-ranging Rhubarb sortie to seek out locomotive movements on the French railways on 26 November. Steam trains were primary targets for these operations and the pilots located a well-loaded goods train, which was successfully attacked and probably destroyed. Following the rail line for another target, they reached the River Seine, where a tug vessel was seen. Both Spitfires turned and commenced an attack when unexpected and intense light flak ranged upon them. Pilot

Officer Bogdan Mijakowski's aircraft was damaged but he escaped the area, making towards the Channel. He was sideslipping but eventually crashed into the water, leaving nothing more than a dirty patch of oil. Flight Lieutenant Tadeusz Koc had escaped unscathed and had followed the stricken Spitfire until it struck the water. He remained over the crash site for some time before he was forced to leave. Mijakowski had been another of the cadet pilots from Deblin.

Zuromski and Karol Marschall took off from Northolt along with ten further Spitfires from 308 Squadron on 6 December to fly a Circus on a diversionary sweep. Meeting the Kenley wing, the sweep crossed the French coast east of Dunkirk. Operations reported enemy aircraft in the vicinity but none were sighted by any pilots. All aircraft returned safely an hour and forty minutes later. Another ten Spitfires departed Heston on 12 December, flying with 302 Squadron to create another diversionary sweep into France. On this occasion Zuromski and Marschall were required to remain in the air for air-sea rescue duties supporting the sweep.

The final operation for Zuromski in 1942 was another diversionary sweep on 30 December. He flew to Cherbourg, where a short but robust flak assault occurred. All twelve 308 Squadron Spitfires returned safely. During 1942 the Polish squadrons combined had accrued a most credible figure of around 1,700 operational sorties, many protecting shipping.

The year 1943 began with the sporadic bombing by the Luftwaffe of coastal areas across southern England. On 9 January, 306, 308 and 315 Squadrons escorted twelve Bostons to France but the weather prevented any bombing. Zuromski added another one hour and thirty-five minutes flying into his log book. He was approaching a total accumulative record of 1,000 hours' flying time. The friendship between Zuromski and Marschall ended when Marschall was dispatched to the Officers School at Cosford on 3 February 1943. That day during the Circus 258's attack on airfields in France, the Northolt Spitfire wing fought hard with a group of Fw 190s over

Courtrai. The Luftwaffe strength of fighters was thought to have been between twenty to thirty. The encounter was fierce and endured, with the Luftwaffe engaging well into Channel waters. No. 308 Squadron's pilots took a mauling: Flying Officer Jan Wiejski was killed; Flying Officer Jerzy Zbierzchowski and Sergeant Jan Okroj were shot down to become prisoners of war; while Flight Lieutenant Tadeusz Koc was officially reported missing, having been seen to go down over Dunkirk. Many other aircraft were shot up and damaged. The escorted bombers suffered one loss, while one also force-landed at Manston through combat damage. During the debriefing and intelligence gathering after this costly operation, Squadron Leader Zak and Flight Lieutenant Koc were credited with one probable Fw 190 each. Group Captain Mieczysław Mumler, the commander of the Polish base in Northolt, was accredited with another as damaged.

On 15 February Zuromski made another impressive entry into his log book when he flew his Spitfire on another Circus to Dunkirk. A large German vessel had berthed there and the operation was mounted to attack the port. Nos. 306 and 308 Squadrons were ordered to fly in the forward position led by Wing Commander Kolaczkowski, with 303 with 315 Squadrons operating as support over the target led by Squadron Leader Szczesny. Zuromski penned in red ink 'One Fw 190 damaged', illustrating another swastika on the log book page. The combat report reads:

> Half way back across the channel I heard Highway Squadron saying that they were being attacked by FWs. The squadron turned left, making off in the direction of the French Coast. As I had not sufficient room to turn with the squadron I turned right, climbing as I did so, and saw above me, at about 20,000 feet many aircraft milling round and streams of tracer fired by enemy aircraft. I saw four FW190s above me so I climbed and attacked two of them, giving two short bursts to each enemy aircraft,

range 600 yards as enemy aircraft climbing and banking, results were unobserved. Soon after, I saw seven FWs positioning to attack Highway squadron which I warned, thereupon three FWs turned north and the other four dived away towards Cap Gris Nez. I heard a pilot saying over R/T that he could see a parachute in the sea between Cap Gris Nez and Sangatte. Coming back, about ten miles from Dover, I saw first two FWs at approximately 15,000 feet at the same time as I got a warning from operations that enemy aircraft were at 22,000 feet, then I saw another five between 15/19,000 feet turning right. As I was above them, I dived down, two enemy aircraft turned left, the three remaining, turned right. While one FW was still turning left, I delivered a beam attack giving it a three second burst with more than two rings deflection, whereupon the hun immediately stopped turning, started weaving sluggishly, slowly losing height. I followed it down for approximately 2,000 feet hoping to finish it off but I had to break off the chase as streams of tracer started to fly past my port side. I turned right very steeply and went down to 9,000 feet. I heard warnings that enemy aircraft were near Dover. The Wing Commander ordered aircraft to converge on Deal which I did, but as my fuel was running low, I landed at Rochester with five gallons left in my tanks. I claim one FW damaged.

Circus 299 Northolt Polish Wing 15 February 1943.

Flying Officer Zuromski

A debriefing to the squadron intelligence officer took place and details were subsequently recorded within both the squadron summary of events and record of events. Warrant Officer Piatkowski also submitted a combat report with identical times and similar locations. He likewise was unable to rejoin 308 Squadron and had returned alone but with sufficient fuel to reach Northolt. Zuromski was flying a Spitfire Mk VB. The suffix B after the aircraft type, denotes that it was fitted with two 20mm cannon guns and four machine guns. Officially, Piatkowski's combat was confirmed as probably destroyed, whilst Zuromski's combat report, submitted as having damaged a Fw 190, was not officially accepted. These circumstances appear difficult to understand as the only differing circumstance would be Zuromski's decision to peel away turning right because he was of the opinion insufficient space was available to turn in with the squadron strength. The author is left wondering if that action was interpreted in a different perspective by person or persons unknown. The events are recorded in the squadron daily and summary official records but the combat action against the Luftwaffe fighter pilot is not officially endorsed or credited to Zuromski.

The Sikorski Museum archives A.V.44/11/22c holds a document where the claim of inflicting damage on an Fw 190 on 15 February has lines drawn across in red and 'Not Admitted' has been typed. The understanding of this situation may be made clear by the fact that fighter pilots could claim an enemy aircraft destroyed, probably destroyed or damaged, with the bar of proof set high in all instances. For a claim of destroyed, the incident had to have been witnessed by an independent person and seen to crash, to have crashed in flames or to have broken up in the air, or the pilot to have taken to his parachute. Any aircraft spinning away trailing smoke or flames but not seen to crash, explode, or the pilot escape by parachute could only be claimed as probable. The intelligence officers could not endorse a claim as destroyed even if the reporting pilot saw it crashing without corroboration. The one exception was gun camera film, which had to reveal damage so heavy that it was highly probable that the enemy aircraft had been destroyed.

Dunkirk appeared once more on the operational briefing for Circus 270 on 18 February 1943, however the operation was cancelled shortly after the Northolt Spitfires had formed up for crossing the Channel.

The following morning, 308 Squadron flew a battle formation exercise, which was completed after ninety minutes. Zuromski duly entered the details in his log book, unaware that this was to be the last entry he would make while serving with 308 Squadron. Two days later there was jubilation on the squadron when Flight Lieutenant Tadeusz Koc unexpectedly arrived at Northolt. He had survived his parachute escape on 3 February over France and had been fortunate in gaining assistance in escaping capture. The French took him on to Gibraltar and he was shipped to England after just eighteen days.

For Zuromski there was disappointment and possibly confusion when he was instructed to depart 308 Squadron, having been posted to join a non-Polish contingent fighter squadron. Orders were for him to report to 66 Squadron at Skeabrae in the Orkneys. As he departed, the commanding officer and the 'B' Flight senior officer both signed his log book and applied the official 308 Squadron Polish rubber stamp impression on to the page once the flying hours were completed and signed.

Polish squadrons were stationed at Northolt throughout the war and a Polish liaison officer was appointed at the group's Uxbridge bunker to liaise directly with Polish Air Force High Command. The Headquarters 11 Group Fighter Command at Uxbridge co-ordinated responsibility for organising fighter aircraft at airfields in the south-east of Britain. This posting for Zuromski appears isolated and it certainly was not commonplace to post a Polish pilot independently on to a non-Polish contingent squadron like 66 Squadron. The 308 Squadron daily record page for 23 February 1943 simply reported, 'Flying Officer Zuromski and his dog are posted to 66 Squadron.' The mascot was called Jumbie and it appears to have become Zuromski's companion, whereby after more than fifteen months together they were regarded as inseparable.

CHAPTER 8

66 SQUADRON SKEABRAE AND CHURCHSTANTON

On 9 February 1943, 66 Squadron relocated to Skeabrae in the Orkneys, where they would provide air cover for Scapa Flow. As the Royal Navy's main fleet anchorage, it was without doubt one of the single most important expanses of water in Europe. These waters faced the German seaborne forces across both the North Atlantic and the North Sea. The sea basin of some 120 square miles has navigable shipping entrances to the east, west and south between the islands of Hoy, Flotta and South Ronaldsay, irrespective of weather conditions.

No. 66 Squadron had joined 13 Group Fighter Command and was destined to fly in the wild Scottish weather conditions in the Orkneys. When the squadron pilots arrived at Skeabrae airfield, they were no doubt disappointed by the age and worn appearance of the Spitfire aircraft that confronted them. The engineering officer, however, gave them an endorsement of fitness to fly to protect the fleet anchorage at Scapa Flow from Luftwaffe reconnaissance flights. The squadron would also fly merchant shipping convoy protection sorties, which would be undertaken to the extremities of distance possible. The Arctic convoys delivered millions of tons of vital military supplies across treacherous, often freezing seas. Tanks, fuel, ammunition, raw materials and food were shipped to the Soviet Union's northern ports of Arkhangelsk and Murmansk.

Zuromski flew the length of the country before he arrived at the northern tip of Scotland and on to the island of Skeabrae. His log book records that he flew de Havilland Dominie X7345 in company with a Flight Sergeant Douglas on a two-day flight from Edinburgh Turnhouse before reaching Skeabrae on 2 March. It would appear that the Dominie biplane was to become the resident hack and jack of all tasks at the airfield. No. 66 Squadron was welcoming, with pilots from New Zealand, Australia and Rhodesia. The available records make no mention of Zuromski's black dog arriving with him, however it was common for pilots to be accompanied by a trusty mascot and it may well not have been noteworthy. Zuromski was, however, the only Polish pilot at Skeabrae.

Zuromski almost immediately took to the air in a Spitfire to reconnoitre the terrain and seas. The perils of the weather were illustrated within a few days after his arrival. On 12 March, Flying Officer William Horatio Donald failed to return from a sector reconnaissance. His Spitfire had lost all communication and was assumed lost in unknown circumstances. He had only recently arrived at Skeabrae. Zuromski undertook a search of ninety minutes in an effort to locate the missing aircraft but found nothing to report. An assumption was that the recent storm weather front had been responsible for his demise and neither the aircraft nor the pilot have never been located. Donald was an Irish volunteer from Stillorgan, County Dublin, in the Republic of Ireland. His life is commemorated on the Runnymede Memorial.

The following day, Zuromski flew a dawn patrol, followed by army co-operation exercises, while an inconclusive emergency scramble took place towards the end of the month. These scrambles were nearly always connected to intrusion flights by the Luftwaffe but frustratingly for the Skeabrae pilots they often passed without sight or contact. A radar station was present at Orkney, part of the defences for Scapa Flow, and an extension of the radar Chain Home network capability on the south and east coast of mainland Britain. The actual radar site was at Netherbutton, 4 miles east of Kirkwall. Initially, Netherbutton had been linked to the operations room at Wick but from late 1940 the station relayed information on approaching enemy aircraft to the combined gunnery and sector operations room at Kirkwall. From there the anti-aircraft guns located around Scapa Flow were controlled. The squadron scrambles were instigated by radar contacts by the Netherbutton site.

On 4 April 1943, Sergeant Harries took off with Squadron Leader Harold Bird-Wilson and Flight Sergeant Arthur Hill to escort a Dominie with engine trouble back to Skeabrae. Bird-Wilson, the commanding officer of 66 Squadron, was an ace Battle of Britain pilot. He had signed Zuromski's log book, confirming his flying hours and the dawn and dusk patrols he had undertaken in March and April 1943.

On 14 April, 66 Squadron was separated when 'B' Flight relocated to Sumburgh, the more northerly island on the Shetlands, while 'A' Flight with Zuromski remained at Skeabrae. He continued to fly the regular dusk patrols but on 1 May a high patrol with Flight Sergeant Hill covering Scapa Flow took place. They reached 30,000ft searching for expected intruders but found nothing. That day the newly promoted Flight Sergeant Harries suffered an incident when he struck the ground with his propeller tips during a low-flying exercise and was most fortunate to survive. Zuromski flew his last convoy patrol in the war-torn Spitfires on 5 May. A large and impressive convoy of around thirty merchant vessels escorted by two destroyers were making westwards to Pentland Firth.

New Spitfire Mk VIs arrived at Skeabrae, with expectations high among the station. These Spitfires were equipped with pressure-sealed cockpits and extended wingtips that were much more sharply contoured, as was the tail fin. These were performance-enhancing measures to enable the Spitfire to gain and attain greater heights in the sky required to counter the high-flying German reconnaissance aircraft over Scottish waters. Various types of German reconnaissance aircraft flew over Scotland from bases in Norway and Denmark. The Ju 88D-1 was the Luftwaffe's most effective long-range reconnaissance type, powered by Junkers inverted V12 engines that gave a maximum speed of around 295mph and a range of over 1,500 miles. The large Focke-Wulf Fw 200 Condor became synonymous as a truly long-range reconnaissance bomber and acted as the eyes and ears for the German Kriegsmarine vessels and submarines.

The Spitfire Mk VI was undeniably capable of dealing with the threat posed by the high-flying intruders. The powerful Merlin engine was fitted with a four-bladed propeller. However, fewer than 100 Mk VIs were built between December 1941 and October 1942. The pilots of 'A' Flight undertook their first air experience flight on the new type on 7 May. The Perspex cockpit canopy would require the pilots to undertake a rather more complicated method of opening in any emergency, a rather thought-provoking but necessary situation because of the pressurisation. Zuromski flew nearly three hours during three flights undertaken that day. He engaged in aerobatics, and tested the cannon, guns and cameras. He later flew a height test in one of the new Spitfires, reaching 38,000ft.

Squadron Leader Keith Temple Lofts took command of the squadron in May. He was an ace Battle of Britain pilot who also signed Zuromski's log book and thereafter endorsed his operations and flying records. Pilot Officer Henry Furniss-Roe arrived at 66 Squadron on 1 June 1943. He was a newly commissioned officer who had been posted from his operational training unit. He flew with Zuromski on 14 June, flying a dusk patrol between 2350 hours and 0110 hours. Flying the Spitfire at night was challenging; the exhaust outlets either side of the aircraft engine illuminated brightly, reducing the pilot's ability to see clearly in any darkening sky. The two pilots flew together again on a shipping convoy sortie on 17 June, flying between 0435 hours and 0605 hours. Furniss-Roe would later become renowned for two escapes from France after his Spitfires went down. Both incidents saw him escaping and evading capture, a most notable achievement.

On 18 June, 66 Squadron received news that it was going to be posted away from the Scottish island with a move southward to Churchstanton in Somerset. The idea of leaving the misty rain, squalls and inclement cloud for better flying conditions was most welcome to the pilots. Meanwhile, orders were received to carry out practice sweeps, a sign of duties that would in all probability be coming their way. The Czechoslovak 313 Squadron took over the Scapa defensive duties from 66 Squadron.

On 28 June, the pilots at Skeabrae flew their Spitfires to Peterhead in the far north-east of Scotland, where they were provided with a Handley Page Harrow transport for their onward journey to Churchstanton. The flight at Sumburgh were required to leave their Spitfires on station and arrangements were in hand for their transit to Churchstanton. The squadron's first two days at Churchstanton were spent flying sector reconnaissance flights across the Somerset and Devon borders. The landscape presented good opportunities for landmarks and navigation as they progressed towards flying convoy patrols in the Bristol and English Channels. Zuromski had now returned to familiar skies as he was not far from Exeter, where he had operated from in 1942. The entire squadron protected two large shipping convoys between 1345 hours and 2325 hours on 30 June. Nominated pilots protected the vessels on lengthy east and westbound shipping routes.

During 1943, offensive patrols over France and the Low Countries were flown primarily by the forty-eight squadrons located south of the Bristol Channel with a line eastward across the country reaching the Wash coastline. A considerable proportion of those squadrons were stationed at airfields of 11 Group in south-east England. The squadrons were usually grouped in two-squadron wings and named after the base from which they operated: Biggin Hill in Kent; Kenley in Surrey; Tangmere in Sussex; Hornchurch, North Weald and Debden in Essex; and Northolt in Middlesex.

No. 66 Squadron was on the westward boundary but well positioned to support the significant escort duties if necessary. The summer weather of July was embraced by the 66 Squadron pilots and it facilitated a lengthy exploration of the Channel to the French coast on 3 July, when they flew for just under two hours searching for a missing Wellington. However, they found nothing other than driftwood. Zuromski then flew two additional search sorties looking for the missing bomber, staying airborne for three and a half hours with flights in Spitfire EP757 and EP752. Once again, he found no trace of the missing aircraft. The search was for Wellington Z1470 from 460 Squadron and its Australian crew, which ditched returning from a raid to Bremen. It later became known the crew had difficulties and four men were still inside the aircraft when it sank. One crew member was fortunate to escape and was later rescued to become a prisoner of war.

The following day Zuromski flew from Churchstanton to Portreath on the north coast of Cornwall. The pilots were briefed for a sweep flight to Ushant Island in the Channel. It was at the north-westernmost point of France directly in line from the French port of Brest.

The day 4 July 1943 brought immense sadness to the Polish service personnel. General Sikorski, Poland's Prime Minister in exile, was killed in a tragic air crash after taking off from Gibraltar. The general was returning to London with his daughter and high-ranking staff officers. The aircraft, flown by a Czechoslovak pilot, had been in the air only a short time before it crashed. Only the pilot survived and great suspicion was voiced about the circumstances of the fatal accident. Flight Sergeant Dobson Hunter was the wireless operator on Sikorski's flight. His remains were not found and his life is commemorated on the Runnymede Memorial. Squadron Leader Wilfred Herring was the co-pilot and his remains were likewise not recovered. Flight Sergeant George Gerry's body was recovered, as was Sergeant Lewis Zalsbery, the navigator, but the remains of Zofia Leśniowska, Sikorski's daughter, were not. She is commemorated by a symbolic grave at the Powązki Military Cemetery in Warsaw. Of the sixteen people killed, two were members of the British House of Commons. General Sikorski's remains were recovered from the crash scene and on 8 July, his coffin, draped in a Polish flag, was carried on board a Polish destroyer for repatriation to the United Kingdom. His successor as commander-in-chief of the Polish forces was General Kazimierz Sosnkowski.

On 8 July there was another flight to Portreath for twelve of the 66 Squadron Spitfires. Zuromski was alongside Flying Officer Deytrikh, his signature appearing on the July summary page within Zuromski's log book. The pilots reported seeing both east and westbound convoys between Bolt Head and Portland Bill. The westbound convoy included the unusual sight of landing craft. Two days later another interesting operation for the entire wing of 66, 504 and 131 Squadrons flying from Hurn took place. They were to protect a stream of American Flying Fortress heavy bombers returning from France. The bombers were picked up near Le Havre and escorted without incident, however severe weather caused an unintended overnight stay at Hurn for the 66 Squadron pilots before being able to fly back to Churchstanton.

Flight Sergeant Harries experienced another close shave while returning from a convoy patrol on 20 July. His Spitfire suffered an engine failure when he was about 15 miles from the nearest landfall, his engine seizing completely just before 1900 hours as he flew over the coastline between Torquay and Exeter. At Kingsteignton, north of Newton Abbot, he pancaked into fields with his wheels up, escaping unscathed having put the Spitfire down with a gentle glide to earth. This was rather more dramatic than his previous bending of propeller tips in May. Also on 20 July, Flight Lieutenant Zuromski was promoted to lead the 'B' Flight pilots. This effectively meant that he was leading half of 66 Squadron's Spitfire pilots and was responsible for their welfare and operational effectiveness, working alongside the equal 'A' Flight commander.

On 25 July, the squadron was deployed across England to Coltishall, Norfolk, to provide close escort for Mitchells bombing Amsterdam. Ramrod 154 departed at 1400 hours and the twelve 66 Squadron Spitfires including Zuromski's joined twelve Mitchell bombers of 180 Squadron. Nos. 66 and 504 Squadrons provided close escort, 302 and 317 Squadrons escort cover, and 303 and 316 Squadrons high cover. The force formed up at Lowestoft at below 500ft and flew to the target area. The Mitchells dropped the bomb loads from 14,000ft but intense flak was experienced over the target. The escort climbed to 24,000ft, while the close escort encountered four Bf 109s identified below the main formation and these were engaged by 504 Squadron. One Bf 109 was damaged and one Spitfire was lost. Near Amsterdam heavy air fighting took place against ten to twenty Bf 109s in loose pairs and fours. However, all the bombers returned safely, as did 66 Squadron.

With no respite the following day, the pilots were briefed again and ordered to provide another close escort, this time to Bostons on a mission to Schiphol aerodrome, approximately 9 miles south-west of Amsterdam. Earlier that day, Ramrod 159 had taken place attacking Courtrai-Wevelgem. Zuromski received a briefing for Rodeo 250, which was planned for late afternoon. At 1934 hours, twelve Bostons from 107 and 342 Squadrons were escorted by the Spitfires of 66 and 504 Squadrons as close escort. Nos. 302 and 317 Squadrons flew as escort cover and 303 and 316 Squadrons both provided high cover at around 22,000ft. Approaching the Dutch coast, one of the bombers turned back, with four 66 Squadron Spitfires instructed to protect its return. As they did so, they spotted an aircraft circling over an air-sea rescue operation in the Channel, which they avoided. Schiphol aerodrome was attacked successfully from around 15,000ft and the bombers were unmolested as no enemy aircraft appeared. The withdrawal element of fighter protection provided by the Canadian

Spitfires of 118 and 402 Squadrons joined the bombers and they flew inland to the Dutch coast. As they did so they were engaged by twelve or more Luftwaffe fighters, one of which was claimed as damaged in the short aerial fight. The bombing operation was regarded as successful. The 66 Squadron pilots were required to be rested overnight in Norfolk. Squadron intelligence officers at several stations undertook the operation debriefings, a complicated task to undertake with many Spitfire pilots undertaking several specific supporting duties.

The following day, the 66 Squadron Spitfires flew to Martlesham Heath in Suffolk to provide another escort cover duty. This time it was an attack in Belgium upon Courtrai airfield, Ramrod 162, and 504 Squadron also joined the escort party for nine Bostons from 88 Squadron. Departing at 1035 hours, the aircraft all crossed the English coast heading towards the Belgian coast at Nieuport, when 504 Squadron was attacked by enemy fighters. However, this was ineffective and limited in duration, leaving no opportunity for Zuromski and the other 66 Squadron pilots to become involved. Completing the operation, the Spitfires returned to Churchstanton for much-needed rest. During the next night, 26 July, Luftwaffe bombers attacked East Anglia and south-eastern areas of England.

Daylight Circus operations attacking key targets with medium bombers such as the Boston were mounted purposely to entice the Luftwaffe fighters into attacking them. This was rather disconcerting for the light bomber crews, who knew they were being used as bait. The significant numbers of escorting Spitfires protecting them were deployed strategically, assumed to always be in a position to engage and be capable of inflicting meaningful losses on Luftwaffe fighters should they attack. Where twelve bombers were involved, the RAF normally formed what were called two boxes of bombers. This was six aircraft in two boxes, each flying in a double formation. Forming up took place over the Channel, with the Spitfires flying low to avoid enemy radar. Only when closing to the target area would they all gain height to around 12,000ft. After the bomb run the aircraft would turn into a diving trajectory.

The close escorting Spitfire pilots on these daylight operations made certain that both sides of the bombers had a flight on each side. The rear of the bomber stream was likewise protected. If the enemy was spotted, the squadron commander would instruct specific fighter pilots to engage, usually with a very tight turn away from the stream. The Spitfires often lost sight of the bombers and the pilots could often thereafter be on their own. This explains how the fighter pilots might well become separated. In some cases, it was possible the fate of a particular pilot was not known should they fail to return because combat and chasing took place in ever-changing circumstances.

Some operations saw differing tactics. Occasionally, the Spitfire close escort and escort cover units were not deployed. Some preferences came to light for protection with top target and return cover. This was where Spitfires flew high and in front of the bombers to the enemy coast. The medium cover was in the target area itself and then some protection to the rear. The medium bombers that operated within No. 2 Group were all proficient at close-formation flying in the box configuration. This was flown in the step position in order to avoid turbulent slipstreams from preceding aircraft. The highly decorated pilot Basil Embry assumed command of No. 2 Group in June 1943. He had been shot down over France and had undertaken an audacious escape from his captors. As an acting air vice marshal, he advocated larger bomber strengths and the Circus operations gradually fell away from the regular schedules that had existed. Embry commanded with tenacity, and he continued to fly operational missions despite his high rank.

On 27 July, the weather was good and Zuromski was aware that the next operation he would fly would be in the afternoon that day. No. 66 Squadron flew to Tangmere on the south coast for a briefing with 131 Squadron. All ten Spitfires from 66 Squadron landed at Tangmere to receive briefing instructions for the escort for eighteen

Marauder medium bombers. Zuromski entered the detail 'Rodeo 164' into his log book. The wing would rendezvous over Beachy Head chalk cliffs near Eastbourne. The target was another Luftwaffe aerodrome, this time at Triqueville west of Paris. The operation was unopposed by flak or enemy fighters and 66 Squadron returned to Tangmere in excellent weather conditions. Following debriefing and rest, the dusk departure for Coltishall did not go well as once in the air the Spitfires were ordered to divert to Tibenham airfield, about 7 miles from Diss. It is assumed weather conditions enforced the diversion. Tibenham was nearing completion for occupancy by the US Army Air Force. The Spitfires landed safely and pleasantries were put in place for the pilots, who managed to rest and sleep before eventually returning to Coltishall in daylight the following morning.

With only three hours rest on the ground at Coltishall, Zuromski and eight other pilots were briefed and took off to rendezvous once more with twelve Bostons tasked to attack the Focke-Wulf aircraft factory at Amsterdam. On this occasion Zuromski entered 'Circus to Amsterdam' in his log book. No. 66 Squadron experienced heavy flak over the target area and guns fired by coastal batteries added to the firepower, as did some defensive guns from an enemy convoy on the Dutch coast. However, good fortune came in the fact that no Luftwaffe fighters appeared at any time. After a busy and long day, the Spitfires eventually landed back at Churchstanton, where another immediate patrol was ordered for Zuromski with a sea search west of Cherbourg. On 28 July Zuromski recorded a total of six hours and forty minutes of operational flying, which was a most unusual amount of flying time for any wartime Spitfire pilot.

The next day did not provide much rest. Zuromski took his Spitfire up for a thirty-five-minute air test before eventually leaving Churchstanton and flying to Tangmere once more. Orders were received to escort eighteen Marauders to the Netherlands, his log book stating 'Rodeo 166'. On that day, Marauders of the USAAF's 323 Bombardment Group were to attack Schiphol airfield, however the operation was cancelled and the aircraft were recalled. Also, that day Zuromski has a log book entry that states: 'Roadstead, six Beaufighters to Zeebrugge in Belgium'. The code Roadstead relate to dive bombing and low-level attacks on enemy ships at sea or in a dock situation. These shipping targets were dangerous, comprising deadly German flak ships, often former small fishing vessels and trawlers, which constantly moved position to unpredictable locations. Each flak ship carried significant anti-aircraft firepower and they were very capable of shooting down any aircraft attacking a port facility or vessel. The Beaufighter was a favoured and most effective Coastal Command aircraft that carried rockets and torpedoes.

It must be remembered that Bomber Command's heavy bomber force was consistently operational in their night-hour bombing campaigns. Targeting primary targets in central Germany was always fraught with danger and they were always undertaken without fighter escorts. The Command's loss of air crews were substantial, especially when penetrating to Berlin. They published quarterly reviews of performance, and review No. 61 of July 1943 quoted:

The destruction of Berlin without a much heavier weight of attack than Bomber Command alone can produce, is an extremely difficult problem. It is the target which above all, the Luftwaffe has to defend, and no chances will be taken with it even if this involves leaving lesser places like Stettin and Hanover relatively lightly protected. The penetration of enemy-held territory necessary to reach it is large. Finally, its mere size −18,000 acres of closely built-up area as compared with 8,380 at Hamburg − means that no noticeable impression can be made on it except by a large force. None of the three attacks made on it during this quarter was an unqualified success, though two of them caused extensive and important damage. The first attack fell

A Polish PZL P11c aircraft, a type flown during the September 1939 invasion of Poland. The leather-clad Polish pilots are wearing flying uniform of that period. (*Norman Franks*)

Julian Zuromski standing third from right among 308 Squadron personnel at Northolt. The group includes high-ranking officers and ground crew among several pilots who often used the large gasometers at South Harrow and Southhall as landmarks flying into what was a well-camouflaged aerodrome. (*Guillaume Hirsch*)

Above left: Portrait of Julian Zuromski when entering Polish military service. (*The Polish Institute and Sikorski Museum LOT.A.IV.1/47B-001*)

Above right: Zuromski with Jumbie, the 308 Squadron mascot. This little dog was a constant companion for him while serving with the squadron. (*M.P. Sikora*)

No. 308 Squadron personnel in December 1941. The squadron mascot sits upon the Spitfire, with Zuromski standing third from right. The pilots had little knowledge of the English language and regular lessons and the use of gramophone records with prepared literature assisted greatly with their vocabulary. (*M.P. Sikora*)

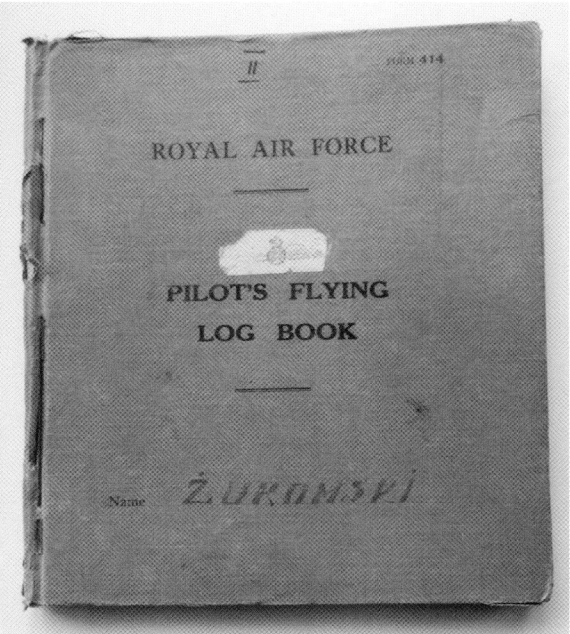

Above left: Zuromski's Royal Air Force pilot's flying log book. The consistent use of the book resulted in the use of heavy stitch repairs to hold the pages together. Thick twine or thread binds the spine in several places. (*Author's collection*)

Above right: An operational Royal Air Force station unveiling the Polish standard flag, which was required to be flown beneath the Royal Air Force standard flag.

Sergeant Nowakiewicz of 302 Polish Squadron with his Spitfire at Exeter in Devon in November 1941. The Polish chequerboard on this Spitfire is in an unusual position. The pilot, wearing leather cold-weather clothing, gives a victory sign before climbing into the cockpit. (*Author's collection*)

A Royal Air Force Fairey Battle aircraft painted with bold identification markings while deployed for target-towing duties. (*Author's collection*)

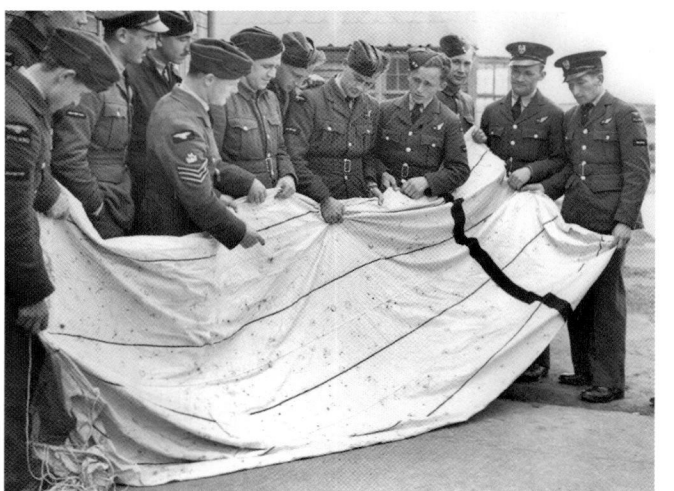

Above left: Polish air gunnery students examine the fabric target drogue that had been their target. Penetrating bullet holes recorded their gunnery accuracy. Live ammunition was expensive but was necessary for training. The Air Ministry announced to the public in 1943 that a five-second burst of ammunition from a Spitfire consumed ammunition that cost the country the then significant sum of £75 to manufacture.

Above right: Karol Pniak, a former pupil with the Air Force Cadets School at Deblin, commissioned in August 1939 and served with both 306 and 308 Squadrons. His Spitfire is displaying the Polish chequerboard below the engine manifolds. Pniak was recommended for the British Distinguished Flying Cross, having destroyed six German aircraft with 306 Squadron in July 1941. Northolt's Station Commander, Group Captain T.N. McEvoy, endorsed the award. (*Author's collection*)

Patriotic stamps created by the Polish forces in exile. The Minister for Wartime Production initiated the idea of presentation aircraft as a morale incentive in Britain. A financial target of £5,000 was created, which was considered to be a representative amount of money for a donor to raise for a Spitfire aircraft to be named after the town or institution that raised the funds.

Patriotic Polish Air Force messages printed upon stamps issued in 1941. (*Author's collection*)

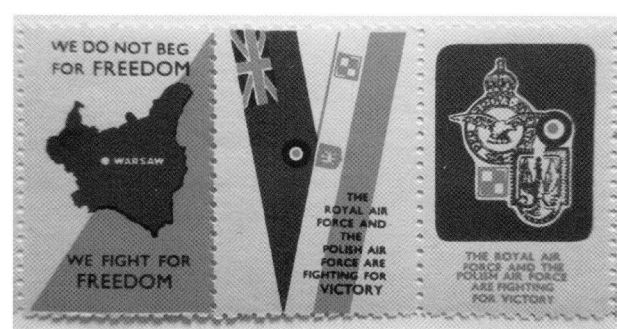

A flying log book page recording combat against the Luftwaffe flying from Exeter with 308 Squadron on 25 April 1942. Zuromski flew for two hours and ten minutes that day. Squadron Leader Nowierski, the squadron's commanding officer, applied his signature to the log book page shortly after the entry had been made. Imperial War Museum combat film illustrates this aerial engagement, reference CGC101-199. (*Author's collection*)

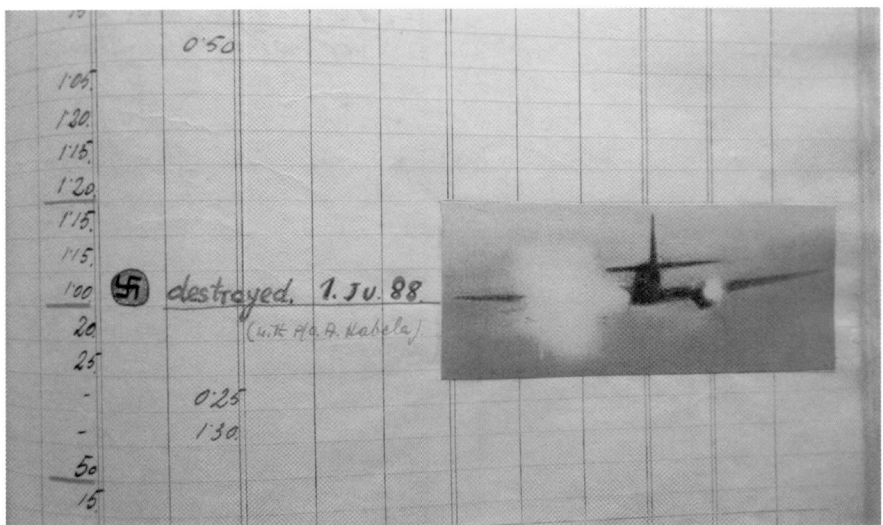

The flying log book entry of Zuromski recording his combat with a Luftwaffe Ju 88 that was probably destroyed on 24 July 1942 when flying from Hutton Cranswick in Yorkshire. Squadron Leader Zak, in command of 308 Squadron, applied his signature endorsing this record on 1 August 1942. The Polish Cross of Valour, Krzyż Walecznych, military decoration awarded to Zuromski was given for his operational sweeps in April and July and for the destruction of this Ju 88.

The flying log book entry made by Zuromski recording the damage inflicted upon an Fw 190 on 15 February 1943 flying from Northolt. That day he flew for just over two hours, Squadron Leader Kornicki, in command of 308 Squadron, applied his signature upon the flying log book page endorsing the entry. (*Author's collection*)

The full log book entries in February 1943 endorsed by the commanding officers. It appears that Zuromski anticipated the move to Skeabrae in Scotland early as he recorded an additional six sorties after calculating his flying hours. These were entered below his summary, which required amending to show the total hours flown that month. The second Polish Cross of Valour, Krzyż Walecznych, military decoration in the form of a 'bar' to his original medal was awarded to Zuromski in early 1943.

The 308 Squadron record of flying for December 1941 from Northolt. The Polish squadron official stamp and commanding officer signatures are clearly seen. Zuromski occasionally applied pasted cuttings from the *Flight* periodical, as seen on this particular page. (*Author's collection*)

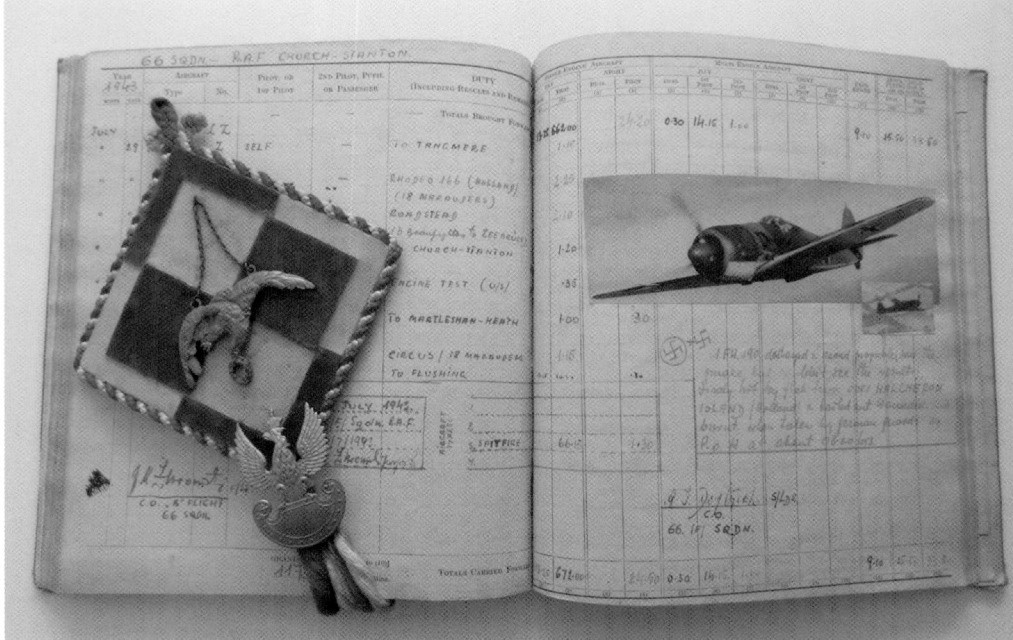

The impressive log book entry recording the events of 30 July 1943 while flying from Churchstanton in Somerset with 66 Squadron. The Polish Air Force chequerboard with chained pilot's wings and cap badge beneath were often gifted to recipients by Polish airmen throughout the war. Many had personal notes of appreciation written on the reverse of the chequerboard.

Above left: A Royal Pakistan Air Force Tempest displaying identification symbols on the tail fin. On 16 December 1949, 14 Squadron was placed under the command of Squadron Leader Julian Zuromski. On 24 March 1950 it flew to Miranshah on the banks of the Tochi River, where missions were flown against the insurgency of the Faqir of Ipi. (*Author's collection*)

Above right: Polish pilot Boleslaw Kaczmarek wearing the uniform of a Royal Air Force pilot officer and his Polish squadron badge. Kaczmarek was an accomplished veteran of 306, 316 and 302 Squadrons. As an instructor in the Royal Pakistan Air Force, he lost his life when his 5 Squadron Fury crashed near Maripur at Karachi on 25 October 1951.

well to the south-west of the centre of the city in the area of Charlottenburg and Marienfelde. The second was spoilt by unexpected meteorological conditions and caused damage only in the outlying suburban area in the south. The third, which, though the smallest in numbers was in some respects the most successful of the three, caused heavy industrial damage in Siemensstadt and the north-west of the built-up area. The area of damage resulting from these and earlier attacks approaches 500 acres and is thus about three-quarters of what the enemy succeeded in doing to the larger area of Greater London in a series of attacks extending fairly continuously over nine months. This, however, serves only to indicate the size of the whole job. It can be done, but it is not easy. Probably the most important result of these attacks was their effect on German morale. The first is said to have produced panic evacuation comparable to that experienced in Hamburg. The others added considerably to it. Firefighting services again proved inadequate to deal with the results of large-scale incendiary attacks ... The evacuation of towns affected by the air raids is proceeding in a very disorganised manner and there seem to have been no prepared evacuation plans for the civil population. People are being evacuated to wherever space can be found to Poland, Pomerania, Silesia, the Baltic States and even Denmark and Holland. Large numbers of evacuees from Hamburg were sent to Danzig, thus creating a crisis in living accommodation. Relatively few refugees from Hamburg have been sent to the Baltic States. Many have been sent to Poland very much against their wishes, as Poland has the reputation of being the most unpleasant and dangerous country for German settlers. Relations between Poles and Germans are extremely bad and the Poles seem to be becoming more and more daring in their dealings with the local Germans.

It is surprising to read that German civilians were being sent unwillingly to Poland for accommodation purposes. The German forces were undertaking mass deportations from Warsaw in the summer of 1943. It is possible that this may have influenced an opportunity for repurposing shelter and accommodation.

The day 30 July would be a momentous one for Zuromski. At 0550 hours, in company with five other 66 Squadron pilots, he flew to Martlesham Heath for an operational Ramrod briefing. The briefing disclosed the target to be Woensdrecht aerodrome, a Luftwaffe fighter airfield in the southern Netherlands. The Spitfires were escorting twenty-one Marauders of the US 386th Bomber Group. It was their first operation conducted from RAF Boxted, near Colchester, Essex. The briefings disclosed that the American unit had recently undergone extensive training to develop new tactics that involved higher-altitude flying, however this operation would be described as a medium-altitude operation. On the morning of the operation a Marauder crashed on take-off but the accident did not affect the remaining bombers leaving off successfully. They were to be escorted by six squadrons of Spitfires: twenty-one of 453 and 616 Squadrons from Ibsley for close escort; twenty from 66 and 504 Squadrons from Churchstanton as escort cover; and twenty-four of 129 and 222 Squadrons from Hornchurch as high cover.

The attack on the Luftwaffe fighter base in the Netherlands naturally carried a high probability of the target being well defended. The attack was to be among the first medium-altitude operation by Marauders in Europe. Zuromski and the entire fighter protection flights experienced a significantly detailed briefing. The bombers flew to Orford Ness on the Suffolk coast to rendezvous with the Spitfires at 0628 hours. Below them was the impressive and extensive shingle banks where developments in radar were secretly taking place. Once the aircraft formed up together they started making for the Dutch coast. The Luftwaffe, however, had detected that an operation was under way, most probably by the many wireless transmissions. On reaching the enemy coast, evasive actions commenced in an attempt to disrupt the tracking system of the enemy anti-aircraft gun layers. It was approximately 0650 hours and the Fw 190s at Woensdrecht were scrambling into the air. They climbed rapidly for height into the rising sun. As the bomb run began, heavy flak caused damage to several aircraft. Once the bomb run had been completed, the Marauders commenced to turn away. As they did so, approximately twelve Fw 190s appeared, diving from height out of the sun and engaged in pairs as they selected their targets. They attacked both the bombers and the escorting Spitfires. One Marauder was seen going down on fire and one Fw 190 was seen to burst in flames, the result of defensive fire from the bombers. The Luftwaffe pilot managed to get out of his cockpit but was unable to deploy his parachute as he fell. Having left the immediate target area, the 66 Squadron escort cover flew slightly behind and roughly 1,000ft above the bombers. They were then simultaneously attacked by two Fw 190s from astern. Zuromski was radioed to warn him to break away as it looked like he was a probable target but his Spitfire was hit by the attacking Fw 190's gunfire and pieces were seen to fly off as he took evasive action. Zuromski called on the radio, reporting that his engine had been damaged, but he was also fighting in an aerial battle with a Fw 190. A fellow 66 Squadron pilot had been able to get in a short burst of gunfire on the enemy fighter from astern at a distance of 600 yards. This attack was probably against the second Fw 190 from the original pair who had singled out Zuromski. Despite the squirt of gunfire on the Fw 190, little if any damage was seen to have taken place on the Luftwaffe fighter. Another Fw 190 appeared in the proximity and remained in sight before it also peeled away. This all took place over a very short period of time.

The 66 Squadron written summary of action is worthy of quoting, completed after the debriefing process had taken place and at a time when Zuromski's fate remained unknown:

During the withdrawal which commenced at approximately 0720 hours the squadron was flying behind and above the close escort at 14,000 feet on a westerly course. The sun was directly behind the formation and at the same level. At 0730 hours two enemy fighters were sighted closing in rapidly on the formation and Red 3 Flying Officer Zuromski was at the time astern of Red 1 the leader of the formation and was warned by R/T that he was being approached by a FW 190 and told to take evasive action. The R/T was jammed during the whole of this operation and it is most likely that the message passed to Red 3 did not reach him. The enemy fighter continued to close in on Red 3 whilst the rest of the formation took evasive action but did not break on account of their small number and the possibility that more enemy aircraft were still behind in the sun. Red 3 was seen to have had a burst of about two seconds fired at him at close range but nothing was seen to be out of order with his aircraft as he took violent evasive action to avoid enemy fire and was seen attacking this aircraft whilst it was doing its breakaway to his port. Red 3 was called by the leader of the formation but did not reply immediately. At approximately 0735 hours Red 3 was heard to call up on his radio saying that he had been hit in the engine and was steering for home on a course of 270 at 1,400 feet or 400 feet, the R/T was very indistinct. The leader of the formation went off on 270 and had a good look round but could not find Red 3 and was unable to contact him over R/T owing to severe jamming and background so continued home and reported the incident to operations and to the air-sea rescue flight. The position of the attack was about 10 miles south-west of Woensdrecht and if Red 3 flew on his course of 270 this would bring him home flying parallel to the Dutch and Belgian coast for about twenty minutes. In all probability if he had no one with him he would glide down and make a forced landing in enemy territory. It is known that after the attack Red 3 was quite alright himself and if he had no further interferences from enemy aircraft it is highly probable that he is still alive.

Squadron Leader Lofts, Pilot Officer Furniss-Row, Flight Lieutenant Denville, Flight Sergeant Lonnen and Flying Officer Deytrikh returned to base at 1215 hours. Zuromski and his Spitfire, BL436, were recorded as missing.

During the next few days, Deytrikh made the final entries in Zuromski's log book, recording his last operation and he calculated the flying hours summaries to completion. Pilots lived sometimes three to a room and one of the most disturbing things for them was the loss of a fellow pilot and friend. Often the roommates would pack up the missing man's personal items and it appears certain in this instance that Deytrikh undertook this. He signed the log book and it appears that he kept custody of it as it was not dispatched to the RAF central depository. It has to be assumed that the log book was retained by the squadron or possibly his friend who endorsed his book with such care.

The assumptions made by Squadron Leader Lofts upon the bearing of flight provided by Zuromski had been relevant and in later years proved to have been accurate. It later became known that his Spitfire had been attacked and damaged by the Luftwaffe pilot H. Munch, flying with 3/JG 26 stationed at Woensdrecht. Zuromski had retained height after his Spitfire was damaged and managed to fly in a south-westerly direction, assumedly observing the Dutch coastline. He then approached the Schelde Delta where the Rhine and the Meuse rivers meet the North Sea. The Dutch islands at that location were heavily defended with German gun batteries and flak positioned on all of the primary island bodies of land. The German Marine Artillerie Abteilung 202 was at that time located on the island of Walcheren. There were different batteries spread out on the western coastal areas, the term *abteilung* being a battalion equivalent of the Wehrmacht Army. Below him lay the small village of Domburg on the coastline of Walcheren. The German defences at Domburg were strong, the Marine Artillerie Abteilung consisting of a coastal battery with four 150mm guns and four 220mm guns. Flak anti-aircraft guns and a radar position enhanced that location. Walcheren was bristling with a significant defensive infrastructure and in all probability they targeted his Spitfire, which sealed his fate.

Zuromski was faced with a situation where he was losing control of the Spitfire and an emergency parachute escape was likely to have been the best option he could take. In all probability he had the ability to turn the Spitfire fuselage sufficiently and unclip his Sutton harness to allow him to fall away from the cockpit. This would have reduced the possibility of him sustaining further injuries. Having fallen clear, he pulled the parachute rip cord to stream the parachute, which opened and inflated correctly. Zuromski's Spitfire crashed at Roosjesweg, easily still in sight of him as he descended and not far away from the beach line. His parachute decent landed him safely and in sight of the burning remains of his Spitfire. The German troops from the gunnery positions had followed his decent and were quickly on the scene. He received first aid from his captors, having suffered some minor facial injuries and slightly more significant burns from the flames swept back into his cockpit from his engine fire. Ironically, he was then taken to the air base at Woensdrecht, the target of his operation that day. The airfield was approximately 40 miles distant from the crash location. The following day he was transported under guard to Amsterdam, where he was detained for three days while arrangements were made to transport him as a prisoner of war to a Dulag Luft, which was a Luftwaffe interrogation camp.

The events that befell Zuromski are revealed by returning to his log book. It remains unknown when he regained possession of it, however a retrospective entry was made against the 30 July operation. He once again illustrated it with a red swastika and noted:

> One FW190 destroyed a second probable saw the smoke but could not see the results finally hit by flak over Walcheren Island Holland and bailed out. Wounded and burnt when taken by German guards as a prisoner of war at about 0800 hours.

CHAPTER 9

DULAG LUFT, OBERURSEL

The name Dulag is an extraction of the German word *Durchgangslager*, or entrance camp, aptly named for Allied air crews who entered the Luftwaffe structure of detention camps. However the term Dulag Luft, has become synonymous with interrogation. Not long after the beginning of the war, the Luftwaffe set up several locations for prisoner of war interrogations. At Oberursel, near Frankfurt, the authorities used the infrastructure of redundant buildings from mid-November 1939. Major Theodor Rumpel, a man who spoke several languages, was the commandant of this, the main Dulag Luft, between June 1940 and November 1941.

The camp had three separate areas: the accommodation blocks for staff and guards; the interrogation facility, officially in the town district of Oberursel; and the camp hospital, located at Hohemark, a mile west of the interrogation camp. In the spring of 1940, a transit camp was also set up, fenced and secured with guard towers, with three barracks, two of which served to house up to 150 prisoners. Throughout the war, the prisoners in Dulag Luft were almost exclusively military airmen from the forces of the Western Allies. The official title of the camp by 1941 was *Auswertestelle West*, or Evaluation Centre West. The Luftwaffe were aware that air crews and pilots were valuable sources for information, as was the aircraft wreckage that fell in occupied territories. Steps were taken to control any looting from crash scenes, with the German People's Court empowered to deliver death sentences by guillotine for the looting of military assets from the Luftwaffe. An infrastructure existed for airmen prisoners to be transited to the interrogation camp expeditiously by rail stock via the Frankfurt am Main rail station and on to Oberursel station. At Dulag Luft the Luftwaffe permitted a select few prisoners to be resident and known as 'permanent staff'. The concept was to provide newly arriving prisoners with men who were able to settle fears and advise of the procedure for the camp's processing of airmen for onward movement to the transit camp facility and then into permanent prisoner of war camps. Some permanent staff prisoners performed daily tasks in the canteen or kitchen controlled by the camp's senior British officer, who was also resident. It becomes obvious that these privileged prisoners, as permanent staff, were in certain circumstances likely to be viewed with suspicion and as having questionable loyalties. Jealousy and ignorance were always capable of influencing the mindset of men who had endured trauma injury and the ignominy of capture by the enemy.

At the instigation of Hermann Göring, the transit camp was relocated to a newly constructed facility built in the proximity of Frankfurt am Main, not far from the main railway station. Oberstleutnant Otto Becker, having been an interrogation officer in Oberursel, became the commandant at Frankfurt in September 1943. It became a common assumption that this move had been an intentional one to deter the Allied bombing of Frankfurt. The transit camp would later be moved again to Wetzlar following the bombing of Frankfurt on 23 March 1943. Wetzlar was where the significant Ernst Leitz optical factories were located. The German war industry required a great many optical devices, many of which came from Leitz Wetzlar.

By March 1943, admission figures into the interrogation camp had risen significantly. Several prisoner collection centres known as *Auffangstellens* had been created across the occupied Reich territories where airmen were collected together and held until arrangements were made for them to be accepted at Oberursel. The intakes notably included many men who had been wounded or injured when shot down or after they made an emergency parachute descent. In May, Doctor Ernst Waldemar Ittershagen became the chief medical officer at Hohemark hospital. He lived in the hospital grounds and it is highly probable that Hohemark would have figured in the initial medical reception of Zuromski. The burn and facial injuries he sustained are not known in detail, but they were worthy of mention in various reports, indicating they were not superficial. It was not uncommon for aircrew prisoners to arrive at the interrogation camp suffering from burn injuries. Escaping from any aircraft that was on fire was likely to have caused hand or facial burns to differing degrees of intensity. It was common practice for any airman suffering from significant burns to be taken directly to the Hohemark hospital. Should the burns be regarded as slight, the prisoner would most probably have been taken to the hospital after reception and identification had taken place. Doctor Ittershagen would visit the Dulag Luft camp whenever requested to do so, the red cross markings on prisoner cell doors placed by a medical orderly indicating to Doctor Ittershagen where a medical examination was necessary.

There were between four to six medical orderlies at any one time working in the Dulag Luft camp, often attending to the bandaging and basic treatment of wounds. The hospital ward for prisoners of war was on the second floor of the hospital and comprised various rooms accommodating sixty-five beds. The only guards were the German medical orderlies. Wounded men were rarely interrogated at the hospital, however the better-equipped single and double rooms were places where high-ranking Allied airmen could be interrogated in circumstances considered appropriate to their rank.

In early May 1944, the highly decorated pilot Ivelaw-Chapman, the base commander at Elsham Wolds airfield, elected to fly with his men. Air stations were usually commanded by a tour-expired group captain or veteran career officer, and a typical bomber squadron had a wing commander and squadron leaders responsible for individual flights of approximately eight aircraft and their crews. Ivelaw-Chapman's decision to fly may have been to enhance morale or possibly simply to experience the operation to bomb the German ammunition dump at Aubigné Racan, north of Le Mans. It was not a deep penetrating operation into central Germany but regardless of that he was forced to escape by parachute from his damaged Lancaster while over France. He landed safely and was on the run, evading capture for several weeks before his luck ran out on 8 June when the Gestapo arrested him with his French helpers. Ivelaw-Chapman already carried shoulder injuries from his parachute escape and he was then brutally treated and interrogated over three days, sustaining back injuries in the process. Eventually it was accepted that he was a British airman, he was passed into Luftwaffe custody and eventually arrived at the Dulag Luft interrogation camp. Placed into a cell with a red cross mark, the next day he was taken to the hospital at Hohemark, where he exchanged his civilian clothes for whatever uniform was available. He was admitted into the hospital, his captors unaware he had been the Director of Policy within the Directorate of Plans for the invasion of northern Europe. The sensitive and secret information he retained was well guarded during his interrogation, which as a high-ranking officer took place over several days.

At the time of his capture, Ivelaw-Chapman was effectively an air commodore and was the most senior Bomber Command officer ever to be captured by the Germans. He remained resident in Hohemark hospital and after gaining his fitness he worked in the wards. Hauptmann Hoffmann was the welfare officer at the Dulag Luft camp and visited the hospital frequently, well aware of Ivelaw-Chapman's long-term employment in the hospital. The hospital had a secure fence compound around the grounds, which were available for exercise for those prisoners who were regarded as free and not requiring any guardianship. Following Ivelaw-Chapman's release, in

July 1945 he returned to France tasked with helping those who had assisted Allied aircrew to evade capture. His work resulted in the formation of the Escaping Society, of which he was appointed vice president.

The Dulag Luft camp was the principal intelligence facility for the Luftwaffe's western theatre of operations. It operated as a military service and Oberstleutnant Erich Killinger was appointed to command the camp in November 1941 and he did so until late 1943. Killinger had served in the Imperial German Navy as an observer in seaplanes patrolling the Baltic waters. His plane crash-landed in the sea in 1915 and they were captured by the Russians. Killinger was imprisoned in St Petersburg, Russia, but later escaped from a train travelling the Trans-Siberian Railway. An extensive escape route saw him endure travelling through China to reach Japan. He crossed the Pacific to the west coast of the neutral USA by ship, travelled to the east coast, boarded a Norwegian-bound vessel and returned to Germany after an eleven-month experience. His experience placed him in one of great understanding for the men in the camp he commanded, several of whom held the same desire for escape.

Killinger had refused to join the Nationalsozialistische Deutsche Arbeiterpartei in 1933. The National Socialist German Workers' Party was more simply known as the Nazi Party which frowned upon such refusals. However, as Germany embarked on military conflict in 1939, Killinger was recalled for military service within the Luftwaffe. At the Dulag Luft interrogation camp, his senior interrogation officer was Major Heinz Junge. He was another First World War aviator who had also been shot down and had likewise experienced being held as a prisoner of war by the French and British forces until 1919. He had joined the Nazi Party in 1932. The Dulag Luft camp was entirely under the control of the Luftwaffe. The SS or Schutzstaffel, commanded by Heinrich Himmler, had little intervention at the camp until 1943, when the Gestapo made their intentions known that some interrogations should be undertaken by them and not Luftwaffe officers.

The SS were the ultimate defenders of Nazi ideology and they terrorised both civilian and military personnel who threatened Hitler's far-right, totalitarian, socio-political ideology. In doing so, the SS created fear by reputation and appearance within both Germany and the German-occupied territories. The presence of the SS in Dulag Luft was infrequent and was restricted to the carrying out of political interrogations. There were instances where detention or arrest of a suspect wearing civilian clothing was sufficient to suspect them of being an agent, spy or saboteur dropped by the RAF. The Gestapo often claimed them but the majority of evading airmen wearing civilian clothing were easily identified at interrogation. Major Alexander Heimpel was head of counterintelligence for all German prisoner of war camps. His intelligence work in each camp was carried out by a comprehensive structure of reading or censoring incoming and outgoing mail.

The only outgoing mail from Dulag Luft was the first report cards, which had minimal room for content. The Kriegsgefangenenpost Postkarte was a simple card that was addressed to the writer's next of kin. There would be no other types of mail sent from the Dulag Luft camp. The obverse side of the Postkarte contained the pre-printed message:

Dulag-Luft Germany

Date

I have been taken prisoner of war in Germany.

I am in good health – slightly wounded (*Cancel accordingly*)

We will be transported from here to another camp within the next few days.

Please don't write until I give new address.

Name and Surname

Rank

Detachment

Article 36 of the Geneva Convention evidenced the right of a prisoner of war to have a set amount of correspondence per month with his family. At the established prison camps an efficient process was in place whereby communications were always cross-referenced against the interrogator's forms and stamped *Gepruft* (Checked) in red ink.

The primary function of the Dulag Luft camp was to obtain information of an operational nature relating to Allied air forces through the interrogation of captured crews. The Geneva Convention of 1929 created two particular article sections relevant to the tasks undertaken by the German Luftwaffe interrogators. Article Two provided that prisoners must at all times be treated humanely and Article Five expressly provided that no pressure of any kind may be used to obtain from them information relating to the armed forces of their country or the general situation therein.

The number of prisoners being processed at the time when Zuromski arrived in August 1943 was approximately 750 to 800 men a month. The interrogation officers at that time numbered around forty. The main camp consisted of four large wooden barracks, two of which were connected by a passage that contained approximately 200 individual detention cells. The cells had a double window that opened from the inside and situated above was an opening flap window. In order to prevent conversations between prisoners, the only window that opened was the flap. Below the window was a tube heater with an enclosed sealed heating element controlled by a switch in the corridor of the cell block. The cell walls were lined by thickly insulated fibre board. The cell door was also insulated and close fitting, creating a soundproof environment. An indicator arm was fitted outside each door that could be operated by the prisoner if he wished to call the guard.

The administrative headquarters were located in the third barrack and the fourth building was a large unusual-shaped barrack that housed the interrogating offices and administration. The German personnel were all Luftwaffe. Interpreters all took part in the interrogations of Allied airmen, regardless of the rank held. Hauptmanns Hans Vollman and von Thaiental are two identified interpreters employed at the Dulag Luft.

All prisoners of war were stripped and searched on arriving at the camp and the normal prisoner administration included taking fingerprints, portrait photographs and recording identifying details on an index card system. At the time of Zuromski's admission, the administration had been under Otto Boehringer since 12 January 1943. He had requested additional English-speaking officers and other ranks, which were necessary to deal with the increasing numbers of prisoners of war arriving at the camp. Boehringer also requested English-speaking female staff to deal with other administrative matters and assist the numerous visitors that were often shown around the camp. Security officers were required to visit the cells regularly and an orderly officer was instructed to carry out inspections with an interpreter available to communicate with the cell occupant. There were no free association areas for prisoners at the camp. The cell structure was the primary accommodation and only if removed from a cell to be walked for interrogation did any association take place. The average cell was 10ft long, 6ft wide and 9ft high. There were facilities for washing in communal facilities that required escort and supervision by the camp staff. Boehringer was promoted to the rank of major in July 1943.

When Zuromski arrived at the camp, he was issued prisoner number 350. This low number may well indicate there were separate numbering principles applied to captured Polish men. The prisoner's number would quite often change when there was movement between camps but in the case of Zuromski he retained his initial identifying number throughout his time in custody. At the Dulag Luft, following the initial process of identification, the prisoners retained the clothing in which they arrived and were then placed in solitary confinement cells. The period of confinement frequently lasted four to five days. At Dulag Luft the confinement in an overheated cell was something that did occur, as did the restriction of food. However, those malpractices were only present during two short periods of time in 1943 and 1944.

It has to be recognised that political influences within Germany were capable of infiltrating everywhere. However, it should also be recognised that the majority of an estimated 40,000 prisoners of war who passed through the Dulag Luft camp did so without undue interference and they received respectful treatment as Allied airmen. The interrogation often commenced in a very subtle way with a person posing as a Red Cross official offering cigarettes and chatting with the prisoner, assuring him that he had no interest in any military information that the prisoner may have. A Red Cross form was inevitably presented to the prisoner to be completed and signed by the prisoner.

Another approach might well have been applied to Zuromski. Being of Polish nationality, the Luftwaffe officers were aware of their resentment towards Russia because of its historical treatment of the Poles. The commandant would himself occasionally engage in interviews of men like Zuromski, and his staff always sought out prisoners with indications of political or racial resentment. This tactic often explored sensitive areas, exposing to the prisoner that they were very sympathetic to whatever opinion he was voicing. Simply asking why a prisoner's country was at war with Germany was often a route to open conversation.

The primary objective at Dulag Luft through the interrogation processes was to simply gather intelligence in the widest sense. A press department evaluated the English and American press every day and the Luftwaffe operations staff and German listening service all reported into the camp administration. The camp staff effectively gathered what were often seen as minor comments or partial components of conversations among the prisoners to such an extent that when collated together over time they knew more about the workings of the RAF than the prisoners did. For example, the Luftwaffe interrogators had possession of the central allocation of service serial numbers of RAF pilots. Once a prisoner gave his serial number, they were able to tell him on or about the date it had been issued. The German interrogator would often reveal knowledge, informing the prisoner of the answers to questions they posed. This created a situation in many cases where confusion existed, the interviewee assuming that other prisoners must have divulged much detailed information. The majority of men being interviewed always wanted their families to be notified they were safe. The men were informed that if they co-operated, then the cap authorities would confirm to their families that they were alive and well and that they would be well looked after. It does become reasonable in some circumstances to see how a prisoner confronted with his captors who apparently knew so much would engage in some communication to ensure his family were contacted about his survival, knowing that they were likely to have simply been advised they were missing over occupied Europe somewhere.

Pearl Joyce Vardon was a native of Jersey. Following the occupation of the island, she formed a liaison with a German officer, and she volunteered to act as interpreter for a German building firm operating there in August 1941. In 1943, she decided to go to Germany to not be separated from her friend. Passage was to be arranged on condition that she agreed to work on German radio. She was employed as an announcer of musical programmes and became a speaker on the transmissions, which consisted of reading letters written by British prisoners of war to friends and relatives in Britain. That material was no doubt secured in the camp censoring of mail and used in the broader sense of propaganda purposes. At the Central Criminal Court in London in February 1946, Vardon pleaded guilty to six counts of assisting the enemy by broadcasting propaganda, and received a sentence of nine months' imprisonment.

Allied airmen were all instructed that the only legal obligation of disclosure if captured was their true name, rank and number. They were also advised that there was nothing that prohibited their interrogation providing no pressure was deployed to extract information. In normal circumstances, the head of the interrogation department received a list of new prisoners and throughout that day received the reception forms, often referred to as Red Cross forms. The name, rank and number of the prisoner was present, sometimes the squadron number and, in the case of a bomber crew, the names of fellow crew. The rear of the form held comments or notes about the prisoner.

Squadron Leader Eric Douglas Elliott was a prisoner frequently in company with Heinrich Eberhardt, the camp reception officer. The post-war questionnaire report of Elliott states he was captured near Arras on 21 May 1940. He arrived at Dulag Luft in October 1940, having spent four months in a hospital in France. He was resident in the camp for some considerable time, serving by request of the commandant as the senior British officer until September 1943. Zuromski was in his presence during the last two months of his time at the camp.

Several incidents caused some prisoners to view Elliott with concern, however the post-war questionnaire composed about him in April 1946 noted that he may be recommended for an award for his conduct in the German camp because he had communicated on numerous occasions with the War Office's MI9 by secret means. The post-war investigating officers into collaboration by prisoners of war later established that he had in fact composed letters with coded messages.

MI9 had been formed in January 1940 for the purpose of engaging with all matters pertaining to British prisoners of war, and in particular to engage in intelligence gathering. MI9 also operated in the guise of the Prisoners Leisure Hours Fund from 66 Bolt Court, Fleet Street, London EC4. Books, games and entertainment items were sent to prisoner of war camps with instructions to communicate directly to request other items. This opened opportunities for information exchanges. MI9 created an intelligence school for selected operational personnel to be give an awareness of the existence of the department.

They provided instruction on the use of secret letter-writing codes for prisoners of war. The first code used was one that could only operate in conjunction with a dictionary. A second, less complicated one was then devised and taught. The RAF had been well advised upon the first code and when France fell in 1940, there were hopes of a positive response to coded letters arriving. However, no communications came through from any prisoners of war until November 1940. Thereafter, MI9 received coded letters from several RAF prisoners, and the secret means of communication was established within the German Stalag Luft camps. Any captured prisoners of war who had been taught an official code were aware they should inform the senior British officer of the camp but it should not become general knowledge. The skills of using codes and the actual codes used developed as the war progressed.

Squadron Leader Elliott may well have been an officer who had been instructed upon the skills of code writing and little doubt exists that he had used a code to communicate with MI9 about some concerns he had about both Sergeant Raymond Davies Hughes and Zuromski. His concern about Zuromski appears to be related to him wearing civilian clothing, and there is no information available about his comments on Hughes.

The author feels compelled to comment upon the circumstances of Elliott's activity. The evidence of his communication to MI9 on what was rather meaningless subject matter connected to Zuromski puts in question his motivation to report such inferior intelligence. Elliott openly associated with Luftwaffe intelligence officers and was capable of reporting on many other valuable aspects of intelligence, so his behaviour becomes highly questionable.

Elliott's questionnaire from April 1946 contained another comment dated 26 April. It advised that he was the subject of enquiries concerning his own conduct when a prisoner of war. He was certainly required to answer several areas of questioning, primarily from evidence provided by other prisoners who observed and reported upon his conduct. However, the words of the Judge Advocate General uttered on 4 November 1946 were definitive, ignoring those factors. This influential sentence within the overall statement of the Judge Advocate General is rather telling in its direction:

> In view of the fact that Group Captain (He had been promoted) Elliott sent such (coded) messages to the Air Ministry, I do not think a court martial would convict him on any charge of misconduct whilst serving as a prisoner of war.

Decoding a message from within a prisoner of war letter required the decoding officer within MI9 to have the writer's full name, the last letter of which would be the writer's 'spelling' letter. The decoding officer would mark out a square in accordance with information obtained from the first two words of the opening sentence of the letter. The decoding officer would underline the words in frequency positions, remembering that if the word 'the' appeared in a frequency position, coding would start after the next full stop. With the start of a new paragraph, frequency positions would start afresh as at the beginning of the letter, but at the beginning of the paragraph instead of at the start of the first full line. The transfer of all code words recorded in their respective squares left the interpretation of spelling the text as the last action to undertake. The message could be read off diagonally from the right bottom corner of the decoding matrix.

Prisoners of war held at the main camps could send their letters containing a coded message to any address in England. MI9 was responsible for intercepting all coded letters, even if addressed to an entirely fictitious address, which did occur. The decoding would not entail delay in the delivery of letters from prisoners of war. The information Elliott sent or the MI9 decoding messages are no longer available for scrutiny.

The messaging that had taken place was certainly not unusual. It actually became fairly prevalent within prisoner of war camps, but in this case it appears to have had a major influence on the Judge Advocate General's decision-making when assessing Elliott's behaviour in the camp. It appears to put aside the accusations and evidence secured in the investigations that had been made based upon reports by others. The squadron leader's frequent association with Heinrich Eberhardt understandably held little weight in any respect and it could be easily explained. Some of the letter content written by the squadron leader to the camp commandant that had been exposed in the investigation was less easily explained. The most obvious question to contemplate is why Elliott engaged in reporting Zuromski. He was the well-established senior British officer and he was well aware of many aspects of events taking place in a most important intelligence-gathering Luftwaffe establishment. Simply reporting a Polish pilot being given civilian clothing appears rather meaningless among other intelligence matters that could easily have been reported.

One of the most telling matters of exposed information involving Elliott came from the post-war statement of Squadron Leader George Tench. He found himself at Dulag Luft in 1942, having experienced the trauma of ditching his Wellington bomber into the sea. He had previously received the Distinguished Flying Cross, and another prisoner with that distinguished medal was Wing Commander Anthony Eyre, a member of the Auxiliary Air Force, commissioned in 1938 and shot down in February 1942. These officers and another, Squadron Leader Ian Cross, all found themselves together in Dulag Luft but, despite their rank, Elliott appears to have avoided any communication with them.

The three high-ranking officers immediately noted the Nazi tendencies and utterings of a fellow prisoner, Pilot Officer Benson Railton Metcalf Freeman. The camp commandant was aware of Freeman's alleged British fascist and anti-Bolshevik opinions. Cross,

Tench and Eyre collectively saw Elliott, informing him of their concern, which also involved another prisoner's suspicious activity who was unidentified to them. An unexpected outcome prevailed after their disclosures, with little if any definitive action taken. Freeman was a permanent staff member at Dulag Luft and he was clearly very well known to Elliott. Tench was moved to Stalag Luft III within a week of his meeting with Elliott.

Following the special investigation completed upon Elliott in 1946, the letter previously mentioned became somewhat challenging for him to explain. The letter directly connected him to Freeman and was submitted as evidence to the air commodore in charge of the Judge Advocate General's office. The letter had been dated 23 June 1942 and read:

> Dear Oberst Lt Killinger,
> We send this note to thank you very much indeed for granting us the facility of such a marvellous walk, together with the much appreciated 'Betriebsol'.
> Your countryside is so beautiful that we shall not want to leave it when the war ends.
> I hope that you will agree with us and decide that such walks are also most beneficial for the health and potential energy of Luftwaffe officers!
>
> Yours sincerely,
> E.D. Elliott, B.R.H. Freeman and R. Hardy.

The Dulag Luft reception officer Eberhardt, who was in frequent company with both Elliott and Freeman, had been a school teacher before the war. This was a position that represented a state official, requiring membership of the Nazi Party. Eberhardt had studied in England and had a good command of English. He was initially employed at the Dulag Luft camp as a civilian, censoring mail and distributing parcels. Men with special linguistic or technical skills but lacking in necessary military training were referred to in military service as *Sonderführer*. They wore standard military uniforms and held authority within the area covered by their occupation. Eberhardt wore the blue Luftwaffe uniform, his position being the receptionist engaged in checking every prisoner's reception form and examining it against a card index system that held thousands of names of RAF personnel. He was assisted by an elderly civilian and four temporary staff who processed about thirty to forty new prisoners each day. In each case, the reception form had a unique number that often related to an aircraft crash site. The next check undertaken was by the casualty recording department, where all the crash numbers and crew numbers were recorded on a card index. Any information on any other prisoners from that crash were noted in detail on the form provided to the interrogators. The interrogators would go to the department of evaluation of documents and provide the crash number to see if any documents were found at the scene. These records were often of incidental value but target maps were often found revealing specific details. The interrogator built his knowledge further by going to the intelligence room, where the various interrogations and evaluations of documents were co-ordinated and collated to create current information. Crew sheets, methods of attacking targets and maps were pinned to the walls. The squadron histories files contained the names of senior officers and photographs of airmen of that squadron who had previously been processed, as well as newspaper clippings reporting men from that squadron as missing. These combined to create a well-collated and accurate intelligence base of valuable information.

One of the most valuable and regular sources of intelligence came from the small portrait photographs that were carried by captured airmen. These were issued to assist in any evasion as they enabled false documents to hold correctly taken identity images. The various but consistent use of poses, along with other identifying features, allowed the document evaluators to establish the aerodromes where the images were produced. These photographs fitted exactly in Dutch, Belgium and French identification cards, full face for French, left profile for Belgium, and right for Dutch.

The interrogators, which numbered around thirty men, were all specifically tasked for interviewing fighter pilots, bomber crew, pathfinders and also aerial mine-laying pilots. Gustav Bauer-Schlichtegroll was a Nazi Party member and interrogator who was specifically engaged in extracting any technical aspects of the RAF. He was also an interrogator of bomber crews and special duty flying crews. Hanns Scharff was an interrogator with a specific responsibility for interrogating American airmen. His son, Claudius, assisted the author with personal aspects of research concerning the Dulag Luft operating system. During the day, the interrogators would report the events of the interrogation. In some cases, authority was immediately given to move the prisoner into the transit camp ready to be transported to Frankfurt or Wetzlar and on to the numerous Stalag Luft prisoners of war camps for airmen.

The Dulag Luft camp received daily teleprinted messages reporting upon the night bombing attacks. Often prisoners could be easily referenced to having been engaged on a particular raid. Any crashed bomber was examined and occasionally a log book would be found that provided important intelligence. Heinz Junge, the senior interrogator at Dulag Luft, in his post-war evidence reported that in 1943 he estimated 8,000 prisoners were processed in the camp, rising to 29,000 in 1944. During 1944, because of the number of men captured, only half were interviewed with the remainder, simply passing through and onwards to the prisoner of war camp infrastructure.

The Dulag Luft camp deployed every means it had, including every known device for covert listening in order to extract information from the captured airmen. The camp was very important to the intelligence section of the Luftwaffe, and it was without doubt a most effective centre for gathering intelligence. The interrogation staff were well aware that an air gunner was much less likely to have information of value than a pilot. Therefore, a young gunner may well have experienced a short interrogation, while a pilot of experience might be interrogated more than once a day over several days. It becomes quite possible that during lengthy interviews Zuromski openly exposed his prejudices against the Bolsheviks to his interrogators and he became a prisoner of more significance to them because of that.

The Polish had defeated the communist invasion in 1920 and Germany was prepared to use that same resolve for its own purpose against the Russian forces fighting alongside the Allies. Any prisoner who showed any inclination to talk would be retained at Dulag Luft in the hope they could be turned by the Germans and used as an informant. Any prisoner who spent more than a fortnight in Dulag Luft was suspected of some type of involvement with the Luftwaffe staff, especially if they were open about their perks of food and cigarettes.

The Reich Ministry of Public Enlightenment and Propaganda attempted to demoralise the Allied public's resolve by broadcasting political propaganda in its Anzac tattoo radio programme made by the Büro Concordia in Berlin. They also chose to announce the names of recently captured servicemen during the radio transmissions, giving their name, address and sometimes service number. This alone became a strong reason for the airmen's loved ones to listen with intensity.

Zuromski was present in the Dulag Luft camp between 4 August and the 30 September 1943. This was a lengthy time period in comparison to the norm, but it was not exceptional. Flight Sergeant Townsend was a Spitfire pilot who as a prisoner of war had direct contact with Zuromski during his interrogation at the centre. His documented prisoner of war repatriation report composed in 1945 is indisputable evidence of his contact with Zuromski.

Anthony Edward Townsend was born on 17 February 1921, and originated from Brighton, Sussex. Having worked as a clerk for

Southern Railway, aged nineteen years, he enlisted into the RAF in January 1941. As a sergeant under air crew training, he eventually qualified to fly single-engine fighters and was posted as a flight sergeant to 222 (Natal) Squadron, with whom he would later fly Spitfires.

In March 1943, the squadron became an early member of the 2nd Tactical Air Force, and Townsend joined it in late May or early June. The squadron was at that time operational at Hornchurch, deployed as an offensive fighter unit. The Hornchurch Spitfires also flew escorts for daylight bomber missions as well as fighter sweeps, which often accompanied bombing raids into central France. These were the same type of operations that Zuromski had undertaken. Between 1941 and 1943, more than 100 Hornchurch pilots had lost their lives, with many others injured or, like Townsend, captured after being shot down. He had flown thirty-eight operations between 24 June and 8 September 1943. On his final sortie the Hornchurch wing took off to act as high cover to seventy-two Marauders attacking Lille-Vendeville airfield in France. The operation was given the reference Ramrod S41.

Over the target area around twelve Fw 190s attacked the bomber stream and engaged with the defending Spitfires, which were flying high cover positions. Townsend, flying Spitfire IX MH389, was one of two shot down by enemy fighters over Lille. He escaped with his life by parachute and was captured almost immediately to become a prisoner of war. Townsend was taken to Dulag Luft and placed in confinement for five days. He was then placed in solitary confinement for a further nine days and was subjected to interrogation during that time period. Townsend reported in his repatriation report that Staff Sergeant M. Trick of the United States Army Air Force was with him during interrogation. He later reported that Trick was seen in civilian clothes at Dulag Luft and he also noticed several other persons in civilian clothing and in possession of German money. The only comprehensive details he could remember was one person, a Flying Officer Zuromski from Poland, who was reputed to be from Fighter Command and had been shot down over Flushing in June 1943. No doubt it was the unusual name Zuromski that Townsend recalled when he was debriefed in 1945. The American uniformed man identified as Trick by Townsend does appear elsewhere in special investigations interviews. However, in the author's opinion insufficient evidence exists to speculate further upon this person's identity with any certainty.

Townsend departed Dulag Luft following his interrogation and was taken to Stalag Luft 6 at Heydekrug, where he remained until June 1944. A move to Stalag Luft 4 at Tichow followed, where he remained until February 1945, before being transported to Stalag Luft 11B at Fallingbostel until 10 April. In April the prisoners from that camp were force marched in long columns towards central Germany. This mass evacuation of camps was ordered by the German High Command in order to prevent the prisoners falling to the Russians advancing in the East. During the march, Townsend saw an opportunity to escape together with Warrant Officer Nettleton and Warrant Officer Jones as they were approaching Lüneberg. The three escapers eventually located a company of the 15th Royal Scots on 19 April and at that time they effectively became liberated prisoners among Allied forces.

Townsend's repatriation report, compiled in 1945, has provided provenance of Zuromski's time spent at the Dulag Luft camp. This evidence on the surface appears compelling in that Zuromski was acting for the Luftwaffe within the camp. However, it provides no evidence or mitigation of motive as to why this took place. It simply places Zuromski in civilian clothing and unchaperoned. It has to be accepted that, by means unknown, Zuromski had agreed to be complicit with the Luftwaffe and had become engaged in various duties under their direction within the camp. Townsend's prisoner of war debriefing document established firm evidence of Zuromski's presence in the camp while wearing civilian clothing and in possession of German currency. It does not provide evidence of anything more substantive than those facts.

During August and September 1943, around 1,600 captured airmen arrived at the Dulag Luft facility. Zuromski was within the camp structure during this time and among the prisoners were several high-ranking RAF officers, including Group Captain Douglas Ernest Lancelot Wilson and Squadron Leader George Robert Carpenter. The latter was a mature forty-three-year-old pilot and to his friends, in keeping with his family name, he was known as 'Chippy'. Having been shot down over the Netherlands on 25 July 1943, he had escaped by parachute, with his Lancaster crashing on to the Cleefswit estate in Elsendorp. Good fortune saw him assisted in evading by several brave civilian underground resistant operatives. On 2 August, after a train journey using a false name and papers provided by the Dutch underground, he arrived at Weert in the Netherlands. Carpenter was then placed in a safe house in the Brussels suburb of Woluwe-Saint-Lambert. The main underground contact was a man called Prosper de Zitter, who spoke perfect English and was trusted by both the underground operatives and local priests. Group Captain D.E.L. Wilson, a forty-five-year-old Australian, was already in the safe house when Carpenter arrived, as were the evaders Flight Sergeant Hansen from New Zealand, a Canadian Sergeant Poudrier and a Sergeant Weir.

However, during July and August 1943, de Zitter was actually using the safe house at 369 Avenue AJ Slegers in the Brussels suburbs as part of a fake escape line. De Zitter had developed connections to genuine escape organisations in the Netherlands and other parts of Belgium. His plausibility induced priests and other religious officials who were likely to engage with evaders to confide in him. The priests, believing de Zitter to be genuine, would contact him with details of an evader in hiding. Those escaping airmen would inevitably be met at a Brussels railway station by a car driven by de Zitter or his mistress, who described herself as his secretary. Carpenter after, leaving the safe house, entered the same car on or about 15 August but was taken to the gates of the notorious Saint-Gilles Prison in Brussels. He had become one of more than seventy escaping airmen that de Zitter had led into Gestapo traps from safe houses in Brussels. Many Belgian helpers and agents were also betrayed by him, primarily for money as each captive resulted in a financial settlement of some significance for de Zitter. The trapping was so successful that cells were kept available in the prison at Saint-Gilles for the regular delivery of his captives. Carpenter's cell also held two of de Zitter's other recent captures: Sergeant F. Jackson, who had been shot down on 11 August 1943, and the Canadian Sergeant T. Froats, shot down in late July.

The connection between Wilson and Carpenter within the safe house appears to be the catalyst for retrospective reported suspicion placed upon both men. They may have asked questions about inappropriate subjects among a group of escaping airmen, which gave rise to concern that they may be informers. Wilson was without doubt a person in possession of an unusual character. He and Carpenter both spent a few weeks in jail before arrangements saw them taken to the Dulag Luft camp. At the height of betrayals both in Antwerp by a traitor called Van Muylem and de Zitter in Brussels, regular transits of captured evaders were taking place to the camp.

Carpenter and Wilson found themselves among several other ranking officers in the camp. Among them was Squadron Leader Carlton Orme Bastian, who had been shot down in a Stirling heavy bomber on 22 June. Collectively these men were held there for around three weeks. It was to be a coincidence, but one of significance, that Zuromski would meet these men in that relatively concentrated period of time. Another prisoner to engage with at the same time was Sergeant Raymond Davies Hughes from Wales. This is the name that Squadron Leader Elliott had included alongside Zuromski's in his previously mentioned coded letter to MI9. Hughes had been shot down with his crew on 17 August 1943. During his interrogation at Dulag Luft, circumstances were exposed that indicated to the Luftwaffe interrogators that Hughes was likely to willingly assist or help with intelligence gathering for the German staff. It appears Hughes was used by Heinrich Eberhardt, the camp reception officer, to obtain information gleaned by the use of the fraudulent Red Cross forms. Working closely together, it appears likely that the two men became proficient in administering the reception processes. Hughes and Carpenter would also feature significantly in events of commonality with Zuromski when they were all jointly selected to be moved from the interrogation camp to another camp in Berlin. Clearly there had to have been some inducement deployed for these prisoners to undertake the move of camps but this remains unknown.

In September 1943, Wilson was released from Dulag Luft and when he arrived at Stalag Luft III it ended Wing Commander Day's position as senior British officer there. Wilson, by rank alone, became the senior and he remained in that position until the camp's evacuation in January 1945. The group captain was apparently mistrusted and disliked during this long period of time. He was suspected and investigated for aiding the enemy, with his name appearing in the statements of two post-war collaborators who were convicted of offences in relation to assisting the enemy. However, on 4 July 1945, the Judge Advocate General decided that in Wilson's case no offence had been committed.

It remains unknown if Zuromski associated with Wilson during his time in the interrogation camp in 1943. Carpenter and Zuromski left the Dulag Luft together on 1 October, both wearing civilian clothing and under the supervision of Lieutenant Bonninghaus, one of the camp's political interrogators. Hughes also left the camp towards the end of November. Heinrich Eberhardt was detailed to take Hughes to Berlin, and it appears Hughes was required to use the name Baker thereafter. It has to be assumed that Zuromski, Carpenter and Hughes had volunteered to be moved to the Berlin prisoner of war camp IIID. It is unknown if this move was an inducement to be engaged in propaganda work, but it has to be a distinct possibility.

In September 1944, the Sicherheitsdienst des Reichsführers office in Frankfurt, which was the intelligence branch of the SS and the Nazi Party, alleged that Killinger and his senior staff at the Dulag Luft camp were undermining the morale of the Wehrmacht by fraternising with and being too lenient towards the prisoners. The accusations placed before the camp leaders at Oberursel were of Anglophile tendencies, defeatism and transgression of service rules. Reichsführer Heinrich Himmler ordered a Luftwaffe special court investigation into charges relating to those claims. The investigation took place on 7 December 1944 but an accusation that Killinger had harmed the striking power of the Wehrmacht was not upheld. Likewise, claims that he violated his duty of supervision were dismissed. The deputy commander, Major Junge, was found responsible for some infringements, but both accused men were advised that punishable acts were unable to be found in each case.

Three camp interrogators were identified in the special court investigation. They were First Lieutenant Birmele, Lance Corporal Schwartz and Sergeant Weil. Lieutenant Colonel Kienitz was the advisor of the outcome of the investigation. In his summary after the hearing, he questioned if the interrogators possessed the necessary qualifications to carry out their work. There was little doubt that the informant to the Sicherheitsdienst office in Frankfurt that instigated the investigation was the SS. It is possible that the camp leadership's resistance towards the SS having access to certain prisoners detained in Dulag Luft may well have instigated the subsequent court investigation. The British Air Ministry Weekly Intelligence Summary No. 323, dated 12 November 1945, published the German official report of this outcome.

CHAPTER 10

CAMP IIID BERLIN

The High Command in Germany decided in May 1943 to establish a special prisoner of war camp identified as Stalag IIID with a sub number 999 for men of officer rank in Zehlendorf, Berlin. A second camp, identified as Stalag IIID sub number 517, was located at Genshagen, south of Berlin, for non-commissioned prisoners. These were generic camps where prisoners from all services could be accommodated, an anomaly for pilot and aircrew prisoners as in general airmen from all Allied forces were primarily segregated into Stalag Luft camps and guarded by Luftwaffe personnel.

The two IIID camps were approximately 11 miles apart. Zehlendorf was also the location of a sub-camp of prisoners from the Sachsenhausen concentration camp, which had been built in the summer of 1936. A high proportion of female Polish workers, among thousands of others, were deployed daily from the sub-camp into the capital city. Sachsenhausen had been the first concentration camp to be established following the appointment of Reich Leader SS Heinrich Himmler. During the war, the camp infrastructure was responsible for the deaths of many thousands of people. More than 100 satellite or sub-camps were set up to provide a constant supply of undernourished, shaven-headed concentration camp internees as workers in the German armaments industry. The camps were located near arms factories such as those of AEG (Allgemeine Elektricitäts-Gesellschaft) and Siemens in Berlin.

The political interrogator Bonninghaus from the Dulag Luft camp had taken Carpenter and Zuromski into Berlin and they were thereafter officially registered and regarded as prisoners of war in Stalag IIID in Zehlendorf. The post-war examination of documents, in particular statements obtained in special investigations, identifies Zuromski's place of residence as the Auto Hotel building on Saldernstrasse, a main road in Berlin. This was roughly 6 miles away from Zehlendorf, therefore it has to be accepted that prisoners documented as being in Stalag IIID were in many cases not actually held in secure camp environments. They were effectively paroled against agreements not to escape from the Berlin districts.

At a later time Bonninghaus took Raymond Hughes from the Dulag Luft to the Auto Hotel, where they met Carpenter and Zuromski, who were resident and living in adjacent rooms. According to a later statement made by Hughes, Bonninghaus advised they were now to be addressed as Herr Carter and Herr Kowalski. The name Kowalski, or interpretations of that name, are referenced in other documents and connected directly to Zuromski.

This evidence clearly illustrates that Stalag IIID was quite different to a conventional prisoner of war camp. Although several locations were annexed to Stalag IIID, the central camp was a main prisoner of war facility in the geographical area of the German capital city. It also had loosely attributed locations, which were apparently no more than different residences away from the camp structure. Zuromski was later relocated as a resident at the porter's lodge in the sports ground at Charlottenburg in Berlin.

The concept of selecting Allied prisoners of war identified with possible prejudices or grievances against certain political or religious beliefs was embedded into the German prisoner of war camp structure. More radical individuals identified in the process were to be given the opportunity to join Hitler's British Free Corps. This appears to have been one of the primary outcomes sought by Germany in creating Stalag IIID. The British Free Corps was a unit of the Waffen SS that consisted of British and Dominion prisoners of war. The British Free Corps was a creation of an Englishman, John Amery. He was the son of the Conservative Cabinet minister Leo Amery, who apparently embraced the fascist doctrines of Nazi Germany as well as that of communism.

In 1936 John Amery left Britain and joined Franco's Nationalists during the Spanish Civil War. The Republicans supported the democratically elected government, which was at that time openly supported by the Soviet Union. The Nationalists, however, were supported by Nazi Germany and those military forces overthrew the government under the leadership of General Francisco Franco. Amery was decorated by the Nationalists while serving as an intelligence officer. He met the French fascist leader Jacques Doriot in Spain and Amery and Doriot later travelled together to Austria, Czechoslovakia, Italy and Germany before residing in France under the Vichy government. Amery desired to return to Germany and meet with the German English Committee. With the help of Hauptmann Werner Plack, a Nazi propaganda official, Amery obtained the authority to travel to Berlin. In September 1942, Amery spoke to the German English Committee, a select group that in advance of the invasion and occupation of Great Britain was preparing for its future administration by Germany. The committee was also interested in finding English collaborators to combat Bolshevism. Amery suggested to the committee that the Germans should form a British anti-Bolshevik legion. They were impressed by Amery and allowed him to remain in Germany as a guest of the Reich. He later engaged in writing and delivering a series of pro-German radio broadcasts to Britain.

Amery's concept was for an independent British force to fight within the Nazi regime against the communists. Amery aimed to recruit 50–100 men and from the Nazi perspective this would be a valuable propaganda opportunity. The Waffen SS had already raised some military renegade units made up of foreign nationals. Once Hitler had sanctioned the recruitment, Amery visited British prisoner of war camps to begin his recruitment drive for the organisation, which he named the British Legion of St George, later simply becoming the British Free Corps.

When visiting the camps and other establishments, he distributed recruitment material. The prisoner of war camps occasionally received a basic, flimsy newspaper called *The Camp*, printed by an editorial office in Wangenheimstrasse, Berlin. The paper included official German communiqués and extracted British newspaper articles, including notifications of military awards taken from *The London Gazette*'s public announcements. The most influential articles printed in *The Camp* were open letters sent to the editor from men held in prison camps across the Third Reich territories of occupation. When published, the contributor was often readily identified. There were obvious German propaganda objectives achieved by deploying the news sheet. Among them was the inducement of the 'Editor's Competition', whereby rewards could be won. This ploy potentially created contacts by individuals from within the prison camp structure. Sergeant William Stogdale from 99 Squadron was most derogatorily identified by a fellow prisoner of war in his repatriation report composed in 1945. Stogdale had submitted a letter that was published in the newspaper titled 'His friends in the Luftwaffe'. It is possible this submission, used as propaganda, was no more than an attempt to receive a reward. However, it certainly has insufficient merit to be regarded as collaboration with the enemy, despite the suspicion it may have raised.

Thomas Haller Cooper had been a member of the pre-war British Union of Fascists. Having German parenthood on his mother's side apparently became an issue of non-acceptance in British society, and his applications to join both civil and military services in Britain were rejected. In 1938, the Hammersmith Branch of the British Union appears to have established his mindset that his rejection for service was rooted in prejudice incited by the so-called Jewish Conspiracy. In early 1939, as a fluent German speaker, Cooper sought employment in Germany. He was employed at the Reichs Arbeits Dienst (RAD or German Labour Service) in Stuttgart. His mother had ensured he carried the required documents classifying him as an ethnic German by parenthood. He later voluntarily enlisted into the German Army and after several postings, which included attending the SS training school at Lauenburg in Pomerania, concluding in May 1941, he found himself fighting on the Eastern Front against the Russian forces. He was badly wounded in February 1943, and because of his injuries, he was transferred to the newly created British Free Corps and assigned to a transit camp for new recruits at a villa in Grunewald, in the western district of Berlin.

By October 1943, the Waffen SS decided Amery's services were no longer needed in recruiting. His ambitions had been thwarted by his low recruitment of willing individuals and he was regarded as ineffective. The emphasis on the procurement of prisoners of war to join the British Free Corps became the primary objective at Stalag IIID. English-speaking guards had been recruited who would also act as information gatherers.

When prisoners arrived in Stalag IIID, Thomas Cooper and other pro-Nazi operatives specifically sought out any fascists and openly sought conversations about attitudes towards the communists. Men like Roy Courlander, the son of a Lithuanian Jew and an English mother who had been serving in the New Zealand Army when captured in 1941, were identified. He openly expressed extreme anti-Russian views. Francis George MacLardy of the Royal Army Medical Corps and Edwin Barnard Martin of the Canadian Essex Scottish Regiment were also recruited. It must be remembered that the men sent to Stalag IIID had already been vetted as likely candidates for political reasoning by the Germans. MacLardy was later tried and sentenced to life imprisonment, reduced on appeal to fifteen years. This man is also identified as Frank MacLardy with an alias of Wood. He was released from custody in 1953 to live in Germany. Courlander would eventually appear before a New Zealand military court, where he was sentenced to fifteen years' imprisonment.

There was also another primary outcome sought in Stalag IIID, the desire for Germany to enhance its subversive propaganda. This was to be achieved by using Allied prisoners of war with anti-Bolshevik tendences or other racial grievances who were likely to be of use in broadcasting from central Berlin into Allied and neutral countries via a number of 'black' radio stations. These presented themselves as though they were run domestically by internal dissidents but were actually broadcast from Berlin by the Büro Concordia, or Concardia. This enterprise operated under joint control of the German Foreign Office and Propaganda Ministry, and employed many more civilians than it did military personnel. From 1942 to 1945 Hans Fritzsche was the head of the radio department of the Reich Ministry of Propaganda. He was also the political director of German radio. Fritzsche, with other officials of the Propaganda Ministry, engaged with the Concardia.

The German Reich also promoted the Volksempfänger domestic home radio set, which was part of a programme induced by Germany to make radio receivers cheaply and be available to the vast majority of the public. The Nazi government saw the use of radios as a means of disseminating Nazi propaganda to millions of people. Germany was proactive in making the availability of radio receivers to the populus as well as broadcasting to listeners throughout Europe and beyond.

The Concordia radio stations had come on the air in the spring of 1940. Initially the Concordia was based in a building known as Villa die Grosse close to the Rundfunkhaus in Berlin. Then in July 1941, it relocated to the Third Reich's 1936 Olympics sports Reichssportfeld stadium complex in Berlin, with offices located below ground. Doctor Anton Winkelnkemper lived in nearby Charlottenburg. He was the director of Concardia, having previously been appointed regional head of the Rhineland propaganda department. As an SS officer, he had been appointed acting director of the shortwave station on 1 January 1941. He ultimately became not only responsible for the foreign language programmes of Nazi radio, but also for the secret broadcasting channels. The British press enthusiastically published extracted details from many transmissions, ostensibly to 'expose' them as enemy propaganda stations. Stories on the Concordia transmissions appeared in almost every British newspaper, including *The Times*. The Olympic stadium was in relatively close proximity to the Auto Hotel at Saldernstrasse where Zuromski resided.

Herbert Krumbiegel was an electrical engineer employed at Concardia, recording talks on magnetophone bands and transmitting the recordings on specific metre bands. Talks and music were recorded on to magnetophone bands, which enabled them to be played back over a cable to a transmitter for broadcasting. Krumbiegel was often present when the speeches or talks were composed. When interviewed in 1945, he recalled a Polish speaker called Kowalski or Kolawski. This is without doubt Zuromski. The Concardia required speakers and script writers who had, by deliberate intention or by misfortune, found themselves deployed in this subversive activity. The station was understaffed with competent English-speaking scriptwriters and efforts were always in place to recruit British prisoners of war who were willing to co-operate in return for benefits and freedom.

In September 1944, Allied bombing operations saw Concardia move into the bunker at the Funkhaus in Berlin, and finally in April 1945 it relocated to Helmstedt.

Allied intelligence, and in particular the British MI5, were aware of Stalag IIID and the British Free Corps recruitment. The National Archive AIR 20/2336 document identifies prisoners of war at the Stalag IIID location and records it as a prisoner of war camp. Among references in this text, Zuromski's name is present. It was in 1944 when MI5 commenced collating information about what they referenced as British Renegades. A section in MI5 known as S.L.B.3. was created and tasked with the provision of evidence should any of those individuals be prosecuted at a later time. There were two sections, military and civilian investigations. The British Renegades list was collated and within the names were many broadcasters as well as the men who openly admitted membership of the British Free Corps, most of whom were informers. Generally, the term informers related to men from prisoner of war camps who were gathering information and intelligence for Germany. In British terms they were classed as stool pigeons.

SS Officer Hans Werner Roepke was made commander of the British Free Corps in November 1943. He held an excellent command of the English language and although he commanded low numbers, the volunteers were prepared to fight Bolshevism. The Germans had hoped to create at least a single infantry platoon of thirty men, none of whom were to be engaged in any action against British and Commonwealth forces, nor could they be used for intelligence gathering. There was no requirement to swear an oath of loyalty to Hitler, nor were the volunteers subject to German military law. They would receive pay equal to the German soldier and wear standard SS uniforms with appropriate identity and insignia.

The Concardia community of workers were engaged in writing political scripts, making broadcasts and to some extent recruiting for the British Free Corps. In 1943, the German propaganda broadcasting strategy was simply to cause a rift between the eastern and western Allies by providing the populations of Europe with visions of predicted Bolshevik tyranny. Erich Hetzler was a prominent propaganda minister in control of Concardia. His rank was Hauptsturmführer, and he served on the SS General Staff and managed the anti-British propaganda section. That section became operational before French, Russian, Polish and Yugoslavian sections followed. Interestingly, the Polish section only commenced broadcasting in 1943. Hetzler was personally responsible for ensuring all manuscripts prior to transmission had been overseen by the Propaganda Ministry and Foreign Office. Additionally, needed to allocate time in the radio studios in order to maintain the effectiveness of broadcasting continuity within the agreed schedule.

The British personnel who worked for the Anti-British Propaganda Section in Berlin had their identities published in the post-war case enquiry, The National Archives KV2861. They were listed as writer and announcers John Brown, Miss Bothamley, Spillman, Kenneth James and Lander. The latter was Kenneth Vincent Lander, who had lived and worked in Germany as a teacher of English since 1933. He became attracted to National Socialism, and despite the imminence of war, sought to obtain German naturalisation. His application was officially refused in January 1940, however he was invited to Berlin and offered the opportunity to engage in broadcasting from a secret radio transmitter in the city, the concept of which was that it should appear to the listeners that it was being transmitted from England.

Also listed were Jones, writer and announcer; Humphreys, announcer; William Griffiths, announcer; Bowley, announcer; Richard Clark, writer and announcer; William Winter, announcer; Dorothy Eckersley, writer and announcer, and one other only identified as Vernon, who engaged as both writer and announcer.

The British soldier Lance Corporal Ronald Spillman had been recruited while a prisoner of war and taken to Berlin in April 1943. Apparently unaware of exactly what was required of him, at Stalag IIID he was given better clothing and introduced to script writing and assessed for voice compatibility in broadcasting. William Winter, the announcer, looked after Spillman and introduced him to John Brown at the Concardia complex. The announcer William Griffiths had been a prisoner of war since 1940, and was broadcasting on the communist station Worker's Challenge, which focused upon working-class listeners. He had been provided with accommodation at the East Gate of the Reichssportfeld. Griffiths was later tried and sentenced to seven years' imprisonment for his involvement in the German propaganda engagements. That same sentence befell Ronald Spillman, an acquaintance of the writer and announcer Kenneth James. Spillman, a Channel Islander civilian whose true identity was Charles Patrick Gilbert, was employed at Concardia but lived as a married man in Berlin. Corporal Francis Maton, a Royal Artillery gunner, was another British prisoner of war who found himself moved to Stalag IIID. Captured in Crete and injured, he was later sent to work in Dresden on working party duties while attached to Stalag IVA. Maton became a fluent German-speaking individual, who later found himself sent to the Berlin camp under the guise of being rested from the manual working parties. Arriving at Stalag IIID on 3 August 1943, the camp's true identity became obvious when he was openly approached about the British Free Corps. The Germans increased their Jewish propaganda programme in 1943 with a new and ferociously anti-Semitic freedom station. Peter Adami's Radio National began operating in July and Corporal Francis Maton started broadcasting on this channel under the identity Manxman.

Francis Maton was accommodated in a building detached from IIID. He was resident in that building when Lieutenant Colonel Stevenson, a member of the South African Royal Corps of Signals, arrived. Stevenson later spoke to Maton of having been taken with other prisoners of war to Katyn. He reportedly witnessed the Germans and other representatives investigate the finding of a mass grave of thousands of Polish officers. The duties for Stevenson and the others who accompanied him to Katyn remains unknown. Credibility of this information is established by the fact that it had been in February 1943, when Professor Gerhard Buhtz, a forensic pathologist, formerly Professor of Forensic Pathology and Criminology at the University of Breslau, had been instructed by the German forces to investigate the reported mass grave. Work had commenced in late March and an interim report on 10 April reported that from a single grave, workers had uncovered twelve layers with some 250 corpses within each layer. An estimated total of at least 3,000 dead were present, many being Polish Army officers.

On 11 April, Goebbels's public propaganda effort began with the first mention of the discovery of the graves by the German news agency Trans-Ocean. Two days later Germany broadcast across all German radio stations reporting the discovery in the Katyn Forest near Smolensk of the massacre of Poles by Bolsheviks. On 15 April the Soviets denied the report, denouncing it as a vile fabrication made by German-fascist murderers. On 16 April William Joyce, better known to the British public as Lord Haw-Haw for his anti-British propaganda on Station Breslau, broadcast his personal thoughts to listeners:

I am used, of course, to the fact that Bolshevism is criminal, remorseless and unscrupulous. There is no account of any Jewish-Bolshevik atrocity which would be brought before me that could surprise me, and yet there does seem to be a particularly macabre element in this discovery. The work of exhumation has been carried out by Poles. These men must be wondering as they go about their gruesome task how much British guarantees are worth. For after all, the pledges given to Poland by the British Government did not specify that Polish sovereignty was to be protected against Germany but surrendered to the Bolsheviks. So far as the Poles knew, the guarantee was perfectly general. It is not merely that Britain is the ally of the Soviet Union, the associate of these Jewish-Communist murderers whose character, if it has changed at all in the last quarter of a century, has altered for the worst. Never has there been a more flagrant abuse of human credulity than the Jewish attempt to convince the British people that Bolshevism is harmless. How harmless it is the thousands of corpses

dug up in that pine forest near Smolensk will testify, with
a silence more expressive than words could be.

Breslau appendix IV Transcript 187

The Polish government in exile on 17 April 1943 issued a statement of
grave concern that condemned the murders but also denounced German
hypocrisy in consideration of German crimes against Poland and the
Poles. The Polish Red Cross, despite reservations and concerns about
being used for German propaganda purposes, did send a commission
with its secretary to Katyn. They witnessed an International Commission
invited by the Germans consisting of forensic pathologists from
twelve German allies or states occupied by Germany, seven of whom
conducted autopsies on the exhumed corpses.

The German Foreign Office released a significant book titled
Amtliches Material zum Massenmord von Katyn. It held 331 pages
consisting of affidavits, reports, photographs, and a detailed listing
by name of 4,143 recovered bodies. Some images in the book
apparently showed Lieutenant Colonel Stevenson. He was later
identified by that means by Francis Maton during his post-war
interrogation and prosecution for being a member of the British Free
Corps. A propaganda pamphlet from 1943 reproduced the report of
the International Physicians Commission and a collection of stark
photographs from the site were illustrated in that pamphlet.

At Stalag IIID, Maton, having been provided with a false name,
was known as Patrick MacCarthy and given identity documents in
that name. He was requested to read all available newspapers and
then comment and broadcast short reports on the Radio National
channel. Taken to the Reichssportfeld, he obtained a Rundfunk pass
that allowed access into the Concardia complex. It was there that
Maton saw two individuals he reported to know as Carpenter and
Kowalski. Maton later provided evidence that he was aware that
Carpenter had refused to be involved in broadcasting and clearly the
person he knew as Julien Kowalski was Zuromski.

With the recent German disclosure concerning the Russian atrocities at Katyn and the exceptionally strange circumstances of Lieutenant Colonel Stevenson's first-hand account disclosures, it seems remarkable that Zuromski was present and in company with a person at Stalag IIID who had personally witnessed the place of execution of his father. However, there are no transcripts or post-war evidence during any trials to support any theory that direct contact between Stevenson and Zuromski took place.

Carpenter, who had been in close company with Zuromski in Berlin, remained in his allocated accommodation but his activities are not clearly identified. It is known from the archive testimony of the investigations carried out among the identified persons at the Concardia that Carpenter had refused to broadcast or speak on the radio. In early November 1943, he was taken from the Auto Hotel. His generic reference as to his whereabouts remained simply as a prisoner of war at Stalag IIID.

Carpenter was still in Stalag IIID on 27 January 1944, but his removal from the Auto Hotel might be explained by the Special Investigators' Report SIB639/45. This document advises that Carpenter and Hughes had authority to purchase second-hand overcoats. The purchasing of clothing necessitated using authority tickets, a requirement enforced due to strict rationing. While engaged in acquiring the clothing, Carpenter purloined an additional coat and was arrested in February 1944. He was put before the People's Court. No official transcripts appear to exist but the circumstances suggest Carpenter was found guilty and thereafter ordered to a secure prisoner of war camp. As an Allied prisoner of war, it was highly unusual for the German People's Court to engage in a civil offence committed by an offender while under control of the Reich military.

It appears that Hughes, alias Baker, was not involved in the appearance at court. However, his actions were further exposed in translated documents secured after the war within the German propaganda services. One document disclosed that Hughes had recorded a message on 17 January 1944 for a programme called 'Forces Hour'. This obviously occurred around the time of Carpenter's arrest for the coat incident. Hughes identified himself in the programme as Captain Baker. Investigations later revealed that the recording by Hughes had only been transmitted on 10 November and the content included statements about Hitler's newly deployed Vengeance weapons, the V1 flying bomb and the V2 rocket.

Both Hughes and Carpenter would eventually be reunited at the Stalag Luft III prisoner of war camp near Sagan in Lower Silesia. Carpenter was placed in hut 106, where the camp interrogator became interested in his unusual account of events in Berlin. In general, he was treated with caution. Flying Officer Geoffrey Willatt, a bomb aimer from 106 Squadron, who had been the only survivor of a crew led by Group Captain Hodder, the station commander, on 5 September 1943, was tasked to watch Carpenter and was to ensure that no escape activity be exposed to him.

Carpenter had spent approximately three weeks in an assumed escape line safe house, a short spell in the Saint-Gilles prison, three weeks in Dulag Luft and, almost four months in Berlin before becoming a Stalag Luft III prisoner. He was among the assembled group of 300 officers hastily summoned to the camp theatre on 6 April 1944. The commanding officer at Luft III, Group Captain Massey, told them that the camp commandant had just advised him that forty-one officers from the escape at Luft III on 24 March 1944 had been shot by the Gestapo. Massey was subsequently repatriated on health grounds and Group Captain Wilson, Carpenter's safe house partner, took over command. It was Wilson who was to receive the urns containing their murdered colleagues' ashes, which were dispassionately delivered to Stalag III. The ashes would later be stored in a commemorative memorial constructed by the prisoners of war at the camp.

Returning to the information provided to post-war investigators by Raymond Hughes. He stated that he had been in Zuromski's accommodation, where he had seen scripts written mostly in Polish, but one or two in English against the Jews and against Russia. No evidence of those scriptures is known to exist. The statement written by Hughes during the detailed investigations conducted upon the British Free Corps activity and the archives of the Concardia transmissions from central Berlin are relatively detailed and comprehensive. They include some transcripts recorded from the original broadcasts from Berlin.

It would appear that Zuromski had been under instructions to create anti-Russian propaganda and no doubt this was something that he was well suited to have done. Ronald Spillman, in his post-war interviews, declared that he knew of him as Kovalski, the Polish fighter pilot in the RAF, working in the Polish station at Concordia. He described him as unusually standing in the open during bombing raids, looking into the sky and describing what he saw to those sheltering. Spillman was of the opinion that Kovalski's wife and children had been killed by the Russians and he had escaped. This was clearly a misconstrued conversation or assumption as it had been his father who had been murdered by the Russians and his mother's whereabouts were unknown. During the investigations into Spillman's actions of assisting within the German propaganda system, he was the only individual who made reference to the investigators that Zuromski or Kovalski was known as 'Warsaw Willi'. Bearing in mind the significant numbers of extensive interviews that were undertaken by the Special Investigators, and the many evidential reports they composed, is surprising that reference was never made by any other individual.

Zuromski was under the controlling influence of Professor Reinhard Haferkorn, who was the responsible person for the Concardia staff in Berlin. He had been a university professor but now, employed by the German Foreign Office, he was responsible for controlling the English section of the foreign broadcasting department at Concordia. The staff under him included Fritz Hesse, an expert on British matters who had been involved with the von Ribbentrop German-Soviet non-aggression pact. He was responsible for the policy concerning radio propaganda to Britain and the British Free Corps. Other intellectuals included Doctor Springborn, Doctor Edwards and Hiller Ziegfeld. A plethora of journalists, interpreters and linguistics all worked within the Concardia, and of course the politically biased Allied prisoners of war that were brought to his attention were most sought after. Clearly Zuromski had been identified and manipulated to help deliver the German propaganda objectives as anti-communist material was seen as a valuable resource for transmissions.

Reinhard Haferkorn disclosed in post-war interviews that in the latter part of 1943, two men, Carter and Kowalski, were brought to Berlin by Lieutenant Bonninghaus and presented before him. Those men were RAF prisoners of war, Squadron Leader Carter and Flying Officer Zuromski. Reinhard Haferkorn and Herr Adami interviewed the prisoners. Adami was in charge of the Radio National channel, broadcasting music and talk programmes from Büro Concardia. Kowalski, being Polish, was passed to the controller of the Polish section at Concardia. Adami was left to find appropriate work for Carter. Haferkorn was able to say his only other knowledge of Carter was of his known meetings with a man named Hughes, alias Baker. This has to be assumed to have been Raymond Hughes, who had used the alias John Charles Baker or Captain Baker.

Adami took Carter to the underground studios of Concardia on 21 October. He watched the recording of propaganda messages by a person Adami addressed as Wallace. This was the alias of Roy Purdy, a Royal Navy prisoner of war who appeared unrestrained in his opinion having been a member of the British Union of Fascists. Carter was thereafter required to report daily to Adami, having not been engaged with any specific tasks.

Another RAF prisoner of war who took a prominent role at the Concardia was Pilot Officer Benson Railton Metcalf Freeman. Pre-war, Freeman had been an officer cadet at the Royal Military Academy at Sandhurst, obtaining a commission and transferring into the RAF in 1926. He qualified as a pilot, only to resign his commission in 1931. He joined the British Union of Fascists in 1937 and returned to service in 1939. Freeman was posted as a communication and transport pilot, taking supplies to France. On 22 May 1940, over Saint-Omer, his aircraft was shot down by anti-aircraft gunfire. In June 1940, his squadron reported to the Air Ministry that among his personal kit they had located his membership card of Oswald Mosley's British Union of Fascists political party. The party's name had changed to the National Socialists in 1936 and in 1937 to the British Union. It later transpired Freeman's wife was also a member of Mosley's party. As a prisoner of war, his correspondence to his wife was censored and MI9 tested the paper for secret ink messages. Freeman no doubt disclosed his political thoughts to his Luftwaffe captors and found himself moved from Stalag IIA camp in Neubrandenburg to residence at the Dulag Luft interrogation camp. The camp commandant and Heinrich Eberhardt, the reception officer, appeared to have developed a good relationship with him. Haferkorn had seen Freeman at the Dulag Luft camp in February 1941 after it was reported that he was an alleged British fascist and anti-Bolshevik.

Eighteen months later Eberhardt took Freeman to Berlin, where he met Dr Fritz Hesse, a pre-war Nazi diplomat. Freeman, with an alias of P. Royston, was reintroduced to Haferkorn and recruited into the German Radio Corporation, where he took part in collating material for the 'Germany Calling' radio broadcasts. The main presenter of that propaganda was William Joyce, known as Lord Haw-Haw. Freeman's job was to write scripts for Joyce but he also worked on his own scripts using the name Royston. Those scripts and transmissions included anti-Bolshevik material and criticisms of the British government. Freeman resided at the Alhambra Hotel in Berlin and was paid a healthy tax-free salary. Haferkorn ensured access to Red Cross food parcels were readily available to the prisoners who were employed in Berlin. Erich Hetzler, the propaganda minister and SS officer, was in frequent contact with Joyce, who held the commanding position in delivering 'Germany Calling' and the entire programme content. The mornings were reserved for meetings with Hetzler, who also oversaw the broadcasting of the 'New British Broadcasting Station', which was a fake news programme. Freeman became embedded into this network and actually became a Waffen SS officer in 1944.

The British Free Corps came into existence on 1 January 1944 and it is thought that Freeman volunteered to join the unit around this time. In April, the corps was issued its distinctive insignia. The uniform jacket cuff title bore 'British Free Corps' in Gothic script, a three-lion passant collar tab and Union Jack arm badges. However, with the real threat that the unit would soon be of a strength for Eastern Front deployment, Freeman drafted a letter, signed by fourteen other British Free Corps men, requesting they be returned to their stalag camps. In June 1944, Freeman, as the instigator, was swiftly sent to a penal stalag on the charge of mutiny. He escaped the stalag in November 1944, and reached Soviet lines, from where he was eventually repatriated in March 1945.

The Special Investigation Branch document SIB639/45 discloses that Freeman was interviewed about his actions, specifically his activity at Concardia. Zuromski was also the subject of interest by the investigator, identified in the report as Flying Officer Wickham. Freeman was shown several images of individuals, one of which was Zuromski, and was required to identify him. He would not make a positive identification, simply stating if he was a short man that would be him. Freeman admitted knowing a Pole 'Kawawlski' but added no additional information other than addressing him as the 'poor bloody Pole' and made attempts to justify his anti-Russian views as a Pole. Freeman was more inclined to expose the RAF pilot Carter, who was Squadron Leader Carpenter also known as Boyd-Carpenter, adding that Bonninghaus, the political interrogator from the Dulag Luft camp, had revealed Carter was writing scripts for broadcasting and he advised the investigators that a civilian working at Concardia called

Teulischen who spoke perfect English knew more. Erich Hetzler, in control of Concardia, was Carpenter and Hetzler's employer and had instructed a female typist to deal with Carpenter's writings.

Hetzler was a member of Hitler's SS and had been an official of the von Ribbentrop Bureau. Joachim von Ribbentrop had been appointed by Hitler as the ambassador to London in August 1936. His main objective was to persuade the British government not to get involved in Germany's territorial disputes and to work together against the communist government in the Soviet Union. Von Ribbentrop was the significant architect of the German-Soviet non-aggression pact of 23 August 1939, which cleared the way for Hitler's attack on Poland on 1 September 1939.

Another reported member of Oswald Mosley's British Union of Fascists political party was Battery Quartermaster Sergeant J.H.O. Brown of the Royal Artillery. Brown, an Oxford graduate, had been captured in late May 1940 while serving in an anti-tank regiment. He was initially placed in Stalag VIIIB, where he influenced his interrogators by purporting to be a genuine fascist in order to gain advantages. He was sent to Blechhammer forced labour education camp in Upper Silesia. Blechhammer became a sub-camp of Auschwitz where, through punishment and forced labour, political dissidents were to be persuaded to agree with Nazi ideology. This camp expanded into a significant concentration camp. Through his activities and by selection by the German intelligence services, Brown was taken to Berlin and assessed as a potential defector. He reportedly met William Joyce and John Amery in 1942. Returned to Blechhammer, Brown was most fortunate to meet Captain Julius Green, a Jewish prisoner who held the secret coding for letter writing that provided a direct link to MI9. Brown and Green were like-minded in deploying trading and bartering for provisions, effectively black marketeering. Eventually Brown took possession of the code, which became invaluable to his later exploits. In June 1943 he was once again in Berlin, selected to act as a leader at the Genshagen IIID camp.

Brown later obtained some freedom of movement in Berlin and gathered intelligence for MI9. Despite the risk of discovery by the Gestapo, he used whatever means were possible to send back information to London by coded messages through MI9 and on to MI5. The International Committee of the Red Cross inspected prison camps and engaged in a central information agency of information. The Red Cross provided mail facilities for prisoners of war that could be used, and it is thought that the Swiss Young Men's Christian Association was another avenue for contact for Brown. During the Second World War, they worked with prisoners of war and refugees. Known as secretaries, the representatives of the association visited prisoner of war camps in nearly forty countries. During the Nazi period, the movement had been abolished throughout Germany and the occupied territories across Europe. Nazi Germany had merged all youth associations into the single Nazi youth movement.

Margery Booth became a contact for Sergeant Brown. She was a professional soprano singer from London who had frequently performed with the Berlin opera and had married a German, Egon Strohm, who worked as a radio reporter with the Empire Section of Berlin radio. Living in Germany, Margery, who had been recruited by MI9, often sang at the Berlin State Opera House and frequented high society. The Germans recruited the English singer to perform at Stalag IIID in Berlin, their objective being to enhance the chances of British prisoners of war being persuaded into joining the British Free Corps. Brown was present in the camp when Margery finished her act with a rousing rendition of *Land of Hope and Glory*. It was somewhat out of place and he realised he had probably found an ally. Margery performed every fortnight at Stalag IIID and eventually she carried intelligence between Brown and MI5, often concealed in her undergarments. Margery's activity became suspicious when she was frequently seen to be connected to Brown. She was arrested by the Gestapo and Major Heimpel, in charge of prison camp intelligence, received information giving details of the suspicions about Brown's activities. Brown was interviewed but apparently convinced his interrogator that the reports were simply malicious. Margery was interrogated but divulged nothing and with no evidence they released her. Her marriage to Egon Strohm had started to break down and the Berlin Opera House had been bombed in late November 1943. Margery chose to escape from Berlin during an air raid in late 1944. She bravely made her way west, presumably on her own until she was provided safety by the advancing Allied army in 1945. In December 1944 Brown was taken from Stalag IIID and imprisoned in a Berlin jail. From there he went to the prisoner of war camp Lamsdorf and thereafter was force marched towards central Germany until his eventual liberation in April 1945.

In London, the information that Margery had been able to smuggle out of Stalag IIID was used in the Old Bailey treason trials. Little was known about the Wigan-born singer or her actions in relation to Stalag IIID until this came to light when a small photograph of her was found, some sixty years after the war. The image of her standing in a wooded area showed her looking demure. It had been taken on one of her visits to the prisoner of war camp in Berlin. The rear of the photograph was officially stamped 'Freigegeben Stalag IIID' and she wrote on the front in ink, 'With kindest remembrances, Good luck, Margery Booth'. There is a good possibility that this photograph was at one time a gift from Margery to Brown.

Brown received a recommendation for the award of the Distinguished Conduct Medal. It was published in *The London Gazette* on 27 September 1945:

> This N.C.O. was serving with the B.E.F. in France when he was captured on 29 May 1940, at Caestre. After a few weeks at Stalag VIIIB at Lamsdorf, he was sent to Blechhammer, E.3 Kommando, where he devoted his energies to the welfare of the men and general escape work until he was returned to the main camp in January

1942. Shortly afterwards he was transferred to a working camp in Berlin (No. 806 attached to Stalag IIID). Five months later he was again sent to Blechhammer and in June 1943, he was appointed Camp Leader to Genshagen holiday camp. (IIID) Realising that the Germans intended to use this camp subversively for their own ends he was determined to thwart them. Despite the very real danger involved, he pretended to be working for the Germans, whilst at the same time he was really using the comparative freedom accorded him to further the cause of the allies. Even when the Gestapo became suspicious B.Q.M.S. Brown did not hesitate to continue work. Acting as he did entirely on his own initiative, he fully realised that in all probability he might be suspected of betraying his own country. This did in fact happen, but it has now been established without question that he did acquire and transmit to this country valuable information. Through his continuous efforts the British Free Corps, which the Germans hoped to expand from the men sent to Genshagen, gained few recruits and eventually the project became a complete failure. In addition, B.Q.M.S. Brown used the frequent change of personnel at the camp to establish inter-camp communication, passing on information and escape aids. It is remarkable that whilst busy with all these activities, he did not neglect his duties as senior N.C.O. Genshagen which was excellently run and men who had been there have shown marked respect and esteem for B.Q.M.S. Brown. When the camp closed in December 1944, B.Q.M.S. Brown was again sent to Lamsdorf, and with the other personnel was later evacuated to Hehenfels (Stalag 383). On 22 April 1945, this camp was liberated by an American unit.

Sergeant Brown and Margery Booth both later gave evidence at the Old Bailey treason trials, providing evidence against William Joyce and John Amery. In addition, also in the prosecution of Roy Purdy, who was charged with making propaganda broadcasts from Berlin. Amery was cited as a British fascist and Nazi collaborator. At trial, he pleaded guilty to eight counts of high treason, for which he was sentenced to death. He was hanged in Wandsworth Prison on 19 December 1945.

In respect of William Joyce, he continued to broadcast from Germany to Britain until 30 April 1945. Until the very end, he continued to tell his listeners that Germany was undefeated and would recover the initiative. However, he had added a warning that if Germany did collapse 'the Soviet Colossus' would devour all Europe, including the British Isles. Joyce was convicted of high treason and sentenced to death. He appealed, but both the Court of Appeal and the House of Lords both upheld his conviction. He was hanged in Wandsworth Prison on 3 January 1946.

Roy Purdy had been a member of the British Union of Fascists before the war. As a prisoner of war, he broadcast for the enemy and prepared propaganda transcripts. Herbert Krumbiegel, an electrical engineer employed at Concardia, positively identified Purdy as using the name Wallace. Purdy was very adept at being used by the Third Reich; he was later employed by Nazi intelligence as a stool pigeon in Colditz Castle. The Germans liked to boast that there was no escape from the infamous medieval castle near Leipzig. Purdy was planted into the castle in March 1944 with the assumed name of Bob Poynter, a name stolen from a British Naval officer. He commenced to integrate with the prisoners and began hearing of their intentions. He was responsible for thwarting the ingenious measures of escape being planned by informing the camp commandant. In June he returned to Berlin as a propaganda broadcaster and interpreter. Purdy was convicted of treason in 1945 and sentenced to death, later reduced to life imprisonment. However, he was released from jail in November 1954 under a Home Secretary's licence. In retrospect this appears a short sentence for the offences of which he had been convicted.

Thomas Haller Cooper, who had fought in the German forces and had joined the British Free Corps, was located and arrested after the war. He appeared at the Central Criminal Court in London on 8 January 1946 to face five counts of high treason. His charges were:

Joining German forces and serving with them against the Soviet Union during the 1 February 1940 and 10 June 1943.

Prepared leaflets for use by the Germans as propaganda for use among British prisoners of war during the 10 June 1943 and 14 June 1943.

Spreading German propaganda among British prisoners of war during the period July 1943 and June 1944.

Purported to become a naturalized German citizen on 12 August 1943.

Joined, served and assisted with the recruitment for a German unit known as the British Free Corps.

Cooper, who denied the charges, was found guilty of counts one three and four. Presumably, following points of law, arguments counts two and five were not proceeded with. He was sentenced to death on 11 January. Although his appeal was dismissed on 11 February, his death sentence was commuted to life imprisonment. The mitigating circumstances of Cooper not being a leader in treason were assumed to have been influential in attaining the commuted sentence. Cooper was released from prison in 1953.

In September 1945, a decision was made to charge Pilot Officer Benson Railton Metcalf Freeman under section 4(5) of the Air

Force Act with voluntarily aiding the enemy while a prisoner of war and, under section 40 in accepting a salary from the enemy while a prisoner of war.. He was found guilty on three out of four charges, one of which was that of serving as a Waffen SS officer. It is believed that he served his full-term sentence of ten years in Leyhill Prison, Falfield, Gloucestershire.

The majority of military cases were prosecutions for having joined the enemy forces or for acting as informers to the Germans in prisoner of war camps. Some seventy civilians were arrested by MI5 investigators, the majority of whom had been employed within the German broadcasting service. The Director of Public Prosecutions became the authority in decision making for all civilian prosecution cases. Erich Hetzler, the SS manager of the anti-British propaganda section in Berlin, was arrested on 13 May 1945. He was detained and held in an internment camp.

Zuromski and Carpenter were both investigated by the Royal Air Force Special Investigation Branch. These were investigations referenced as A5 by MI5, Ref 308.039/SLB3 and SIB case 639/45 for Zuromski and investigation by MI5 Ref 308.017/SLB3 and SIB case 639/45 relevant for George Carpenter. On 20 May 1946, the Special Investigation Branch at Princess Gate Court, Kensington in London, published to the Air Ministry a list of all RAF personnel who had been suspected of improper conduct while prisoners of war. Thirty-five men were listed with various outcomes. Only Zuromski and Carpenter were noted with the comment, 'No further action'. The correspondence between the Judge Advocate General and the Special Investigation Branch on 21 November 1945 was not disclosed.

The Judge Advocate General's Office at the War Office was the central point for legal advice on matters of military law and in 1945 became the focal point for legal questions concerning the prosecution of cases of war crimes committed during the war. The Judge Advocate's findings induced the RAF to withdraw charges of suspected of improper conduct whilst prisoners of war against both Carpenter and Zuromski. Apart from the previously mentioned Sergeant J.H.O. Brown of the Royal Artillery, there was one other British Army prisoner of war who made reference to Zuromski in PRO record WO 71/1131; Signalman William Colledge, who had been captured in the Mediterranean theatre in 1941. He experienced varied periods of time in several locations as a prisoner of war and had undertaken tasks requested of him by his captors. Under suspicion of 'assisting the enemy', he was connected to Camp IIID in Berlin and the Concardia, where he was coached in radio technique by Margaret Joyce, wife of William Joyce. During the investigation of Colledge he described the Pole Kowalski, working on the Polish section, as fanatically pro-British and anti-Russian, and an acquaintance of Carter. This without doubt refers to Zuromski and George Carpenter. Colledge was eventually charged and brought to trial. After he was convicted he was sentenced to servitude for life. This was later mitigated by the Army Council to one of seven years' penal servitude. His contact in Berlin, Margaret Joyce, was a German national and therefore ineligible for any similar charges.

During 1943, Zuromski was still effectively a prisoner of war in Berlin. It is accepted that he and many others had enjoyed a position of freedom, and to a certain extent a privileged existence when compared to that of the many thousands of prisoners of war at that time. However, central Berlin was a prime target of bombing in 1943 and in particular the extensive night bombing campaign by Bomber Command had seen many concentrated raids by significant numbers of heavy bombers.

On 28 May 1945, Zuromski put his signature to a report outlining his escape from Stalag IIID to an officer of the British Directorate of Military Intelligence, Section 9 or simply MI9. That department undertook prisoner of war questionnaire reports from anyone thought to possibly be in a position to provide intelligence on individuals who had assisted or thwarted escape or evasion in occupied Europe. It especially focused on the collection of evidence for the prosecution of war crimes. The questionnaire recorded basic information about the serviceman, including his name, rank, number, unit, home address and date and place of capture. It also recorded all prisoner of war camps the serviceman was captive within and the corresponding dates. This was followed by a series of questions relating to medical treatment, escape activity, sabotage and war crimes. The liberated prisoners were required to sign the questionnaire once completed.

Under question three on the form, 'Escape Attempts', Zuromski wrote:

> Escaped from the Stalag IIID during heavy Royal Air Force raid on Berlin at night 22/23 November 1943. Was about three weeks' east of Berlin … Muggelsee … with civilian foreign workers got false identity papers and before xmas 1943 went to Poland.

The bombing of Berlin on the night of 22 November 1943 was a raid that engaged the greatest force of aircraft sent to the German capital thus far in the war. Some 764 heavy bombers dropped their bomb loads in what were fairly severe weather conditions. Fifty-three bombers were lost to the defences that protected he capital. The bombing destruction stretched from central districts westwards into Tiergarten and Charlottenburg. The RAF sent 383 bombers back to attack Berlin the following night and an additional 443 returned to Berlin on 26 November. The confusion in Berlin owing to the intensity of raids was significant. Charlottenburg, the district where Zuromski had been living, had suffered terrible destruction of houses, flats and apartments, which forced many thousands of people on to the streets, now effectively homeless. The German administration officer or Kreisleiter, a Nazi Party title for county municipal government men, issued those affected with an *Ausweis fur Fliegergeschadigte*, or identity document for bombing victims, within a few days of the raids. The occupant was required to state that their house was completely destroyed and not inhabitable. A payment of Reichsmarks was issued from the War Damage Office, assumedly to pay for accommodation if it could be found. Zuromski mentioned Müggelsee in his intelligence report. This is a district in Berlin and the circumstances he reported are corroborated by the operations logs of Bomber Command at that time. The 22 November raid also destroyed the Berlin Opera House. It is an interesting correlation of facts that opera singer Margery Booth also took advantage of the bombing to undertake a most similar escape from Berlin.

After his escape, Zuromski reported to his interviewers that he had evidence of war crimes having been committed. He disclosed and confirmed by his signature that he wished to bring these to notice, but they had to be given to the Polish government in London. These matters unfortunately remain undisclosed and unknown. His behaviour illustrates a strong desire and loyalty to report directly to the Polish seniorities, and it may be that it related to the information he held upon the revelations exposed to him while he was a prisoner of war concerning the Russian atrocities that involved his father's execution. However, they will undoubtably remain undisclosed.

CHAPTER 11
ESCAPE THROUGH EUROPE, NOVEMBER 1943 TO MAY 1945

Having taken advantage of the night bombing operations in Charlottenburg, Zuromski left the area after the air raids in November 1943. He appears to have had an objective to make towards Kraków, approximately 450 miles away. It may be assumed the identity documentation provided to Zuromski while in Berlin that permitted travelling, in addition to the authorisation documents to purchase food and clothing, will have aided him in that objective. Within Germany there was a general requirement for the majority of subjects to be in possession of a certificate of approved residency. However, as the bombing campaign had destroyed thousands of residences, that registration process had become ineffective. Displaced person movements were significantly high and any cursory inspection of the documents possessed by Zuromski would in all probability have sufficed basic scrutiny.

A report exists that provides further details of Zuromski's movements in 1944 and into 1945. This is the Escape and Evasion report MI9/S/PG/LIB/769, written for the intelligence services when Zuromski was interviewed at the Great Western Hotel London in 1945. Zuromski's report was written after he had been interviewed at length by Squadron Leader Thomas of the RAF Investigations Branch based at the Air Ministry building in Exhibition Road, London. Unfortunately, the MI9 document is undated and frustratingly has some date references that do not appear consistent to the events detailed. However, it was a retrospective report, and was made following the more detailed interview process undertaken with Thomas. Zuromski stated that he was resident at the Auto Hotel, Berlin, between October 1943 and February 1944. Having clearly stated in the prisoner of war liberation report that he left Berlin in November 1943, there is a discrepancy of between ten to twelve weeks.

The Bomber Command operation of 23 November was a directed attack upon central Berlin. Some 383 heavy bombers carried out this raid in inclement weather between 1930 and 2112 hours. The government quarter, Charlottenburg, Moabit and the district around the zoo bore the brunt of the attack. The bombing created widespread fires and induced a partial failure in electricity and water supplies. There was considerable damage caused by the dropping of 130 mines, 900 high-explosive bombs, 200,000 incendiary bombs 20,000 phosphorous bombs and 60 flares of various kinds. The Air Ministry translations of German raid reports composed after the operations on this night detailed the death of 1,757 people. In addition, 6,923 were injured and 180,000 were made homeless. Apart from domestic properties, among the buildings hit or destroyed were the Chancellery Ministry of Finance, Propaganda Ministry, Transport Ministry, Foreign Office and railway sidings with Hitler's special train. Also the Gestapo office and the Air Ministry building in the Schillerstrasse. The Charlottenburg district where Zuromski was resident suffered significantly, with the Siemens and Halske, Daimler-Benz, AEG and Schlegelstrasse Albrecht armament works destroyed or badly damaged. The German communiqué issued at 1300 hours on 24 November 1943 reads:

On the evening of 23 November, the Reich capital was again attacked by strong British formations. This terror raid caused more damage in several districts. In addition to residential districts, numerous public buildings, including churches, welfare institutions & cultural monuments were destroyed. Fighter formations & A.A of the Luftwaffe in spite of difficult conditions for defence shot down 19 E/A.

The next discrepancy in the statement that Zuromski made was that of him leaving Charlottenburg on 15 September 1944 with the help of Polish and Czech workers he had known there. This date must be an error in typing or recording as it has no context to any sequence of events, least of all the bombing of Berlin. The report adds that with the help of friends, he reached Kraków on 5 March 1944. Estimating from the dates of the bombing in Berlin, the journey had therefore taken approximately fifteen weeks. Feasibly this establishes he had on average walked approximately 5 miles each day. In Kraków, Zuromski made contact with an address given to him by a Polish girl worker, and he stayed with an elderly woman at that location for several weeks. Reportedly, he met a Czech foreman factory worker, who supplied him with papers to enable him to go to the small town of Lovosice on the Protectorate border above Czechoslovakia. The Czech foreman was unidentified in the report but he had apparently been responsible in helping other workers to escape. The timescale of events relating to Lovosice are vague. Zuromski added in the report:

> I could not stomach staying in Poland for I saw that the Partisans who were being murdered by the Germans would ultimately be murdered by the Russians. It was horrible. I reached Prague about the middle of June 1944 and stayed there a few days. Until 17 December 1944 I worked as a driver for Allgemeine Elektrisitat Gesellschaft – Transport Abteilung headquarters at Ober Schoneweide about twenty miles from Berlin. The Czech

gave me papers of introduction, stating that I was working previously with Siemens and Halske at Oranienburg, and that I had become redundant and displaced due to bombing.

Allgemeine Elektricitäts Gesellschaft (AEG) and Siemens in Berlin were significant manufacturers of electrical equipment for Nazi military use. They deployed forced labour in the numerous factories, all of which were producing various radar and radio equipment and components. Siemens relied increasingly on forced labourers to maintain production levels. These labourers included people from territories occupied by the German military. A large number of the factories in the Berlin area were destroyed by aerial bombardment. As a result, Siemens had transferred and relocated nearly 400 facilities to more rural districts by the time the war ended. Zuromski's statement in his escape report certainly relates to these circumstances and it is certainly something he was able to take advantage of with the assistance he was given.

Siemens now acknowledge and openly regret that during 1940 to 1945, at least 80,000 forced labourers worked within its production facilities. The industrial company IG Farben became the subject of a war crime trial when twenty-four leading members of the business were charged with actively collaborating with the Nazis, primarily by using slave labour from concentration camps. The trial took place between 27 August 1947 and 11 June 1948. Thirteen of the defendants were found guilty and received prison terms from one and a half to eight years in prison. The convictions were for planning and waging aggressive war, committing war crimes, and crimes against humanity by looting public and private property in occupied countries. Also, for the use of slave labour, participation in the SS and participation in plans to commit crimes against peace.

Returning to Zuromski and his employment in Berlin during the period from mid-June to 17 December 1944. His statement indicates that he was employed as a driver for six months at a factory on the outskirts of Berlin. No doubt the identity or reference papers supplied to him enabled this to take place. There is no mention of where he was living during that period, but there is mention of him receiving a salary of 180 German Marks. Zuromski added in his report:

> On 17 December 1944 I went back to Prague and had bribed my fellow mechanic with cigarettes and food to hide my absence. On 8 October 1944 I had married in Prague a Polish girl whom I had known from boyhood in Poland.

The Air Ministry personnel form 1406 holds details of Zuromski, stating that the date and place of his marriage was 8 October 1944, Prague, Czechoslovakia. His wife was identified as Maria Hanka Krzywicka. Once again, the course of Zuromski's life in late 1944 is little known. The only means of gathering information on the events across war-torn Europe were political leaflets and radio transmissions. Zuromski states he was in Prague in early October 1944, when the domestic insurrection to take control of Warsaw was at its height. No doubt the German authorities broadcast those events. Germany reported that the three-month campaign by the Polish Home Army fighters had failed to seize control. The Germans broadcast that the Soviet army had chosen to witness these events without intervening. The uprising's failure effectively allowed the pro-Soviet Polish administration to gather strength, while the Polish government in exile in London collectively lost control. At the height of the Warsaw Uprising, the Russian position was made clear to the British and American Allies with this message:

> The Soviet Government cannot of course object to English or American aircraft dropping arms in the region of Warsaw since this is an American and British affair.

But they decidedly object to British or American planes, after dropping arms in the region of Warsaw, landing on Soviet territory, since the Soviet Government do not wish to associate themselves either directly or indirectly with the adventure in Warsaw.

Churchill had made several appeals to Stalin to allow Allied planes to use Soviet-controlled airfields, but he repeatedly refused. On 2 October, Warsaw's Home Army formally surrendered and during the following three months German forces demolished much of the city and deported an estimated 650,000 civilians to labour camps. Soviet troops finally liberated German-occupied Warsaw in January 1945. Zuromski was at that time still in Prague. His Escape and Evasion report added:

I stayed in Prague again until 15 January 1945, when I went to Werder halfway between Potsdam and Brandenburg. Here I stayed with a market gardener until about 26 January 1945. This man had previously done black market transactions with me.

From there I decided to go westwards as soon as possible. I sent a telegram to my wife to come and join me immediately and fortunately she left Prague on the last train. She brought a lot of food and cigarettes. On 26 January 1945 we left for Magdebourg but the train could not go beyond Brandenburg, the tracks being bombed out. I purchased a bicycle with cigarettes and with the wheels made a cart on which we put our luggage. At the end of February, we got to Magdeburg where we managed to stay two nights. The town was in a very bad state.

There are no details of events between the end of February and 12 April. On that day, Zuromski and his wife Maria were reputedly walking towards Hanover when they came across American troops between Braunschweig and Helmstedt. This indicates that they had walked approximately 30 miles from Magdeburg over the six-week period before reaching the American forces.

The situation of displaced individuals with dubious identification must have been commonplace when the Allied forces pushed into central Germany. It remains unknown how Zuromski proved his identity as a Polish pilot serving in the RAF. An assumption has to be made that he was still in possession of his identity tags, or a prisoner of war identity tag. Another assumption has to be his retention of the certificate of marriage in Prague. Clearly, it was a highly unusual situation for a prisoner of war to marry in such circumstances and then have to validate his position of having been newly married.

It appears from the log book records that Zuromski returned to flying duties almost immediately. Clearly these entries must be retrospective, unless his log book had been reunited with him relatively quickly. Group Captain Stansfield's signature appears in the log book at that time. He was the commanding officer for the garrison at Brussels. Wing Commander Wilson's signature as commanding officer for the maintenance unit in Brussels is also present. Zuromski returned to flying, undertaking formation and aerobatic practice in a Spitfire on 7 May 1945. The following day was officially Victory in Europe day and Zuromski flew two air displays, each of just over two hours. He flew over Evere near Brussels and the airfield B56 Haren-Evere where large crowds were celebrating the Allied victory over Germany. The ringing of church bells was to be a running theme across Brussels and celebrations abounded everywhere.

Upon Zuromski's return to England on or around 30 May 1945, there are several areas where more detail would normally have been sought during the interview and completion of his Escape and Evasion report. The investigating officer from MI9 remains unidentified as the report holds no signature. In the knowledge that Squadron Leader Willian Percy Thomas of the Royal Air Force Special Investigation Branch had previously interviewed Zuromski, the lack of names and details not being fully documented becomes understandable as the unknown composer of the report saw no reason to develop those particular areas of detail knowing they had previously been investigated.

In the United States, the victory came in the shadow of the recent death of President Roosevelt. His successor, Harry S. Truman, dedicated the day to Roosevelt and ordered that flags should be kept at half mast. He broadcast these words:

> The western world has been freed of the evil forces which for five years and longer have imprisoned the bodies and broken the lives of millions upon millions of freeborn men. They have violated their churches, destroyed their homes, corrupted their children and murdered their loved ones. Our armies of liberation have restored freedom to those suffering peoples, whose spirit and will the oppressor could never enslave.

The Soviet Union, which had first attacked Poland as Hitler's ally in 1939, had seized the entire Polish territories. The triumphant Allies witnessed this and condemned Stalin's actions, but for the Polish people everything was lost. Poland was regarded by many as the spoils of deceit by the Russians. The years 1944 to 1947 saw resistance from Polish pro-independence partisans and the Soviet occupiers chased down and murdered anyone who advocated for an independent Poland. Terror ensued in the territory occupied by the Soviets and concentration camps for civilians were constructed to suppress anti-communist insurrection. There was no freedom in Poland, simply a robust oppression of a most brutal kind.

The Russians had subscribed to the Atlantic Charter in January 1942. The first three principles of this charter, ratified by Britain and the United States in 1941, were as follows:

> First, their countries seek no aggrandisement, territorial or other. Second, they desire to see no territorial changes that do not accord with the freely expressed wishes of the peoples concerned and third, they respect the right of all peoples to choose the form of government under which they will live, and they wish to see sovereign rights and self-government restored to those who have been forcibly deprived of them.

Much of Eastern Europe had fallen to Soviet forces. The joint statement issued by the three leaders at Yalta on 11 February 1945, known as the Declaration on Poland, became one of the key protocols of the Yalta Agreement and to some extent reflected the reality of the situation. It stated:

> A new situation has been created in Poland as a result of her complete liberation by the Red Army. This calls for the establishment of a Polish Provisional Government which can be more broadly based than was possible before the recent liberation of the Western part of Poland. The Provisional Government which is now functioning in Poland should therefore be reorganized on a broader democratic basis with the inclusion of democratic leaders from Poland itself and from Poles abroad. This new Government should then be called the Polish Provisional Government of National Unity ... This Polish Provisional Government of National Unity shall be pledged to the holding of free and unfettered elections as soon as possible on the basis of universal suffrage and

secret ballot. In these elections all democratic and anti-Nazi parties shall have the right to take part and to put forward candidates.

The terms of the Yalta Agreement had stipulated that all Soviet citizens living on Soviet territory on 1 September 1939, must be repatriated, regardless of whether they wish to go or not. An estimated 5 million citizens classified as Soviets were returned to Russia between 1945 and 1947. The forced repatriation of Russians was on many occasions a violent and uncompassionate affair that led to many choosing death by suicide in preference to what lay ahead under communist rule. These circumstances of forced repatriation had not been anticipated and they were disturbing in every aspect of their delivery.

The term 'dissident displaced persons' was specifically allocated to the Poles from Ukraine. The British Foreign Office collated and recorded these displaced persons by their names, date and place of birth, and most importantly where they had lived on 1 September 1939. They had originally been of Polish nationality, but post-war they were regarded as Russian. In response to Soviet complaints about the treatment of Soviet nationals by Polish forces while under British command, the British Foreign Secretary Ernest Bevin advised the Soviet Ambassador in September 1945 that Ukrainians living outside the boundaries of the USSR in September 1939 would be allowed to return to their home country if they wished to do so. However, those who did not wish to do so would not be repatriated against their wishes.

CHAPTER 12

INVESTIGATIONS, INTERPRETATIONS AND LEGALITIES

The Air Ministry had developed five broad principles for dealings with matters that involved the management of the joint Allied air forces. These principles, created in 1942, were advisory and embraced a vast array of diverse matters that included discipline, and they were published as a mission statement on the treatment of the Allied air forces. One of the principal matters was that of fundamental legality, with the understanding of both the British and Allied service laws. Clearly all Allied airmen were serving a joint cause and it was impossible for control and management of personnel to be conflicting and subject to different sets of regulations and punishments.

Reflecting upon Zuromski's circumstances, he had been instructed and educated in Polish Army discipline. He then attempted to embrace French Air Force guidance, and then received significant education on the RAF methods of both combat flying and in British laws and military rules. All European Allied airmen effectively became a member of the Volunteer Reserve. The British authorities felt that RAF law should therefore apply as the primary default of understanding by all ranks. However, many of the Allies tried to retain some control over their own matters of discipline. In some instances, there were remonstrations that it was unfair for Allied personnel to be subject to legislation with which, initially at least, they were unfamiliar. Without doubt, in some elements there were differences and in some instances British law was considered as being more lenient in respect to the sentencing of guilty parties. These conflicts required compromises that took time to be embedded with understanding.

Courts martial would only be convened with RAF officers, with interpreters and lawyers relevant to the offender's country of origin provided where needed. Of utmost importance was the agreement that while serving within air force units, or on stations commanded by a RAF officer, all Allied personnel were subject to RAF law. The only exception was that of a squadron staffed and commanded by another nation. In those instances, their own regulations were permitted or arbitrated together within the discipline structure.

It is not difficult to see how difficulties existed, and that compromise management was likely to be required. The integration of bomber crews, in particular, often saw Commonwealth and European airmen operating harmoniously together. In many cases some of the Allied airmen were keen to gift or present their nation's brevets and badges to British personnel as a token of respect or friendship. There were regulations imposed upon the wearing of insignia and uniform and in early 1943 the issue was laid before the Air Council for a decision. The guidance was that flying badges should not be exchanged and worn. This finding appears to endorse the Air Ministry's mission statement of the RAF being primary in administration and that it had overall control of the Allied airmen serving within it.

The Polish officer Ludwik Maria Emanuel Szul, working for the RAF, provided a post-war report on the Polish service records of Zuromski. The report he submitted, when looked at in the context of the advocated British authority's statement that RAF law had to be applied as the default, appears to be controversial in its content. Szul had been a Polish Army colonel who was awarded the Cross of Valour and the Air Medal multiple times and the Officer's Cross of the Order of the British Empire. From 1935, he became the secretary of the Editorial Board of the Aviation Review and was promoted to the rank of major with seniority from 19 March 1937. He served in Britain as a Polish advisor and reported on Zuromski's service during the immediate post-war years following his request for a permanent RAF commission. Szul commented on the confidential commission application made by Zuromski under Air Ministry Order A571/47:

> He (Julian Zuromski) was awarded summarily seven days house arrest for criticism regarding an order received from a superior officer in 1940. He was sentenced by a Polish Air Force Court Martial to two years imprisonment and cashiering on charge of broadcasting for the enemy – Germany whilst a prisoner of war during the last war. The administrator of the Polish Forces under the British Command has ruled that proceedings against Zuromski be dropped.

There is no evidence about the criticising of an order within the RAF records. Neither is there reference to Zuromski having being placed on house arrest within the Polish Air Force service documentation, and no evidence of the information cited by Szul can be found. This may well suggest that the early incident in 1940 had been properly dealt with within the RAF disciplinary process.

The events that Szul outlined about Zuromski when he was a prisoner of war are well investigated and evidenced. Additionally, The National Archives file KV2/3581 describes a letter written by Lieutenant Colonel V.H. Seymer within MI5 on 27 March 1945. The final paragraph notes:

> In addition to a number of British civilians, the following service renegades have been employed in editing, writing scripts and broadcasting for the enemy ...

Zuromski's name was not on the list of nine servicemen identified within that document. For further clarity in May 1946, the RAF Special Investigation Branch at Princess Gate Court, Kensington, London, published for the Air Ministry, a list of all RAF personnel who had been suspected of improper conduct while prisoners of war. Thirty-five men were listed with various suspicions of their activity and the outcomes of investigations. Zuromski's name was present within that list. He had been investigated but was noted within the document as 'No further action' as directed by the Judge Advocate General in correspondence dated 21 November 1945.

These facts appear to confirm the correct protocol of discipline matters had been administered by the RAF. However, the Polish statement by Szul stated that a Polish court martial had been held. The personnel file for Zuromski holds no evidence of any trial. Zuromski held a temporary commission in the RAF. Therefore, the previous legal standing agreement that had elevated the RAF as having precedence in matters of court martial hearings must have been upheld and the findings of the Judge Advocate General's actions had been definitive. The RAF, with primacy over discipline, accepted the Judge Advocate General's guidance to withdraw any proceedings against Zuromski. Therefore, he was not guilty of any offences committed during his time held as a prisoner of war by the Luftwaffe. However, it appears that the above circumstances and statement by a Polish officer, namely Szul, significantly and detrimentally influenced decision making with regard to Zuromski within the RAF's post-war administration processes.

The Air Ministry Order A571/47 has distinct relevance as it relates to an application by Zuromski for an extension of his commission. Szul, as the Polish advisor for the RAF, recorded comments on that document that undoubtably influenced the Air Ministry or at least Group Captain Valentine Brice Jepson, who received the application and made the decision to not offer any extension to the commission.

That decision induced Zuromski to offer his resignation from the Polish Resettlement Corps.

As previously stated, the decision as to whether or not any military personnel who was a suspected renegade should be prosecuted after investigation rested with the Office of the Judge Advocate General. By August 1946, there had been thirty-seven convictions of offenders within the military services charged with offences of acting for the enemy. Some were for wearing German uniforms, others for operating as informants within prisoner of war camps and others for propaganda broadcasting. The Director of Public Prosecutions had also authorised the arrest of seventy civilians. Twenty-four went to trial and twenty-two of these were convicted of assisting the enemy. Those convictions were imposed by the Defence Regulation Act 2a of 1939 amended 1940 for: 'An act likely to assist the enemy or prejudice the public safety or the defence of the Realm or the efficient prosecution of the war.'

For clarity, it needs to be reiterated that Zuromski resigned his commission as an officer in the RAF. He did so without any disciplinary sentence or conviction of any description imposed by the RAF as he had been exonerated of suspicion by the Judge Advocate General. It has to be stated that on a date unknown within the post-war period, issues of discipline regarding Polish service personnel were handled by Polish military courts. They appear to enforce the rules that a Polish serviceman was required to be in uniform and he was required to obey his officers. However, no doubt exists that Zuromski resigned his commission as an officer in the RAF, therefore the above circumstances, which had evolved from military agreements signed by the British and Polish government in London, were not relevant. In July 1945 the British rescinded recognition of the Polish government in London in favour of the embryonic provisional government in Warsaw.

CHAPTER 13

THE TRIALS

At Oberursel the predictions for the ending of the Second World War gained reality and the Dulag Luft camp began to disperse in March 1945. The senior British officer Air Commodore Ivelaw-Chapman had overseen the dying days of the interrogation centres. He was taken with the commandant Killinger among others in a bus to Buchenbach in central Germany on 18 March. Other groups did similar as the rear party, leaving destroyed piles of documents behind. In mid-April Killinger and a significant number of camp staff were detained by the liberating US troops. Ivelaw-Chapman was extracted and officially became a liberated prisoner of war.

The advancing Allies reached Oberursel on 25 March. Dulag Luft was basically intact and the Allies restored it to functionality and it became a camp to hold Nazi war criminals and other ranking captured German officers. Among them was Oberstleutnant Erich Killinger, who now experienced the confinement aspects of Oberursel from a differing perspective. Among the Allied forces' immediate investigations including evidence gathering, the need to locate high-ranking Nazi officers and those who had committed war crimes was evident. In February and March, the reality of the crimes that the German Third Reich had committed in Auschwitz and other concentration camps became evident. The Polish commission, created by the Russian communist government in Warsaw in 1945, engaged in the investigation of German war crimes in Poland. The commission had the vision to submit some metal components of the gas chambers at the concentration camps to be analysed at the Institute of Forensic Research in Kraków. They revealed the presence of hydrogen cyanide and its compounds. Gradually the extent of the mass extermination that had been carried out by the Third Reich across occupied Europe became clear.

German staff from Oberursel were later brought before a British military tribunal charged with the suspected mistreatment of British prisoners of war in violation of the 1929 Geneva Convention. The main count in the proceeding was the extortion of interrogation statements in violation of international law, through overheating of the solitary confinement cells in the officially titled 'Interrogation section of Evaluation Site West'. Although hundreds of former prisoners of war were interviewed in the investigations leading to the trial, only fourteen statements provided evidence for the breach of the convention. The actual criminal indictment was based on twelve witness statements for offences reportedly committed in 1943. This was the pertinent time when both Squadron Leader Carpenter and Flying Officer Zuromski were resident in the camp. Having been kept in custody and charged with the alleged offences, the defendants were brought to appear at the British Military Court at Wuppertal in central Germany. The trial was listed as Case Nineteen and was scheduled to be heard between 26 November and 3 December 1945.

Erich Killinger, Heinz Junge, Otto Boehringer, Heinrich Eberhardt and Gustav Bauer-Schlichtegroll, all Luftwaffe officers, were charged with committing a war crime in that they at or near Oberursel, Germany, between 1 November 1941 and 15 April 1945 as members of the staff of the Luftwaffe Interrogation Centre known as Dulag Luft, in violation of the laws and usages of war, were together concerned as parties to the ill-treatment of British prisoners of war. It remains unknown why the specific period in 1943 when the overheating of cells took place was not identified in the indictments. It could well have been a prosecution decision to ensure that should additional evidence be disclosed during the trial, it could be accepted within the wider time period captured in the generic charge presented in court. Moreover, the charge did include an extended time period where some evidence was available that suggested a single isolated incident of overheating had taken place on a date in 1944.

The five defendants all pleaded not guilty and their cases were put forward to the court by the allocated defence representatives for each defendant. During the trial proceedings, Killinger, as the commanding officer, honourably took full responsibility for everything that occurred in Dulag Luft from 15 November 1941 to 15 April 1945. According to the trial transcript, there were thirteen specific incidents in which RAF prisoners of war were subjected to being kept in a small prison cell in which the temperature was very high. The periods that the prisoners endured the heat ranged from one to ten hours, and no prisoner went through the experience more than once. Of the thirteen instances supported by evidence, eleven offences were charged. Ten incidents occurred in the summer of 1943, and one in the summer of 1944. There was no evidence available to establish as to how high the temperatures rose, but the affected RAF prisoners were of the opinion that it was very hot. No service personnel from the United States Army Air Corps were subjected to heated cell treatment.

The prosecution and defence testimony established that Killinger did not order the treatment. Also, he did not learn of it until after the fact. With a lack of definitive evidence in relation to the heating of prisoner's cells, no member of the Dulag Luft staff was reprimanded or punished. The trial testimony and transcript evidence did, however, establish beyond doubt that Killinger and his staff had deliberately protected some prisoners of war by registering them as Allied aviators when they were not in possession of any valid identity. Some prisoners that arrived at the Dulag Luft were escaped Allied prisoners of war who had been recaptured without any military identification, while others were suspected of being Special Operations Executive agents, parachuted into occupied France. The false registrations given to those prisoners, although exceptionally low in number, was implemented to prevent those men from being turned over to the Gestapo. Evidence of these factors was presented within the verbal evidence of the last senior British officer at the camp, Air Commodore Ivelaw-Chapman, who by that time was an air vice marshal. Squadron Leader Elliott, the prior senior British officer and once a permanent staff member at the interrogation camp, also gave evidence at the trial. Of the defendant Heinz Junge, he said:

> I know Junge. He was a man who would go out of his way
> to treat prisoners of war in a good way. At times, contrary
> to regulations, he would allow American prisoners to pass
> through without any interrogation. He was an easy going
> man … He like Killinger, always behaved towards the
> prisoners in keeping with military etiquette and I never
> had any complaints about his behaviour …

Despite the mitigating factors, on 3 December 1945, the military court sentenced the former camp commandant, Killinger, and his deputy, Junge, to five years in prison. Eberhardt received a sentence of three years, while two of the accused, Boehringer and Bauer-Schlichtegroll, were acquitted. Those who were convicted were imprisoned in Werl Prison and later granted early release after serving two thirds of the term.

The immediate post-war Germany was divided into four occupied zones: Great Britain in the north-west, France in the south-west, the United States in the south and the Soviet Union in the east. The capital city of Berlin, situated in Soviet territory, was also divided into four occupied zones. Displaced person camps were established in the occupied zones of Germany. The first inhabitants of these camps were concentration camp survivors who had been liberated on German soil. In 1947, they were joined by a further wave of Jewish refugees from Czechoslovakia, Hungary and Romania. It was estimated that the total number of displaced persons in the camps reached 250,000. Registration cards identified the name, nationality and place of residence for each individual.

Investigations continued to try and identify Nazi war criminals in the most trying of conditions. Lüneburg, Hamburg and Wuppertal were within the British occupation zone of Germany, from which a total of 1,085 defendants were tried before British military tribunals and 240 defendants were sentenced to death. In the French Zone, 2,107 defendants were tried and 104 convicted and sentenced to death. The total number of Nazi criminals convicted in the three Western occupation zones between 1945 and 1949 was 5,025, of whom 806 were sentenced to death. Four hundred and eighty-six death sentences were carried out. The remainder were commuted to prison terms of varying lengths.

The heinous war crimes and crimes against Jews defined as crimes against humanity were considered by the International Military Tribunal, commonly referred to as the Nuremberg Trials. This judicial setting tried the senior leaders of the Nazi regime who had been jointly captured by the Allies. The first of the Nuremberg Trials was conducted over a lengthy period, November 1945 to October 1946. Britain, France, the Soviet Union and the United States worked together to prosecute the most heinous war criminals under the Nuremberg Charter. Each country provided two judges and one prosecutor for the Nuremberg Trials. The trial of the surviving Nazi leadership at Nuremberg was the only one conducted by the International Military Tribunal. Later trials, called Subsequent Nuremberg Proceedings or zonal trials, were conducted by military tribunals of the four occupying Allied powers within their own occupation zones.

CHAPTER 14

AFTER VICTORY, SUPPRESSION

When victory in Europe had been achieved by the Allied forces there were fifteen Polish Air Force squadrons operating in fighter, bomber, coastal and special duties units serving in the RAF. Some 14,000 Polish men and women were engaged in a vastly diverse range of employment. A total of 2,408 Polish airmen had been killed in combat or in accidents. The Czechoslovak contingent remained smaller by comparison, with only four squadrons in all commands and out of 2,500 flying personnel a total of 511 gave their lives.

Tragedy continued to befall the brave men and women who had escaped occupied Europe. Having fought for their homelands and contributed to the liberation of occupied Europe, the Russians imposed a communist government grip upon Poland, reneging on the promise at the Yalta Conference in February 1945. The Polish Provisional Government of National Unity had been formally created in Moscow on 21 June 1945, with protests by Russia's then allies proving ineffective. The Polish government in exile also lost that formally recognised status, imposed by the British government on 6 July 1945. Two days previously, as seen in document AIR 8/115, the Air Ministry communicated to all commands that the deteriorating situation in Poland was likely to cause difficulties among the men awaiting repatriation. Propaganda became prevalent among the pro-communist elements and there were many who were distressed at the Russian stance.

The Soviet Union, the United States and Great Britain began to have significant differences during the immediate post-war negotiations, which were undertaken during two conferences. One had taken place before the official end of the war, and one after. These conferences set the seeds for conflict that saw the beginning of the Cold War and which led to a significantly divided Europe. Stalin, with tacit compliance to the Yalta Conference, allowed for elections in Poland, but by that time the Russians had sent in Soviet troops to eliminate any and all opposition to the communist party. The Polish dissatisfaction with the Yalta declaration resulted in Churchill issuing a statement in the House of Commons and a transmission on the Polish Radio Section to confirm that Poles in the United Kingdom would not be forced to return to their homeland. Churchill was very aware that Britain had promoted the defence of Poland in 1939 and that Britain had committed to the Polish government a shared defence cost in doing so. This was a genuine debt within the financial mutual aid scheme at that time. However, the Anglo-Polish agreement of 29 June 1944 significantly impacted upon the financial agreements of 1939. The British recognition of the Polish government in exile in London defaulted upon the then provisional government in Warsaw. Thereafter in the negotiations by the British with the Polish communists over Poland's debt, there appear to be no definitive figures established.

The Poles witnessed helplessly as their country was taken over by the communist regime. Russia had deported hundreds of thousands of Poles during the initial aggression pact with Germany in 1939. It had inflicted impoverished deaths upon a great many people. After the Allied victory in Europe, the Russian occupation of Polish territories simply defaulted back to Russian control that had been imposed in 1939. The Russians viewed all Polish armed forces personnel returning from the West as enemies. They were treated as potential spies due to their adherence to the traditions and will for an independent Poland. These Poles were very much regarded as dangerous to the new communist authorities and therefore persecuted.

The British government recognised that Polish ex-service personnel would in many instances not want to return to Poland. The Air Ministry initiated a suspension of promotions and non-essential training among the Polish Air Force personnel in August 1945. This stabilised the rank structures to assist in managing the Polish personnel and no doubt indicated that opportunities to remain in service were diminishing. A solution to the issue of repatriation followed with the introduction of the Polish Resettlement Corps in May 1946. This was to assist in resettlement and integration for the thousands of stateless people in the United Kingdom or to assist them to begin new lives elsewhere. Several thousand Czechoslovaks and Polish airmen were permitted to serve in the peacetime RAF and some did so until pension status was attained.

The previously mentioned Polish cavalry officer Lieutenant Colonel Kazimierz Bolesław Jozef Halicki, captured in September 1939, had been released after nearly six years of imprisonment by the German forces. His repatriation was to Great Britain, assumedly because of his presupposed marriage to Taisa Zuromski, Julian's mother, before his capture. Taisa Halicki had registered herself as a refugee, leaving France in July 1940. Halicki became employed as a Polish officer within the Polish Resettlement Corps. His and Taisa's home address was recorded as 69 Cleaveland Gardens, London.

The Air Ministry published the conditions of service for the Polish Resettlement Corps on 14 October 1946 and within it were listed three life choices:

> Settle in Britain.
> Emigrate to Commonwealth or other foreign countries.
> Return to Poland.

The RAF had by this time plans in place for all the Polish fighter squadrons to initially relocate to Norfolk for eventual disbandment. Coltishall became the final home for 306, 309, 315 Squadrons, while 303 and 316 flew to Hethel, south-west of Norwich. By April the transport squadrons based at Chedburgh had ceased operations. The pilots, aircrew and ground crew of all these units awaited the final order to disband, which was given in November 1946. Each squadron thereafter marked the occasion with a fly-past and station ceremonies of closure. The formation of the Committee for the Education of Poles in Great Britain became an avenue of education for many Poles. It was an enterprising facility that funded military personnel and their dependents so they could pursue education at British technical schools, polytechnics and universities.

The 1947 compliance election in Poland unsurprisingly consolidated communist rule in Poland, resulting in the recognition of the Soviet-controlled Polish government formally taking place under the manipulations of Stalin. Among the Polish pilots who returned to Poland after the war was Flight Sergeant Wacław Korwel from 308 Squadron. He had been badly wounded on 18 August 1943 flying his Spitfire against Luftwaffe fighters while escorting Marauders over northern France. He lost three fingers from his left hand when a cannon shell struck his cockpit and shrapnel also penetrated into his legs. He managed to cross the Channel and landed near the South Downs. He was treated at the Queen Victoria Hospital, in East Grinstead, West Sussex, and received surgery by Archibald McIndoe, who endeavoured to restore as much function as possible to the injured hand. He became a member of the famous Guinea Pig Club and, despite his permanent disability, returned to combat flying and survived to see the end of the war. Korwel elected to return to Poland in 1947. He gained employment in Warsaw but thereafter the events in his life become unclear. He was detained and kept in the Mokotów prison, which during the Russian dictatorship in Poland served as the main political penitentiary and also became a place of execution.

Between 1948 and 1956, the communist security services buried the remains of nearly 300 prisoners whom they considered particularly dangerous for the state in the Military Cemetery in Warsaw. Their names were deliberately not recorded in the cemetery register. The bodies of the executed persons were transported from the prison and buried hurriedly, usually at night or in the early hours of the morning. In the mid-1950s the ground used for prison burials and the adjacent sections of the cemetery were covered with additional soil and rubble.

Between 2012 and 2014, archaeological excavations were carried out in the cemetery commissioned by the Institute of National Remembrance and the Council for the Protection of Struggle and Martyrdom Sites. As a result, the remains of 198 persons were exhumed. The largest proportion of the bodies showed signs of execution with one or more shots in the back of the head, fired from a handgun. It is assumed that after a trial, Korwel was executed on 24 March 1950. His burial place was in section L of Powązki Military Cemetery. Although his remains have not yet been positively identified, Wacław Korwel is registered as a victim of the multiple events that occurred in Mokotów prison during that regime.

It is estimated that 3,000 Poles from the air force were repatriated to Poland and a further 2,400 emigrated to other countries. By July 1948, some 9,000 Polish Air Force personnel remained as residents in Britain, with at least 5,000 finding civilian jobs. A small number were recruited into the RAF, leaving a minority who were in need of long-term care.

In 1948, the Czechoslovak communists overthrew the government and the Czechoslovak pilots of the RAF were thereafter labelled enemies of the state. The first directive against former RAF service personnel was issued just days after the communist coup. Some of the individuals were persecuted swiftly. As far as the new regime was concerned, anyone who fought with the Western Allies was at best suspect and at worst a traitor. Within days of the coup, leading figures were arrested and tried. The head of the Czechoslovak Inspectorate for the wartime RAF, Karel Janousek, spent fifteen years in jail. After the third wave of communist purges in the spring of 1950 very few remained in any form of military service. Those that had returned home had been persecuted relentlessly, imprisoned or executed, thus removing any threat to the communist state.

During the war the Czech fighter pilot Josef Bryks had been captured and imprisoned in the German prison camp infrastructure. After the war, he married and he and his wife returned to Czechoslovakia together. He had been a prolific escaper and the British government, because of his wartime escapes and the assistance he gave to other escapees, made him a Member of the British Empire. Bryks was refused a visa by the Czechoslovak authorities to go and receive his medal at Buckingham Palace in London. Following the communist coup, he was sentenced to a total of thirty years in prison. He suffered the heaviest depravation during hard labour in uranium mines. His health condition worsened but he was refused medical help. Bryks died as a prisoner on 11 August 1957. His remains were not handed to his family and instead he was buried in secret. His war medals and decorations, including the Medal of the British Empire, were stolen by communist secret police agents during house searches conducted during the purges of persecution at that time. It became commonplace for those men who had retained uniforms or log books to hide them securely or burn them to remove any evidence that could be used against them.

In Great Britain, a Home Office circular dated 4 June 1952 advised legislation was to be revoked and be replaced by the Aliens (Employment) (Polish Forces) (Revocation) Order 1952. The revoked legislation had previously treated many Poles with an alien status where registration and permission to start businesses was covered by statutes passed in the post-war years. The legislation included:

Aliens (Employment) Order, 1948
Aliens (Employment) Polish Forces Order, 1948
Aliens (Restriction) (Polish Resettlement Forces)
    Direction, 1948

In the circular, it was estimated that there were up to 90,000 former service personnel employed in line with the Aliens Polish Forces Order of 1948. They were required to obtain permission from the Secretary of State before engaging in any business activity, profession or occupation for reward other than in the service of an employer. These measures made settlement in Britain problematic for some and it was hoped it would encourage emigration. Those on the reservist list were still required to report according to guidance and not to engage in business or professional activities without permission. To travel outside the United Kingdom required them to pass through registered transit centres and they had to carry what was termed 'refugee passports' as there still remained a large number of displaced people across Europe. Victory had brought with it enormous challenges, with millions of people displaced by the war including liberated prisoners, former slave workers and survivors of concentration camps. Many thousands of people had been extracted from their homes and incarcerated or put to work in the factories of the Third Reich. Those who wanted to return to Poland had to give two months' notice before exit visas would be arranged. The relationship between the British government and the former government in exile became strained as political decision making changed constantly.

By the end of May 1945, Zuromski had been posted to return to the Polish Depot at Blackpool. According to the record of service within his log book, he was resident at Blackpool between 30 May and 25 July 1945. The unit's Polish news sheet, *Wiadomosci Ze Swiata*, was still being used for news distribution among the significant numbers of personnel serving at the Polish Depot. On 19 July, Zuromski completed the Polish form 'Protokol Rehabilitacyjny'. An interview written in Polish was recorded and the translation appears to indicate that the document endorsements suggested further investigation was needed, however the context of this remains unknown.

Zuromski attended a refresher flying course at Hucknall on 26 July, it was the day on which the British electorate gave a landslide victory to the Labour Party and thus removed Churchill, who made way for Clement Attlee to be the new Prime Minister. Zuromski completed his flying course on 5 September. Squadron Leader Mellows, the commanding officer of the refresher flight, signed off the course with an assessment of 'No airmanship which required improving'. The assessment also recorded Zuromski's suitability as a flying instructor as being above the average. He returned to the Polish Depot in order to undertake a special instructor course between 6 and 22 September. This was immediately followed by a posting to Flying Training Command at Carlisle for a lengthy flying instructor's course until 7 November. On this occasion, Wing Commander Tuckford endorsed his log book as above average as a flying instructor.

The aerodrome at Dunholme Lodge became Zuromski's home from 8 November 1945 to 6 May 1946. The airfield closed for operational use in 1946 and housed more than 2,000 displaced refugees from Eastern Europe, many of whom were the families of the Polish airmen based in Great Britain. The British government was about to implement the Polish Resettlement Corps to assist in the integration of the thousands of stateless people in the United Kingdom or assist them to begin new lives abroad. Zuromski moved to the Radlett Fighter Holding Unit on 7 May 1946 remaining until 17 November 1946. These units served no operational function and were purely administrative at the end of the war for demobilisation processing. He moved to the Commeringham Holding Unit on 18 November 1946 and was resident until 27 October 1947.

On 26 June 1948, Zuromski made his final entry in his log book as a member of the RAF. He flew a Harvard trainer, DD711, with a Flight Lieutenant Brown occupying the second pilot's seat on a ninety-five-minute flight across Heston, Hounslow and London. The grand total recorded in Zuromski's log book had reached just over 1,424 hours.

The Polish Resettlement Corps was disbanded in 1949. It had brought about the reunion of families and a significant integration of displaced Poles into British society. For those Polish soldiers, airmen and sailors who fought with the Allies, it effectively provided sanctuary, with the British government allowing them to remain in the United Kingdom with their families. It is worth a moment of thought to remember that Polish pilots had fought in the knowledge of what was taking place in their homeland and this was endured over several years. The German radio broadcasts specifically taunted them with family names announced with accusations of treason and sabotage. The German People's Court administration delivered capital sentences and deportations that were likewise broadcast with the intention of stamping German oppression. What is more, the serving Poles then had to witness the Russian intentions to control their country. All of these factors created a collective experience that was unique. It was the case that many thousands of Polish people had endured years of statelessness in the Second World War, and Zuromski was effectively one of those individuals. However, his story of survival was significantly different to the vast majority.

CHAPTER 15

THE ROYAL PAKISTAN AIR FORCE

The Indian Independence Act was passed in 1947. The act created two independent dominions, India and Pakistan. After the establishment of the state of Pakistan on 14 August 1947, it effectively divided the territory into West and East Pakistan, the latter of which is now Bangladesh. The act repealed the use of 'Emperor of India' as a title for the British Crown and ended all existing treaties with the princely states. Lord Mountbatten continued as Governor-General until he was replaced and Jawaharlal Nehru was appointed as India's first Prime Minister. Muhammad Ali Jinnah became Pakistan's Governor-General and Liaquat Ali Khan its Prime Minister.

India had initially proclaimed that its fighting forces must be Indian first and last, not Sikh, Punjabi, Mahratta, Rajput, Tamil or Telugu organisations. Simply regarded as Indian, the nation was torn apart as the Muslim majority areas of Punjab and Bengal divided into the state of Pakistan. The military assets were likewise partitioned and many men who had flown together representing India for a common purpose in Burma, the Far East and Europe during the Second World War were to be separated.

On 27 July 1947, announcements were made public that Air Marshal Elmhirst had been appointed the first Chief of the Indian Air Force, and Air Vice Marshal Perry-Keene was appointed the first

Chief of the Pakistan Air Force. The Pakistani High Commission in London announced a need for trained technicians and pilots to serve in its air force. They commenced a recruitment process in Great Britain to acquire both pilots and other qualified personnel for immediate military service in Pakistan.

The consultation of partition from India resulted in an allocation to the newly established Royal Pakistan Air Force of twenty-four Tempest II and sixteen Typhoon fighters, two Halifax bombers, eight Dakota transports, twelve Harvard trainers, two Auster light aircraft and ten Tiger Moth biplanes. Not all the aircraft were fit to fly, many requiring maintenance and service. During the ensuing three years, the separation agreement also allocated ninety-three Hawker Fury fighters and a lesser number of Bristol Freighter aircraft to also be delivered. These were to be airworthy and would be delivered to the establishing squadron bases across Pakistan.

The partition in establishing Pakistan resulted in 2,341,040 people movements, mostly on foot by what was known as the Military Evacuation Organisations of Pakistan. The most significant movement of people from East to West Punjab involved 218,405 people being moved by military transport and 1,156,474 by rail. East and West Bengal migration continued for decades after Partition. Religiously motivated exchanges of residency involved East Punjab Muslims, West Punjab Hindus and Sikhs. West Punjab was the Pakistani Punjab and East Punjab was the Indian Punjab. On 1 September 1947, British Overseas Airways Corporation and British air charter companies announced air transport operations would commence for the exchange of populations between India and Pakistan. During the ensuing three months, they transported 43,500 migrating passengers.

The Royal Pakistan Air Force recruitment process for pilots openly offered lucrative service contracts for three years' service with prospectives for time extension thereafter. The RAF put forward a suggestion to Pakistan for Polish pilots and personnel like Zuromski in the Polish Resettlement Corps to be considered. These people inevitably had no passports and any documents issued by the Polish government in exile were unlikely to be recognised in the majority of countries. The majority of volunteers who expressed interest in working in Pakistan were legally stateless persons. One available route to solve the problem was the Nansen International Office for Refugees, who were able to issue a Nansen passport. This was an international substitute passport and allowed stateless persons or those deprived of their national passports to officially transit to enter other countries. Nansen passports were later issued by the Office of the High Commissioner for Refugees, under the Protection of the League of Nations in London.

The India Office holds a file IOR 13330 that discloses Julian Kazimierz Zuromski and Antoni Lbigniew Jedryszek both declared themselves as stateless, and both were provided with a visa to depart Great Britain and enter Pakistan in 1948. Antoni Lbigniew Jedryszek, an RAF engineering officer, and Zuromski were issued visa numbers 818128 and 818129 respectively. These were authorised by the Secretary of State for Commonwealth Relations and once issued were sent by a savingram message to Pakistan. A savingram was a form of correspondence that used informal and abbreviated language in the form of a brief telegram format.

Among the first Poles to volunteer to serve in Pakistan was Władysław Turowicz, who was in company with a group of about thirty other Poles. As part of their service contract, the pilots who signed the contract agreed to fly operationally in defence of Pakistan, which at that time was in conflict over the Kashmir district. After being accepted by the Royal Pakistan Air Force, Zuromski relinquished his position in the Polish Resettlement Corps on 19 November 1948. He officially received his commission into the Royal Pakistan Air Force on 16 December.

The pilots accepted by Pakistan were received at Karachi. It is estimated the Poles numbered between 30-100, including pilots, aircrew and ground crew in various trade qualifications. Many like

Zuromski were married and Pakistan citizenship was available to all of the Polish personnel and wives. Visas were granted by Pakistan to gain lawful entry into the country and this no doubt was applicable to Zuromski's wife and their young daughter Maria, who was born in 1946. However, no evidence of any documentation can be found to support that assumption.

India and Pakistan had gone to war over the predominantly Muslim state of Kashmir in October 1947. Incursions by armed Pathan tribesmen from Pakistan's North-West Frontier Province were motivated by and rooted in the disputed territory of Kashmir. This resulted in a number of Polish pilots flying operationally in the Kashmir conflict against the tribesmen. Maharaja Hari Singh, the ruler of Jammu and Kashmir, had no desire to merge his kingdom with either of the newly divided countries of Pakistan and India. However, by 26 October, the intrusion elements of tribesmen had reached the state capital of Srinagar and Maharaja Hari Singh signed an instrument of accession, making Kashmir an integral part of the Indian Union. This took place barely eleven weeks after the relinquishment of British rule.

The following day India sent troops to Srinagar, the capital of Kashmir, by air and continued to do so until the end of the month. Attacks were made upon Pakistani forces at Poonch, Kotli, Naushera, Mirpur and Uri among others. Indian offensive missions flown during November 1947 indicate that a total of 124 operational sorties had taken place. On 30 October 1947, at Pattan, two Indian Tempests destroyed tribesmen's trucks and a transport column with devastating effect. The Tempests continued attacking ground targets of opportunity. On the following day, 31 October 1947, the Indian Air Force Dakota MA965 was lost after it disappeared in the Srinagar Valley with the loss of its twenty-six occupants.

Armed sorties were flown by both Indian and Pakistani pilots, with many bombing operations and supply flights undertaken to support their ground troops. Indian Tempest pilots flew from Ambala, one of the oldest and largest airfields inherited from the British. Pilots from both newly created nations came under fire and returned it with guns and rockets during the skirmishes.

By March 1948, 12 Squadron of the Royal Indian Air Force had accumulated 3,404 hours of flight, transporting 3.5 million tonnes of cargo, 4,000 troops, and 1,000 casualties. Additionally, they dropped 18,000lb of bombs. Some 10,000 refugees had also been evacuated from Poonch. On 24 May 1948, in response to an urgent request from the Indian Army, a Dakota carrying troops landed in Leh to alleviate a siege.

In 1949, despite the United Nations helping to enforce a ceasefire between the two countries, the Kashmir area remained volatile. The immediate post-independence air forces of India and Pakistan had unexpectantly engaged in the war here. The military award systems for each service had not yet removed themselves from the British infrastructure. These took some time to be established, therefore awards were only made retrospectively in 1950. Unfortunately, records of events are not well evidenced.

Returning to the Royal Pakistan Air Force, a number of Polish pilots were commissioned specifically for senior responsible positions. Zuromski received a promotion to squadron leader and commanded 5 Fighter Squadron. Mieczysław Wolanski commanded 6 Transport Squadron until March 1949, and he supervised the daring night drop missions in the beleaguered Kashmir Valley using Dakotas. Most of the sorties were conducted through Risalpur and Peshawar. Under Squadron Leader Wolanski's command, 437 air drop sorties were conducted across the Bunji, Astore, Gilgit, Burzil and Skardu drop zones. Other Polish pilots undertook instructor flying training positions at Risalpur, where Bolesław Kaczmarek commanded the training squadron. Risalpur was little more than a basic airfield that grew to become a significant college for the development of flying training. It became known as the 'the House of Eagles', a title that resembled the Polish college at Deblin title, the School of Eaglets.

It becomes a fair assumption that this terminology originated from the Polish roots of aviation history.

Zuromski flew in the Royal Pakistan Air Force wearing Pakistani uniform, with the introduction of Polish national symbols to uniforms not considered at that time. The Polish airmen served in Pakistan as contracted officers and they could not be regarded in any respect as a foreign contingent. They were protected by international law; the Hague Convention of 1907 and the Geneva Convention of 1929. The uniform wings of a pilot differed from the British only by the wreath with the letters RPAF instead of RAF. Orders continued to be issued in English. The terms of the deployment of the Polish airmen and the uniforms they wore were decisions made consciously in order to not antagonise the communist rule of Poland by the Soviet Union.

The aerial security of Pakistan at the border with India and Afghanistan in the North-West Frontier Province and Western Punjab fell to 5 and 9 Squadrons. Each squadron had four aircraft on readiness to be dispatched in two flights at all times. In reserve were four aircraft, which despite maintenance, were also available. Following the independence of Pakistan, some armed militant groups in the North-West Frontier that had historically engaged in conflict with the British Raj turned against the dominance of Pakistan, creating further discontent and regional instability.

Squadron Leader Zuromski was issued with the Royal Pakistan Air Force service number 835 and served within the following postings.

9 Fighter Bomber Squadron, 28 December 1948

In July 1947, Squadron Leader Asghar Khan, a member of the Air Force Reconstitution Committee, had insisted that 9 Squadron be officially transferred into the Royal Pakistan Air Force. It became the first operational fighter squadron, equipped with eight Tempests, and was commanded by Squadron Leader M. Ibrahim Khan at Peshawar. The squadron aircraft carried red-painted propeller spinners. Zuromski's name also appears in the log book composed by Czesław Turowski. On 10 February 1949, Tarowski was serving in the Governor-General Communication Flight at Maripur. The flight involving Zuromski and Tarowski was in Dakota H706. Tarowski had served at Deblin alongside Zuromski. An even closer friend of Zuromski within 9 Squadron was Kazimierz Kozak, who had been a pilot in 308 Polish Squadron. He joined the squadron in Pakistan in January 1948.

14 Fighter Bomber Squadron, 16 December 1949

In November 1948, 14 Squadron also served at Peshawar. It was initially equipped with Tempests but later received newly acquired Fury fighter-bombers. No. 14 Squadron was deployed at Miranshah airfield at North Waziristan for counter-insurgency operations and was called upon to fly against several rebel targets. The squadron was short lived following the loss of two Tempests and the subsequent ceasefire in Kashmir. The unit was reactivated on 16 December 1949 under the command of Squadron Leader Zuromski. The squadron left for Miranshah on 24 March 1950 on its first operational deployment against an insurgency by the Faqir of Ipi.

5 Fighter Bomber Squadron, 17 July 1950

This squadron was established as part of the Royal Pakistan Air Force on 15 August 1947, equipped with eight Tempest IIs and commanded by Squadron Leader Zaheer Ahmad. The unit was based at Miranshah and provided cover to the Pakistan Army units at Razmak during Pakistan's withdrawal from the North-West Frontier region. The squadron subsequently converted to fly the Sea Fury, and other operations included ground attacks and patrolling rebellious areas.

Zuromski took command of 5 Squadron in July 1950. During the following month he and the squadron performed an air display at the Dring Road aerodrome in Karachi. This was the first air display of its kind held at the Air Headquarters, and it was attended by the Prime Minister and the Pakistan cabinet. Some 150,000 people witnessed an impressive display of Fury aerobatics. The Polish pilot Bolesław Kaczmarek, a veteran of 306 Squadron, was Zuromski's flight commander. He lost his life on 25 October 1951, flying with 5 Squadron as an instructor in a Fury when he crashed near Maripur airfield in Karachi. A second Fury involved this training accident was flown by Pilot Officer Syed Fazal Hussain Khurazmi.

Another 306 Polish Squadron veteran who served alongside Zuromski in 5 Squadron was Stefan Tronczyski. He carried the Pakistani service number of 841, six digits apart from Zuromski's. Fred Issacs also flew in the same 5 Squadron in 1950. He recalled flying dive-bombing operations from Miranshah in support of the Tochi Scouts in Waziristan against the Faqir of Ipi. In 1948 the faqir had taken control of Datta Khel and moved towards the establishment of an independent state of Pashtunistan. In 1949, he called on Pakistan to accept Pashtunistan's status. In response, and to counter escalating tribal revolts and prevent further conflict, Pakistan undertook operations from Miranshah air base and bombarded the faqir's compounds. Issacs served in the Pakistan Air Force for four years before moving to live in retirement in Canada.

HQ within No. 1 Group, 26 November 1951

No. 1 Group was the operational command in the North-West Frontier Province and Western Punjab, which were particularly important from the perspective of the security of Pakistan as they border India and Afghanistan. This posting for Squadron Leader Zuromski indicates it was possibly an administration role. The Royal Pakistan Air Force delivered the British organisational structure, its military regulations and the nomenclature of British military ranks. However, on 15 April 1953, the Pakistan Air Force Act was embedded into new regulations of service. This was applied to consolidate and amend the service law and discipline of the Pakistan Air Force. The act made aliens ineligible to be considered for enrolment and thereafter any person who was not a citizen of Pakistan required the consent of the Federal Government in writing before being granted a commission or a junior commission, or to simply be enrolled in the Pakistan Air Force.

AHQ Karachi, 15 July 1953

The headquarters of the Royal Pakistan Air Force had been originally established at Peshawar on 15 August 1947. The headquarters moved to Karachi on 1 June 1948 only to return back to Peshawar in 1960.

No. 12 Squadron, 1 September 1953

This squadron was assigned duties as the Air Headquarters communication flight, in addition to its VIP flight operating Viking and Dakota aircraft, which also delivered target-towing capabilities for training. Squadron Leader Zuromski presumably commanded the squadron and no doubt undertook the communication flights, carrying dignitaries of all descriptions.

The contracts of employment for the Polish pilots serving in the Royal Pakistan Air Force expired after three years' service. They were required to make decisions about their future years, with some like Zuromski extending the contract. The fact that they were no longer stateless mean they now had the option of emigration to receptive countries. For example, Ludwik Świerzb, Bronisław Pianko and Henryk Perkowicz spent the remainder of their lives as resident Australian citizens. Konrad Antoni Muchowski was a pilot who like Zuromski served in 308 Squadron and after his contract expired in Pakistan he settled in Great Britain, as did Antoni Lbigniew Jedryszek. Malta became the country of choice for Mieczysław Jan Maksymowicz.

The prefix 'Royal' was removed from the Pakistan's Air Force name when the country became a republic on 23 March 1956.

Squadron Leader Zbigniew Kossakowski became another Polish pilot who lost his life serving in Pakistan, killed on 29 January 1959 in an accident at Rawalpindi. The Pakistani newspapers reported profound appreciation for the service of those Poles who paid the utmost sacrifice while training pilots and that respect never wavered.

The government of Pakistan enriched the lives of many stateless Poles, none more so than Władysław Turowicz and his wife. Like many Poles, he had faced internment in Romania, escaped to France and fought under General Sikorski's command. The husband and wife then faced a complicated escape, whereby Władysław went through North Africa and his wife crossed the Channel. Both reached safety and after the war they travelled to Pakistan, where they contributed significantly to the development of the Royal Pakistan Air Force. In 1959, Turowicz was promoted to group captain, and then again in 1960 to air commodore, after which he joined the Air Headquarters as the commander-in-chief. He retired from the Pakistan Air Force in 1967 and was appointed the Executive Director of Space and Upper Atmosphere Research in Karachi, finally retiring in 1970. Turowicz died on 8 January 1980 and was buried at the Catholic Cemetery in Karachi, with full military honours. In honour of him being the Polish co-founder of Pakistani aviation, a statue of Turowicz was officially unveiled in the main hall of the Pakistani Air Force Museum in Karachi in 2006.

Squadron Leader Zuromski resigned from the Royal Pakistani Air Force at the end of 1953. He had experienced the turbulent years of post-war Asian history and the introduction of jet fighter aircraft as India and Pakistan strove for military authority. Pakistan had appealed to international opinion, arguing for the right of the Kashmiri people to determine their own future, while India continued to consolidate its control over the territory it had secured in the first Kashmir War. Pakistan continued to voice that it was incomplete without Kashmir. When Zuromski left Pakistan, it had been unable to pressure India into giving up its claim on Kashmir, despite the enhanced diplomatic pressure from its alliance with the United States.

The Pakistan Kashmir 1947–1948 medal was designed and struck in English detail. This was the first campaign medal and clasp to be instituted by Pakistan. The decoration is known as the Tamgha-i-Diffa 1947 Medal. The clasp 'Kashmir 1948' was awarded to Pakistani personnel who served in the Jammu Kashmir War between 22 September 1947 to 5 January 1949. Zuromski was entitled to the medal and was able to wear it adjacent to his French, Polish and British campaign medals. Little primary evidence exists in relation to the records of his flying in the first Kashmir War. However, the previously mentioned Kazimierz Kozak, who had served alongside Zuromski in both 308 Polish Squadron and 9 Royal Pakistan Air Force Squadron, retained his personal records. He was able to recall that 9 Squadron flew to Kashmir, where the target was Srinagar, shortly before the truce was signed. The book *The Story of the Pakistan Air Force. A Saga of Courage and Honour*, says: 'Squadron Leader Zuromski, as the commander of the 14th Fighter Bomber Squadron fought with Pashtun insurgents in Waziristan, flying a Tempest Mk II.'

The RAF log book for Squadron Leader Zuromski forms the primary evidence of his war service. The record covers entries between September 1940 to November 1948. The whereabouts of any log book thereafter remains unknown. The presence of the official Royal Pakistan Air Force stamp and signature accepting his RAF log book as being a correct record of his service indicates the probable issuance of an additional log book in Pakistan. No doubt his record of flying within the contracted years offered to him were composed in that subsequent volume.

CHAPTER 16

CIVIL FLYING

Zuromski returned to England in 1955. The post-war period had seen the administration for civil aviation in the United Kingdom become fragmented, with the Ministry of Civil Aviation and the Ministry of Aircraft Production, as well as the Air Registration Board, each having particular roles to administer and regulate. In 1949, new standards had been established for Air Pilot Certificates following the introduction of new grades for professional pilot licences. Civil aerial survey companies flying sorties throughout Europe and beyond were being established and they were seeking experienced pilots.

Zuromski gained employment as a pilot within the Hunting Aerosurveys company, a British aerial photography business. The company had been formed in 1944 by Percy Hunting and was later rebranded under the name Hunting Surveys. Among the aircraft operated was a Percival Proctor and a de Havilland Dragon Rapide. With contracts for aerial surveying for tin mining in Nigeria and for oil in Arabia, Venezuela and Colombia, the company added a Dakota aircraft fitted with two-stage superchargers into the fleet. This was specifically for operations at higher altitudes. Timber surveying in Ontario and aerial mapping in Australia and Hong Kong were other areas of work undertaken. These were significant global contracts; for example, a contract to South Australia required an undertaking of a minimum of 400 hours' flying time.

Aerial mapping began with cameras and was later enhanced with magnetometer surveys. Aerial surveying magnetometers were directly descended from the wartime magnetic anomaly detectors used on anti-submarine aircraft. Tail boom-mounted sensors were fitted on the company's Dakota and it flew extensively for oil and mineral surveys covering the North Sea and other distant and remote areas. Experienced pilots were sought to fly in many countries to deploy the ever-improving sensor technology.

Surveying radars, ground profile recorders, scintillometers, synthetic aperture radars and electro-optical cameras became essential tools for highly accurate mapping, all of which required pilot accuracy. Zuromski embarked on civilian flying and would have been required to record his qualifications to fly the type of aircraft as well as give details of his flying in a civilian pilot log book issued by the Ministry of Civil Aviation. The private pilot's licence was issued annually.

Overseas aerial surveying operations required a crew to be away from home for months, working in countries across many continents. Between 1957 and 1964, Hunting also operated a specially converted Auster for smaller-scale aerial survey work. This was in addition to the de Havilland Dove; Douglas C-47B Dakota; Percival Prince; Percival Proctor; and de Havilland Dragon Rapide, which had been built in 1943 and served in the RAF. That aircraft was fitted with long-range internal tanks to enable the extended flight survey tasks. The Dakota, officially registered as G-ANAF, continued to receive modifications, including long magnetometer tail-booms and extended long-range tanks positioned in the cabin that facilitated twelve-hour endurance flights.

Jacques Peguret was employed by Huntings between 1959 and July 1974, and worked in is French satellite company, Sapa France. He flew with Zuromski during the years 1965 to 1967. The company leased two Prince aircraft in order to fulfil three extensive aerial survey contracts. Zuromski flew Prince serial number G-AMLZ and

Jacques Peguret flew F-BJAI. The Prince was a high-wing, cantilever monoplane with twin engines and metal, stressed fuselage with a retractable, tricycle undercarriage. Both aircraft were contracted to be deployed over Cyprus.

On 20 October 1965, Peguret departed Leavesden, Hertfordshire, for Nicosia, Cyprus. The route was via Luton, Montpellier, Naples, Brindisi and Athens. Zuromski was in company with Peguret on the same route, with both aircraft flown in tandem.

The *Cyprus Mail* newspaper published an article on 26 October 1965:

> An aerial survey for minerals will start in the Nicosia area today. The survey is part of a large exploration programme for minerals and water which the Geological Survey Department has been undertaking for the last two years in association with the United Nations Special Fund. For a period of three weeks, two aircraft will be flying at a height of 500 feet over the hills south of Nicosia, looking for indications of new copper ore bodies.
>
> The aircraft will be easily recognisable from the special equipment attached to the outside. They will cover the county systematically from Peristerona Astromeritis to Larnaca. The equipment carried by the aircraft is similar to radar and has been specially designed to locate big bodies of pyrite similar to the ones already mined in Cyprus. Electromagnetic signals are transmitted from the coils which are carried on the back of the rear aircraft. If there are any electrical conductors in the area, they will produce a signal which is detected by the sensitive equipment which is carried in the leading aircraft and the bird or cylinder which is carried behind the aircraft at the end of a short cable.
>
> When the aerial survey is completed teams of geologists and geophysicists from the Geological Survey Department

and the UN Special Fund Project will continue the work with more detailed studies on the ground which will in turn be followed up by drilling.

Both pilots also flew the same aircraft over the Libyan desert in 1966. On 4 October, Zuromski and Peguret flew individually from Toussus-le-Noble near Paris to Tripoli via Nice, Alghero and Tunis. The aircraft were based at Sebha until November, when they moved to an American Mobil oil base in the middle of the desert. They lived in basic tents and caravans undertaking magnetic, radiation and electro-mag survey flights. This was a contract of employment that ran into 1967. Libya saw significant exploration for resources over several years. It became an independent kingdom in 1951 and developed its mineral rights law through consultation with the large international petroleum companies.

In 1953, Libya granted prospecting permits to eleven petroleum companies. The country was a hotbed of exploration with geological surveys being undertaken by those companies. The Suez Crisis of 1956 and 1957 resulted in the closing of the Suez Canal and impacted greatly upon the events of that time. In 1960 Esso decided that its discoveries thus far required the construction of a pipeline and oil export terminal. The significant 110-mile long, 30in-diameter pipeline gave it a capacity for delivering 200,000 barrels of oil per day for export. In October 1961, the first shipment went to Great Britain.

By the late 1960s, Hunting Surveys had merged with Hunting Geophysics Ltd to form Hunting Surveys Ltd and it merged again with a sister company, Hunting Aerofilms Limited, to become simply Aerofilms Limited in 1987. Jacques Peguret retired from flying and returned to live in Boulogne, France, also the chosen country of residence for Zuromski's daughter, Maria, of whom little is known.

It remains unknown when Zuromski retired from flying. He had anglicised his second family forename of Kazimierz to 'Keith'.

No doubt this was adopted by him for ease and integration reasons during his residence in England and working overseas. Zuromski settled in Manor Drive, Surbiton, Surrey. His mother, Taisa, was living at 69 Cleveland Gardens in London. Census records also list Kazimierz Halicki and Stanisław Wandzilak as resident at that property. Taisa's marriage to Kazimierz had ended and on 1 December 1971, she was remarried, aged seventy-two, to Wandzilak, who was then aged fifty-four. The marriage was witnessed by two Polish dignitaries, Countess Maria Potocka and Count Alexandrowicz, in Richmond upon Thames.

Taisa Wandzilak died in 1993, aged ninety-three with Julian present. Zuromski died six years later in 1999 at the age of eighty-one years, his wife Maria present at his bedside. The announcement of his death was published in Polish. The translation reads:

> Julian Kazimierz Zuromski, Major Pilot of Polish Air Force. Awarded Cross of Courageous, Pakistani AFC and other Polish and British Medals. Member of Foundation of the Polish Airmen Memorial. Born 6.11.1918 died 17.5.1999 in Surbiton, Surrey. Glory be his name.
>
> Published by Association of Polish Airmen in the United Kingdom.

The Polish Air Force Association was founded in London in June 1945. Zuromski had been a long-term member, with his subscription fees paid throughout his life. The association represented all members of the Polish Air Force who served under British command during the Second World War. The association thrived for fifty years but was disbanded shortly after the death of Zuromski on 29 June 1999.

The association later reformed to engage with the membership of families with the principal aim to develop greater awareness of the role of the Polish Air Force during the war. Sponsorship allowed for the basic tasks of supporting numerous projects including the gathering of historical memorabilia for future generations.

Zuromski's stepfather, Stanisław Wandzilak, died in October 2000, aged eighty-three. His ashes were by request placed in his family grave at the Rakowicki Cemetery in Kraków. At the end of the Second World War, the British graves service gathered together graves from all over Poland into three cemeteries, the largest of which is Rakowicki. Among the graves can be found those of airmen who lost their lives during the Warsaw supply drop operations, bravely delivering supplies of medicines, food and clothes to the Polish people fighting for freedom in the besieged Warsaw. On entering any Commonwealth War Graves Commission cemetery, the headstones used to commemorate Polish Forces differ from that of the standard headstone and they become instantly recognisable by the narrow shoulders of stone configuration. There is another poignant and distinguishing feature of those who served in armies in exile, the general absence of personal headstone inscriptions. A decision to exclude these was made to protect the family connected to the deceased. This situation remained relevant long into communist rule and explains why the vast majority of Polish graves commemorate the deaths of Polish airmen but exclude inscriptions of beloved sons, brothers or husbands.

POSTSCRIPT

The objective of the author in writing the account of the life of Julian Zuromski was to portray the hardship he and his family endured in the twentieth-century conflict. Also to establish as much truth as possible, especially in relation to his service as a Spitfire pilot in the RAF and the events he was exposed to as a Polish prisoner of war when controlled by his Third Reich German captors. Some details of this when viewed through different historical perceptions remain in some respects at best murky or possibly distorted.

The years of research and referencing, primarily using the RAF log book composed by Zuromski and official archives at The National Archives, London, and the Polish Institute, General Sikorski Museum, London, will hopefully enable every reader to consider the factual events and understand the very personal influences imposed upon him from adolescence, into the cockpit of the Supermarine Spitfire and as an Allied prisoner of war. The Judge Advocate General's considered advice given to the RAF in November 1945 was to withdraw charges and exonerate Zuromski from the suspicions of having acted as a collaborator or assisting the Third Reich. However, his name in some written debates still carries an association of stigma, which could be regarded as disingenuous to a brave individual who fought Nazi dictatorship and opposed communism in equal measures.

The flying statistics and combat achievements within the RAF log book of Flight Lieutenant Julian Zuromski:

Total hours flying recorded, 1,425 hours and forty-five minutes.

Total operational hours in daylight, 216 hours and twenty minutes.

Total operational hours at night, 3 hours and five minutes.

Total number of operational sorties, 84, entailing 121 hours and twenty-five minutes.

51 operational sorties undertaken within 308 Squadron.

33 operational sorties undertaken within 66 Squadron.

One Luftwaffe Bf 109 fighter aircraft probably destroyed, 25 April 1942. Signature confirming: Squadron Leader Nowierski, 308 Squadron.

One Luftwaffe Ju 88 bomber destroyed, 25 July 1942. Signature confirming: Squadron Leader Zak, 308 Squadron.

One Luftwaffe Fw 190 fighter-bomber damaged, 15 February 1943. Signature confirming: Squadron Leader Kornicki, 308 Squadron.

One Luftwaffe Fw 190 fighter-bomber destroyed, 30 July 1943. Signature applied by Flying Officer Deytrikh, 66 Squadron.

With time the Second World War gradually distances itself from personal memory with the demise of surviving veterans.

Julian Zuromski fought for Polish freedom, as did three Polish mathematicians. Jerzy Rozycki, Henryk Zygalski and Marian Rejewski, who pioneered much of the early decryption work that led to solving the Nazi Enigma military codes and influencing victory. There were many individuals that attained supremacy over persecution, dictatorship and fascism; they all deserve to be embraced and thanked.

ACKNOWLEDGEMENTS

The author would like to recognise the assistance of Sylvia Dodds (née Stacey), Squadron Leader Miroslav Antonin Liskutin, Jacques Peguret, Chris John, Nicholas Lugowski, Adrian van Zandvoort, Jon Eagar, Aleksander Glogowski, Pavel Vancata, Andre Czlapka, Nick Fenton, Oliver Clutton-Brock, David Layne, Gilles Robert – Historique de la Défense France, Bernard Buchwald, Claudius Scharff, Peter Sikora, Usman Shabir Pakistan Air Force, Frederick Issacs, Derek Morris, Amy Schmidt, Wojtek Zmyslony, Bartlomiej Belcarz, Jadwiga Kowalska – Polish Sikorski Museum.

Photographs

Wherever possible, known contributors have been duly accredited. Additional photographs have been included from the author's collection. The terms of the Open Government Licence facilitate the use of historic material from The National Archives, while other material, particularly photographic work, sits within the public domain created by the government prior to 1957.

REFERENCES

Air Historical Branch, AHB6 June 1947, *A Survey of German Air Operations*, dated September 1944.

Air Ministry, *Service and Summary of Psychological Reactions, No. 97*, 3 April 1943.

Bohdan, Arct, *A Group of Great Pilots*, Warsaw, 1966.

Brown, Alan, *Airmen in Exile*, Sutton Publishing, 2000.

Capka, Flight Lieutenant Jo, *Red Sky at Night*, Anthony Blond, 1958.

Clutton-Brock, Oliver, *Footprints on the Sands of Time*, Grub Street, 2003.

Collier, Richard, *Eagle Day: The Battle of Britain*, Hodder and Stoughton, 1966.

Cuddon, Eric, *The Dulag Luft Trial, Vol. 9 in the War Crimes Trials Series*, William Hodge and Co., 1952.

Czapski, Jozef, *Memoirs of Starobielsk*, Rzym, 1945.

Czapski, Jozef, *Inhuman Land*, Warsaw, 1990.

Cynk, Jerzy B., *The Polish Air Force at War*, Schiffer Military History, 1998.

Deighton, Len, *The True Story of the Battle of Britain*, Jonathan Cape, 1977.

Doherty, M.A., *Nazi Wireless Propaganda: Lord Haw-Haw and British public opinion in the Second World War*, Edinburgh University Press, 2000.

REFERENCES

Eagar, Jon, *Squadron Leader Carpenter*, unpublished.

Foreman, J., Matthews, J. & Parry, S., *Luftwaffe Night Fighter Combat Claims*, Red Kite, Walton-on-Thames, 2004.

Franks, Norman, with Muggleton, Simon, *A Fighter Pilot's Call to Arms Defending Britain and France Against the Luftwaffe*, Grub Street, London, 2010.

Gibson, T.A. Edwin and Kingsley, G., *Courage Remembered*, HMSO, 1989.

Gretzyngier, Robert, *Poles in Defence of Britain*, Grub Street, 2001.

Haqqani, Husain, 'Pakistan's Endgame in Kashmir', *India Review*, Volume 2, No. 3, July 2003.

Hijazi, A.Q. (Illustrator), *The Story of the Pakistan Air Force. A Saga of Courage and Honour*, Shaheen Foundation, Islamabad, 1988.

Jaczynski, Stanisław, *NKVD Prisoner of War Camps*, Warsaw, 1995.

Law Reports of Trials of War Criminals, The United Nations War Crimes Commission, Volume III, London, HMSO 1948.

Lisiewicz, Squadron Leader M., *Destiny Can Wait. The Polish Air Force in the Second World War*, William Heinemann, 1949.

Liskutin, Squadron Leader Miroslav Antonin, *A Spitfire Pilot Remembers*, William Kimber, 1988.

Maton, M., *Honor Those Mentioned in Dispatches*, Token Publishing, 2013.

Nemecek, J. and Nemeckova, D., The title translates as *Betrayal*, 2015.

PRO WO 71/1131, Voluntary Statement of William Albert Colledge, 1945.

PRO WO 204/6225, Allied Forces Headquarters, Psychological Warfare Branch Radio Monitoring.

PRO INF 1/292, Home Intelligence Weekly Report on Maton, 26 August 1943.

Rawson, A., *Poland's Struggle: Before, During and After the Second World War*, Pen and Sword Military, 2019.

RAFM MFC77/16/25, Air Ministry Form 1180 for Hurricane W9147, 18 September 1941.

Sikorski Museum London, Personnel documents Julian Zuromski.

Sikorski Museum London, Documents of pilots held in the archives of the Polski.

Stepek, Jan E., *Memoirs Found in Katyn*, Paryz, 1990.

Sarkar, Dilip, *The Story of the Battle of Britain in the Words of the Pilots*, Amberley, 2009.

Sarkar, Dilip, *Battle of Britain: Last Look Back*, Ramrod Publications, 2002.

Sanford, George, *Katyn and the Soviet Massacre of 1940: Truth Justice and Memory*, Routledge, London and New York, 2005.

The Institute of National Remembrance Commission for the Prosecution of Crimes against the Polish Nation.

Public Education Office.

The Berlin Potsdam Conference, 17 July–2 August 1945 Protocol of the Proceedings, 1 August 1945.

TNA AIR 40/2466, Dulag Luft Camp history.

TNA AIR 2/5162, Proposed Agreement with Czechoslovakian Authorities on Employment of Air Personnel in RAFVR.

TNA AIR 2/5196, Employment of Surplus Polish and Czech Fighter Pilots in Fighter Command.

TNA AIR 2/6053, Polish Units Employed with the RAF Rank on Entry and Promotion of Officers.

TNR AIR 40/2297, Letters written by Warrant Officer Hughes.

Toliver, Raymond, *The Story of Hanns Joachim Schraff*, Shiffer Military Books.

United Nations War Crimes Commission, *History of the United Nations War Crimes Commission*, 1948.

United Nations War Crimes Commission, Law Reports of Trials of War Criminals, Vol. 3, Trial of Erich Killinger and Four Others British Military Court, Wuppertal, London H.M.S.O., 1948.

Zamoyski, Adam, *The Forgotten Few: The Polish Air Force in the Second World War*, John Murray, 1995.

INDEX

INDEX

INDEX

INDEX